God's men

from all nations to all nations

the eighth Inter-Varsity missionary convention

Inter-Varsity Press

Bible quotations, unless otherwise noted, are from the King James version. Other versions are quoted by permission:

The New Testament in Modern English, by J. B. Phillips, © by J. B. Phillips, 1958. Used by permission of the Macmillan Company and Geoffrey Bles, Ltd.

The New English Bible (NEB), © The Delegates of the Oxford University Press and the Syndics of the Cambridge University Press. Used by permission.

The Revised Standard Version of the Holy Bible (RSV), © 1946 and 1952 by the Division of Christian Education of the National Council of Churches. Used by permission.

Library of Congress
catalog card number 68-28079

Copyright © 1968, by Inter-Varsity Press,
130 north Wells, Chicago 60606.

Printed in the United States of America

CONTENTS

Part IV

Part V.   Student Work Worldwide
(C. Stacey Woods)

Part VI.   Centennary Tribute
(William McE. Miller, Sr.)

PREFACE

"I have discovered a new element on the scene--student power . . . . Students feel that progress in the world today comes too slowly. They are frustrated. They feel that their elders are not doing a good job. And sometimes they seek to express themselves in perhaps rather violent ways. Students are on the march." With these words in his keynote address, David Adeney set the pace for Inter-Varsity's 8th annual missionary convention.

Men from various backgrounds, countries, and campuses followed through with the clarion call for a demonstration of spiritual power, for turning the world upside down with the gospel of Jesus Christ, by God's men from all nations to all nations. During the last five days of 1967, over 9200 students, graduates, and missionaries met in the assembly hall of the University of Illinois, Urbana, to listen to these men and to consider their claims.

The mammoth convention ran the gamut from rich, insightful studies of 2 Timothy with the Reverend John Stott, of All Soul's Church in London, England . . . to open-faced, open-hearted appraisals of missionaries and mission work by evangelical leaders from Asia, South America, and Africa . . . to impassioned entreaties by missionaries for a positive right-where-you-are witness and for

a commitment to finish the task of world evangelization
. . . to fresh, informative glimpses of student work
overseas through the ministry of International
Fellowship of Evangelical Students (IFES) . . . to
elective workshops with experienced men and women
eager to share know-how and information on their
special fields . . . to small-group dorm Bible study
and prayer times where students interacted and
grappled with personal problems and issues triggered
by messages during the week . . . to "frock," musical
innovation introduced by two young singing guitarists
from two separate continents.

Over 100 denominational and independent
missions sending agencies directed their men and
materials to the convention display area. These
people had wonderful opportunities to individually
counsel and converse with large numbers of delegates
they met at the assembly hall, dining rooms, and
dormitories. The contribution they made to the
entire convention was tremendously significant.

And what is a missionary convention without
representation from other countries? Of the 476
foreign students who registered, most came from
Asia, with Europeans, Africans, and Latin Americans
tying for second place. An Urbana "first" gave
Spanish- and French-speaking delegates respectively
special blocs of seats with simultaneous translations
via earphones.

Another bloc of delegates had the services
of translators for the deaf. Surely the United
Nations would be as proud as Inter-Varsity to have
the Urbana translation team.

Teamwork was evident throughout the week.
There was an awareness of busy people scurrying
behind the scenes to make all systems go. Such
a colossal convention would require months of
preliminary groundwork to establish the structure
and to start things moving. The entire Inter-
Varsity staff and the hundreds of volunteers--
such as Bible study leaders, registration crew,
sales-clerks at the Inter-Varsity Press book stalls--
performed their assignments with enthusiasm.

But all were cognizant that it had to be
God who would tie together loose ends, who would
surmount problems that kept popping up, who would
empower and strengthen during long, weary days
and nights, who would keep sickness at a minimum
in the midst of a flu epidemic in the Midwest,
who would bring delegates to and from the convention
in safety (even providing winter clothing for the
warm-hearted but chilled planeload from Hawaii),
who would prompt delegates to give and pledge
for the project of overseas student work of
International Fellowship of Evangelical Students
($93,000 was given and pledged).

It was he who, by his Spirit, would sweep
over the vast audience . . .

> to touch individuals:
> "I came running from God and His
> demands on my entire life and ran
> straight into Him."

to bring men and women to salvation in
Jesus Christ:

> "I lacked the reality of Jesus
> Christ . . . I had the head
> knowledge but not the heart. I
> began to search for that reality
> . . . my friends prayed . . .
> Saturday night it finally clicked.
> I became tuned in and for the
> first time I really realized who
> Christ was and that He died for
> me!"

to call others to a lifetime of service:

> "I could never leave the convention
> as the same person. Never before
> did I see so clearly my responsibility
> as a Christian, and never before
> did I feel so compelled to tell
> others about Christ."

God did all that—and more. Some results
are recorded in letters in convention files; most
will remain in the annals of God.

"Urbana is a dangerous experience," one

wrote, but it is an experience that can shake the world for Jesus Christ. May Urbana be just the beginning of a movement of God's men from all nations to all nations.

CONVENTION SPEAKERS

Evan Adams, a panelist, is Assistant Missionary
Director, in charge of Foreign Missions Fellowship, Inter-Varsity Christian Fellowship.

David Adeney, keynote speaker, a panelist and
a workshop instructor, is Associate General
Secretary of International Fellowship of
Evangelical Students, Hong Kong.

John Alexander, the evening platform chairman,
is General Director of Inter-Varsity Christian
Fellowship.

Robert H. Bowman, a panelist, Missionary Introduction staff, and a workshop instructor,
is President of Far East Broadcasting Company.

George M. Cowan, Missionary Introduction staff,
is President, Board of Directors, of Wycliffe
Bible Translators.

Robert L. Foster, M.D., Missionary Introduction
staff, is Executive Secretary USA of Africa
Evangelical Fellowship.

Arthur F. Glasser, a panelist and Missionary
Introduction staff, is Director for North
America of Overseas Missionary Fellowship
(CIM).

Michael C. Griffiths, an evening speaker and a
panelist, is general director designate of
Overseas Missionary Fellowship.

Akira Hatori, an evening speaker and a panelist,
is the leading evangelist in Asia today.

Olan A. Hendrix, a panelist and Missionary Introduction staff, is Home Secretary of Far Eastern Gospel Crusade.

J. Philip Hogan, Missionary Introduction staff, is Assistant General Superintendent of Assemblies of God; Executive Director of Assemblies of God Foreign Missions Department.

David M. Howard, an evening speaker, a panelist, a workshop instructor, and Missionary Introduction staff, is Assistant General Director of Latin America Mission.

James Kraakevik, Missionary Introduction staff, and a workshop instructor, is Chairman, Department of Physics, Wheaton College.

Paul E. Little, Assistant Convention Director, is IVCF Director of Evangelism.

Donald A. McGavran, a panelist, is Dean of the Graduate School of World Mission and Institute of Church Growth at Fuller Theological Seminary.

Charles J. Mellis, Missionary Introduction staff, and a workshop instructor, is Secretary-Treasurer of Missionary Aviation Fellowship and missionary pilot in New Guinea.

William McE. Miller, Sr., speaker for the centennary tribute to Samuel Zwemer and Robert Speer, is former missionary in Iran under Presbyterian Church USA.

Emilio A. Nunez, a panelist, is professor at Central American Bible Institute and Seminary.

Olugbemi Olutamayin, a panelist, is a student
at Princeton Seminary and associated with
Sudan Interior Mission, Nigeria.

Waldron Scott, a panelist and Missionary Introduction speaker, is Pacific Area Director,
The Navigators.

Francis R. Steele, an evening speaker, is Home
Secretary of North Africa Mission and member
of the Board of Directors, IVCF-USA.

John R. W. Stott, the morning Bible expositor,
is Rector of All Souls Church in London,
England, and Chaplain to Her Majesty the
Queen of England.

H. Wilber Sutherland, a platform chairman, is
General Secretary, Inter-Varsity Christian
Fellowship-Canada.

George Verwer, a panelist, an evening speaker,
and Missionary Introduction staff, is Coordinator of Operation Mobilization.

Warren W. Webster, a panelist and an evening
speaker, is missionary in West Pakistan with
Conservative Baptist Foreign Mission Society.

C. Stacey Woods, an evening speaker, is General
Secretary of International Fellowship of
Evangelical Students, Switzerland.

Part I. God's Man
morning messages

1. God's Man: The Charge to Guard the Gospel
by John R. W. Stott

Let's open our Bibles at the second letter of Paul to Timothy.

We shall take a chapter a morning. Because they're a bit long, I shall not read them to you every morning, but hope very much that every member of the convention will have read the chapter before we come together.

INTRODUCTION

Before we look at 2 Timothy chapter 1, there are four introductory points about the letter that I think it's necessary for me to make.

First, this is a genuine letter of Paul to Timothy. The Apostle Paul was its author and Timothy was its recipient. And the arguments that have been advanced against the Pauline authorship—historical, ecclesiastical, doctrinal, and linguistic arguments—are not sufficient to overthrow the evidence, internal and external, which authenticates it as a genuinely Pauline epistle. This is number one: 2 Timothy is a genuine letter of Paul to Timothy.

Second, the Paul who wrote it was a prisoner in Rome. He was not now in the comparative freedom and comfort of his own hired house in which the book of Acts takes leave of him and from which he seems to have been set free, as indeed he expected.

But, rather, as Hendriksen puts it in his commentary,
Paul was now in some dismal underground dungeon
with a hole in the ceiling for light and air.
Perhaps he was in the Mamertine prison in Rome,
as tradition has suggested. At any rate, it was
the prison to which a second arrest had brought
him and from which Paul escaped only by death.
So Paul wrote this, his last letter that has
survived to us, under the shadow of his imminent
execution. And although it is a personal communication
of Paul to Timothy, it is also--and consciously
so--Paul's last will and testament to the Christian
church.

Third, the Timothy to whom this letter is
addressed was being thrust into a position of
responsible Christian leadership far beyond his
natural capacities. For over fifteen years Timothy
had been Paul's missionary companion and a trusted
apostolic delegate, and now at the time of Paul's
writing, he was the accepted leader of the church
in Ephesus. And still heavier responsibilities
were going to fall upon him when the apostle's
anticipated martyrdom took place.

Yet, humanly speaking, Timothy was utterly
unfit for the responsibilities that were coming
his way. These were the reasons:

a. He was still comparably young. We
don't know his precise age, but in Paul's first
letter to him, Paul told him that no man was to
despise Timothy's youth. And in this letter that
we're studying, Paul told him to shun youthful
passions. This would indicate that he was still
a comparably young man.

b. He was prone to sickness. In the first
letter to Timothy, the apostle referred to Timothy's
frequent ailments, and recommended that for his
poor stomach's sake he exchange water for a little
wine.

c. He was timid by temperament. Timid
Timothy. He seems to have been naturally shy.
If he'd lived today I have no doubt that we should
have called him an introvert. He shrank from

difficult tasks, so that when Paul wrote to the
Corinthians he had to say, "When Timothy comes,
see that you put him at ease among you, and let
no man despise him." Several times in this letter
Paul told him not to be ashamed but to take his
share of suffering, because God had not given us
a spirit of cowardice--and, in Patrick Fairbairn's
words, Timothy was a man disposed rather to lean
than to lead.

Now this was Timothy--young in years, frail
in physique, retiring in disposition--who nevertheless
was called to accept responsibilities in the service
of Jesus Christ. And I believe there are thousands
of men and women like that here today--young, weak,
and shy. We're not young, strong, and free, as
we sing in one of the hymns, but young, weak, and
shy. And if you feel like that, then this epistle
is addressed to you. If God is calling you to
responsibilities far beyond your natural capacities,
then you're just like Timothy.

And that brings me to the <u>fourth</u> introductory
point. In writing to Timothy, Paul's preoccupation
was with the gospel--the deposit of truth which
has been revealed and committed to the Apostle
Paul by God. You see, Paul was a prisoner then,
but he was going to be a martyr quite soon. Paul's
days of gospel preaching were over. What would
happen to the gospel when Paul was dead? That
was the question that was dominating his mind
throughout this letter. And it was to this vital
question that Paul addressed himself. He reminded
Timothy that the gospel was now committed to Timothy.
Paul was finished. He was on his deathbed. And
Timothy now had to take over responsibilities.
Now it was Timothy's turn to carry on the torch
of the gospel that was about to drop from the
apostle's hand.

In each of these four chapters, the Apostle
Paul seemed to emphasize the different aspects of
Timothy's responsibility. In chapter 1, Timothy
was told to guard the gospel. He was to protect
it, pure and undefiled. In chapter 2, he was told

to suffer for it. In chapter 3, he was told to
continue in it, to abide in it, and not to deflect
from it to the right hand or to the left. And
in chapter 4, he was told to preach it, to make
it known.

THE CHARGE TO GUARD THE GOSPEL

After this introduction, we come to chapter
1 and the charge to guard the gospel. But before
we come to this actual subject which begins with
verse 8, there is an introductory paragraph in
the first seven verses. In these, in a very vivid
way, the characters of both Paul and Timothy, the
writer and the recipient, are introduced to us.
And, in particular, these verses tell us something
of how each of these two men came to be what he
was. These verses throw light on the providence
of God, as we see how God had fashioned Paul and
Timothy to be the kind of men he wanted them to
be.

The Apostleship of Paul

So we'll begin with Paul. Verse 1 (RSV)
says: "Paul, an apostle of Christ Jesus by the
will of God according to the promise of the life
which is in Christ Jesus." Paul claimed to be an
apostle of Christ, and we need to consider that
word.

I am sure you will remember how, at the
very beginning of his public ministry, Jesus
chose twelve men out of the wider group of his
disciples and he himself named these men apostles.
He appointed them to be with him. He deliberately
gave them unrivaled opportunities to hear his
words and to see his works in order that they
might be unique witnesses to Christ of all that
they had seen and heard. And Jesus promised them
a special, extraordinary inspiration of the Holy
Spirit to remind them of his teaching, to teach
them more, and to lead them into all the truth

which it was the purpose of God to reveal to them.

To this select apostolic circle Paul was later added. When Jesus apprehended him and laid hold of him on the Damascus road, he commissioned Paul as an apostle, and Paul could never forget it. Here was Paul, humiliated by men in a dungeon in Rome, awaiting the pleasure of the emperor. Yet, while humiliated by men, he was confident that he was an apostle of Jesus Christ.

The opening verse tells about the origin and object of Paul's apostleship. Its origin was the will of God. "Paul, an apostle of Christ Jesus by the will of God," says verse 1 (RSV). Paul used identical words in two other epistles, and, in nine out of thirteen of his letters, he referred either to the will of God, the call of God, or the command of God through which he had become an apostle. Be clear about this. It was the sustained conviction of Paul from the beginning to the end of his apostolic career, that he was appointed neither by the church, nor by any man or men, nor by himself, but that his apostleship originated in the eternal will and historical call of almighty God through Jesus Christ. That was the origin of his apostleship-- the will of God.

Now the object of his apostleship, the reason why he had been appointed an apostle, was the "promise of the life which is in Christ Jesus." In other words, the great object of his apostleship was to formulate and to preach the gospel--the good news to dying sinners that God has promised them life in Jesus Christ. The gospel offers life, true life, real life, eternal life both here and hereafter. The gospel declares that the only place in which this true life is to be found is in Jesus Christ. And the gospel promises life to every man and woman who is in Christ Jesus.

So that's how Paul introduced himself. He was an apostle of Jesus Christ; his apostleship originated in the will of God and issued in a proclamation of the gospel of God, which is the promise of the life that is in Christ Jesus.

The Making of Timothy

Now we move from Paul to Timothy. To
Timothy "my beloved child," so-called because
Paul had led him to Christ and had become his
father in the gospel. To him Paul sent his customary
greeting, adding mercy: so he sent grace, mercy,
and peace. Grace is shown to the worthless, the
undeserving. Mercy is shown to the helpless who
cannot save themselves. And peace is given to the
restless. God our Father and the Lord Jesus Christ
together constitute the one source from which flows
this threefold stream of grace and mercy and peace.

In verses 3 to 7 came a very personal
paragraph in which the apostle expressed his deep
thanksgiving to God for Timothy. Now I want to
ask you to notice this very carefully. Paul
thanked God for Timothy. And the only reason
he could thank God for Timothy was that he was
quite sure it was God who had made Timothy what
he was. Now Timothy was not an apostle like Paul.
But Timothy was a Christian, he was a missionary
or minister, and he was an apostolic delegate.
And God had been at work in Timothy to make him
what he was. I find it fascinating that in this
next paragraph, directly or indirectly, Paul
mentioned four major influences which had contributed
to the shaping and the making of Timothy.

The first was his parental upbringing. We
skip to verse 5 for a moment: "I am reminded of
your sincere faith, a faith that dwelt first in
your grandmother Lois and your mother Eunice"
(RSV). Now this reference to mother and grandmother
was quite in order, because every man and woman
is the product of his inheritance to a great extent.
There is no doubt that the most formative influence
of every one of us is our parentage and our home.
The Bible taught this long before modern psychology
discovered it. And this is the reason why good
biographies never begin with their subject, but

with his parents and probably with his grandparents
as well. Now Timothy had a godly home. We know
from Acts 16, verse 1, that his father was a Greek,
and presumably an unbeliever. But his mother
Eunice was a believing Jewess who later became a
Christian, and before her, his grandmother Lois
also had been converted. These women had instructed
Timothy out of the Old Testament before his conversion,
so we read in chapter 3, verse 15, that from
childhood Timothy had been acquainted with the
sacred Scriptures. Now this was the first influence
upon Timothy: his parental upbringing, a mother
and a grandmother who were sincere believers and
who taught him out of the Scriptures from his
childhood. Anybody here who has been born and
bred in a Christian home has received from God a
blessing beyond price.

The second influence on Timothy was his
spiritual friendship. After our parents, it is
our friends who influence us most, especially if
our friends are also our teachers. Timothy had
in the Apostle Paul an outstanding teacher-friend.
We already have seen that Paul was Timothy's father
through the gospel, in that he led Timothy to
Christ. But having led him to Christ, Paul did
not desert, forget, or abandon him as we so often
do with new believers. Instead, Paul constantly
remembered him. Three times in this paragraph
he says, "I remember you constantly in my prayers."
"I remember your tears." "I am reminded of your
sincere faith" (RSV). Timothy, I have never
forgotten you. Paul took Timothy with him on his
missionary journeys. When they parted, Timothy
could not restrain his tears. Mindful of his tears,
Paul longed, as Bishop Moule in his commentary
puts it, "with a homesick yearning, night and day,
to see him that he might be filled with joy."
Until Paul could see Timothy again, he prayed for
him unceasingly. And from time to time he wrote
Timothy letters of counsel and encouragement, like
this one which we are studying now. Such a Christian
friendship, including the companionship and the

prayers and the letters which a Christian friendship will involve, did not fail to have a powerful molding influence upon Timothy, strengthening and sustaining him in his Christian life and service.

The third influence in Timothy's life was a special endowment. At this point in his letter, Paul turned from looking at indirect means by which God had shaped Timothy's Christian character--his parents and his friends--to look at a direct gift that God had given him. Verse 6 says: "I remind you to rekindle the gift of God that is within you through the laying on of my hands" (RSV). What this divine gift was we don't know for certain, for the simple reason that we are not told. Nevertheless, we can make tentative guesses. It is clear from this verse and from 1 Timothy 4:14 that whatever this gift was, it was given to Timothy when Paul and the elders laid their hands on him in what we would call his ordination. It was therefore an ordination gift--a gift related to the ministry for which he was set apart. It may have been the ministry itself, which is a great gift of God, as some commentators think. Or it may have been the gift of an evangelist to which Paul referred later in his epistle. Or, since he proceeded at once to refer to verse 7 to the Holy Spirit, it may have been some special endowment, some special anointing of the Holy Spirit at his ordination, to equip him for the ministry to which God had called him. Perhaps we can best sum it up in Alfred Thomas' words: "It was the authority and the power to be a minister of Jesus Christ."

So we have learned that a man is not only what he owes to his parents, his friends, and his teachers, but a man is also what God has made him by calling him to some particular ministry and by endowing him with appropriate natural and spiritual gifts.

The fourth influence on Timothy was personal discipline. All God's gifts, natural and spiritual, need to be developed and used by us. So Paul told Timothy here not to neglect his gift, but rather

to kindle it. The Greek verb _anazopureo_ is used
of a fire. It likens this gift of God in Timothy
to a fire. And the Greek verb contains a prefix
which can mean either to stir up the fire or to
rekindle it if it has died down. This doesn't
necessarily mean that Timothy had let the fire
die down and must now fan the dying embers into
a flame again. It could equally well be an
exhortation to Timothy to continue fanning it.
The J. B. Phillips translation says, "Stir up
that inner fire," and Abbott-Smith says, "Keep
it in full flame." Presumably, this stirring
comes by exercising the gift faithfully and by
waiting upon God in prayer for its constant
renewal. Having issued this appeal to stir up
the inner fire, Paul immediately went on to give
Timothy a ground for doing so--verse 7: "For
God did not give us a spirit of timidity" (RSV),
so you don't need to be afraid of exercising your
ministry, "but a spirit of power" in which to
exercise your ministry, "and of love" in order
to channel your gift rightly. You don't use
your gift for self-advertisement, self-assertion,
or vain glory, but in loving ministry to other
people, and with self-control so as to exercise
your gift with seemly reverence and restraint.

So far in these first seven verses we have
studied what these two men, Paul and Timothy, had
become. We have considered their making--what
made them what they were. Paul claimed he was
an apostle of Jesus Christ by the will of God.
But he said in another place that God did not
give him his grace in vain because he labored as
an apostle. Similarly, a whole complex of factors
had made Timothy what he was: godly upbringing,
Paul's friendship,, God's gift to him, and also
his personal self-discipline.

My friends, I want to urge upon you, whoever
you may be, the conviction that it is exactly the
same with you and me today. The most striking
lesson that we can learn from these verses is the
dovetailing, in both Paul and Timothy, of divine

sovereignty and human responsibility. Paul could say, "By the grace of God I am what I am." But he could add, "I labored." Timothy's mother and grandmother taught him out of the Scriptures; Paul befriended him, prayed for him, read to him, exhorted him; God gave him a special gift; but still Timothy had to stir up the gift that was within him by his own self-discipline. So it is with us. However much or however little we may have received from God, either directly in natural or spiritual endowments, or indirectly through our parents, friends, and teachers, we still must apply ourselves to active self-discipline so as to cooperate with the grace of God and to fan the inner fire into flame. You and I must do this if we are ever to become the men and women God wants us to be.

Responsibility to the Gospel

We come now to verses 8 to 18. Paul turned from the complex factors that had helped make Timothy, to the truth of the gospel, and Timothy's responsibility towards it. He began verse 8, "Do not be ashamed . . . but take your share of suffering (RSV). This is a theme that we will refer to several times. You may be young, frail, and timid, and you may shrink from the tasks to which God is calling you, but God has molded you and gifted you for your ministry. Now don't be ashamed and don't be afraid to exercise it. Paul went on to say, don't be afraid of Christ, of bearing witness to Christ, and don't be afraid of me, his prisoner. Many were afraid, many turned away from Paul when he was arrested, but Paul said to Timothy, Don't be afraid of me. It is possible not to be afraid of Christ, but to be afraid or ashamed of the people of Christ. It is possible to be a Christian on the campus and not want to associate with the Inter-Varsity group or chapter because you are ashamed of them. Paul said, Don't be ashamed of Christ, don't be ashamed of me, and don't be ashamed

of the gospel. These are the three things we must
never be ashamed of. For this temptation is
strong. Every one of us knows it. Otherwise
Jesus would never have warned us, "If any man
is ashamed of me and of my words in this generation,
of him also will the Son of Man be ashamed."

After that introductory exhortation to not
be ashamed, Paul enlarged on the gospel--the gospel
which is committed to Timothy, the gospel of which
he is not to be ashamed, and the gospel for which
he has to suffer. Paul first wrote in verses 9
and 10 what the gospel is, and then in verses 11
to 14 he outlined our responsibility in relation
to it.

Well, what is the gospel? The end of verse
8 says, "Take your share of suffering for the gospel
in the power of God who saved us . . ." (RSV).
Exactly. It is impossible to speak of the gospel
without speaking of salvation in the same breath--
because the gospel is the good news of salvation.
Have we not been thinking of this at Christmas?
"I bring you good news of a great joy, . . . for
unto you is born . . . a savior."

What did Paul tell us about salvation in
these verses? Three things. First, he described
the character of salvation--what it is. What is
salvation? I have to tell you it is more than
forgiveness of sin. The God who saved us
simultaneously (v. 9) called us with a holy calling.
An holy calling is an integral part of the plan
of salvation. Salvation denotes that comprehensive
purpose of God by which he justifies, sanctifies,
and glorifies his people. First he pardons their
offenses and accepts them as righteous in his sight
through Christ. This is justification. Then he
progressively transforms them by the Holy Spirit
into the image of Christ. This is sanctification.
Finally they become like Christ in heaven when
they see him as he is. This is glorification.
I beg you, do not minimize the greatness of our
great salvation. The gospel is bigger than most
of our minds have taken in of it. It is the

transformation of our whole personality, including,
on the resurrection morning, our bodies transformed
into the body of glory that Jesus Christ is wearing.
This is the great character of salvation.

Second, Paul tells us the source of salvation.
Where does it come from? "Not in virtue of our
works but in virtue of his own purpose and the
grace which he gave us in Christ Jesus ages ago"
(v. 9 RSV). If you want to trace the river of
salvation to its source, you have to look right
back beyond time to a past eternity. The J. B.
Phillips translation says, "Before time began."
The New English Bible says, "From all eternity."
Before eternal ages, before history and time started,
the apostle says, it was the purpose of God to give
us his grace which he actually gave us in Christ
Jesus. He gave it to us before we existed; he gave
it to us before history began. And therefore it
is quite plain that the source of salvation is not
our own works. The Father gave us his grace in
Christ before we did any good works, before we
were born and could do any good works--indeed,
before history, before time in eternity. Now,
the doctrine of election seems difficult to our
finite minds, but the doctrine of election is
incontrovertibly a biblical doctrine. It emphasizes
that salvation is due to God's grace, not man's
merit. It is due not to our good works performed
in time, but to God's purpose of grace conceived
in eternity. There is nothing that engenders
gratitude and humility and excludes all boasting
in the presence of God like the doctrine of election.

That brings me to the third teaching here
about salvation. This is the ground of salvation--
that upon which it rests--the historical work of
Christ at his appearing. That this grace that is
given us "in Christ Jesus ages ago, and now has
manifested [historically in time] through the
appearing of our Savior Christ Jesus, who abolished
death and brought life and immortality to light
through the gospel" (v. 10 RSV). This is the
historical outworking, through the coming, death ,

and resurrection of Jesus Christ, of the eternal
purpose of grace that God has given us in Christ
Jesus.

Let us meditate for a moment or two on this
triumphant affirmation that Christ abolished death.
I tell you, if Christians believed that and lived
it out in the world, the world would sit up and
take notice. The world is afraid of death. You
can evaluate a religion almost better than in any
other way when you see its attitude to death. And
only when you see Christian people triumphant in
the face of death do you see Christianity as it
really is. Death summarizes our human predicament
as a result of sin. Death is the wages of sin.
Death is the grim penalty of sin--physical death,
which is the separation of the soul from the body;
spiritual death, which is the separation of the
soul from God; and eternal death, which is the
separation of both soul and body from God in hell
forever. All these deaths of which the Bible speaks
are due to sin. They are sin's just reward.

But Jesus Christ has abolished death and
brought life and immortality to life through the
gospel. Now the Greek verb for "abolish" does
not mean that he has eliminated it, as we know
it, from everyday experience. Certain ones of us
still are dead in trespasses and sins and must be
born again. All human beings die physically, and
there are many who are going to die the final, the
second death. But what is triumphantly asserted
here is that Christ has defeated death. He has
overthrown it. The New English Bible says, "He
has broken the power of death." As Paul says in
1 Corinthians 15, Death is like a scorpion whose
sting has been drawn. It's still alive but it's
harmless because its sting has been drawn. Death
is like a military conqueror whose power has been
overthrown, and Paul can shout triumphantly, "O
death, where is thy sting? O grave, where is thy
victory?" Death is defeated. Physical death is
only a trivial episode in the life of a Christian,
a gateway to fullness and newness of life. When

a man comes to Jesus Christ in penitence and faith,
he is given eternal life and death is passed away.
On the last day, this life will be consummated in
heaven. In these ways Jesus Christ has abolished
death, and through the gospel he has brought life
and immortality to light. This is the revelation
of the gospel. This is what has been brought to
light in the gospel. The gospel is the promise
of life in Christ Jesus with death defeated.

Such, then, is the salvation that is offered
us in the gospel. Its character is man's transformation
into the holiness of Christ. Its source is God's
eternal purpose of grace. Its ground is Christ's
historical appearing and abolition of death.

Our Duty to the Gospel

Now in the last few moments that we have,
we will turn from God's gospel to our duty in
relation to it. Of course, our first duty (which
Paul doesn't mention here but takes for granted)
is to embrace it and believe it. Timothy had
already done that. So in the next verses, Paul
gives Timothy three duties. First is the duty to
communicate the gospel. "For this gospel I was
appointed a preacher and apostle and teacher"
(v. 11 RSV). The apostles formulated the gospel.
Today there are no apostles of Jesus Christ. In
the Christian church's early years, the apostles
formulated the gospel and bequeathed it to the
church. So if you want to find it in its definitive
form, you have to look to the New Testament. Now,
this apostolic New Testament faith is regulative
for the church in every place and in every age.
There is no other gospel. There can be no new
gospel different from what the apostles received,
formulated, and preserved in New Testament Scripture.
However, although there are no apostles of Christ
today, there are preachers and teachers who give
themselves to the work of expounding and proclaiming
and communicating the gospel. And that is our first
duty to the gospel--to make it known.

Our second duty is to <u>suffer for it</u>. See
verse 12: "For this gospel I was appointed a
preacher and apostle and teacher and therefore I
suffer as I do. But I am not ashamed" (RSV). Have
any of you ever asked yourself why is it that people
suffer for the gospel? Why do men hate the gospel
and oppose the gospel? I believe the answer, very
simply, is this: according to the gospel, God saves
sinners in virtue of his own purpose and grace and
not in virtue of their good works. It is just the
freeness of the gospel which offends. The natural
man, who is not a Christian, hates to have to admit
the gravity of his sin and guilt. He hates to have
to admit his helplessness to save himself. He hates
to have to admit the indispensable necessity of
God's grace through Christ's sin-bearing death to
save him, and, therefore, his inescapable indebtedness
to the cross. The natural man hates it.

I remember, when I was a student at Cambridge
University trying to explain to a fellow student
that the good news of Christ is free. Salvation
is a free gift and he could not earn it and he could
not deserve it. And I shall never forget how, as
he sat in a chair in my room there at Trinity College,
Cambridge, he shouted at the top of his voice three
times, "Horrible! Horrible! Horrible!" I thank
God for that experience. I was given a naked awareness
of the hatred of the human heart for the gospel.

Because men hate the gospel which humbles
them, they will oppose and persecute those who
preach it. Every preacher knows the temptation
to trim the gospel and to leave out the unpopular
and unpalatable parts so that he will not have to
suffer for it. But we are called to communicate
the gospel and we are called to suffer for the
gospel.

Third, we are called to <u>guard the gospel</u>.
See verses 13 and 14 (we'll skip verse 12 for a
moment): "Follow the pattern of the sound words
which you have heard from me" (RSV). Paul was saying,
Timothy, you've received sound words--the gospel--
from me. You've heard it in a pattern, on a prototype.

Now follow this and hold onto it. Verse 14 continues, "Guard the truth that has been entrusted to you." The Greek word for this means "deposit." The gospel is a deposit (paratheke). It is a treasure that has been entrusted to us and we've got to guard it. The Greek verb phulassein for "to guard" is a military word that is used of guarding a palace to prevent people from breaking into it. It's used of guarding possessions against their being stolen. It's used of guarding a prisoner to prevent his escape. And it's used of the gospel. We must not allow the gospel to be lost. We must not allow it to be damaged. We are called to guard it. It's a precious treasure. Timothy had to do this because, as the last verses go on to say, all Asia had turned away from Paul and his gospel. Onesiphorus was a bright exception to the general rule. And as all Asia was at this time turning away from Paul, he says, Oh, Timothy, don't you turn away as well. Guard the deposit that has been entrusted to you.

And so I finish. The gospel is good news of salvation. It was promised from eternity, was secured and purchased by Jesus Christ, and is now offered to friends. First, we must communicate it faithfully, we shall undoubtedly suffer for it. And when we suffer for it, we shall be tempted to trim it and to eliminate the elements that provoke opposition. So then, third, and above all, we must guard it against every possible corruption, keeping it pure whatever the cost. Guard it faithfully, spread it actively, suffer for it bravely—that is our threefold duty. These are the gospel.

2. God's Man: The Charge to Suffer for the Gospel
by John R. W. Stott

Let's open our Bibles to the second letter of Paul to Timothy, chapter 2. We entitled chapter 1 "The Charge to Guard or to Protect the Gospel," and we will call chapter 2 "The Charge to Suffer for the Gospel." Although suffering is not the only theme for this chapter, it is the predominant theme.

THE CHARGE TO PROTECT THE GOSPEL

Let me read you now the first two verses: "You then, my son, be strong in the grace that is in Christ Jesus. And what you have heard from me before many witnesses entrust to faithful men who will be able to teach others also" (RSV). That is the stirring exhortation with which the chapter begins. Let us look at it for a few moments. At the end of chapter 1 of 2 Timothy, we were told that all Asia had turned away from Paul except Onesiphorus and his household, who were a bright, outstanding exception. It was in contrast to this multitude who had turned away from Paul and had repudiated his authority that the apostle said to Timothy, "Now you, my son, are to be different."

First, then, there is a call to be strong. Timothy was weak; Timothy was timid. Yet he was called to a position of leadership in the church-- and in an area in which Paul's authority was rejected.

It is as if Paul said to him, "Listen Timothy, never mind what other people say, never mind what other people think, never mind what other people do; you are to be strong. Never mind how shy you feel, never mind how weak you feel; you are to be strong." That is the first thing.

Second, you are to be strong in the grace that is in Christ Jesus. If the exhortation had simply been "be strong," it would have been absurd indeed. You might as well tell a snail to be quick or a horse to fly as to tell a weak man to be strong, or a shy man to be brave. But Paul's calling Timothy to fortitude is a Christian and not a stoical exhortation. Timothy was not to be strong in himself. He was not just to grit his teeth and clench his fists and set his jaw. No, he was, as the Greek literally means, to be strengthened with the grace that is in Christ Jesus, to find his resources for Christian service not in his own nature, but in the grace of Jesus Christ.

This is an exhortation, first, to be strong; second, to be strong in the grace that is in Christ Jesus; and third, to be strong for the ministry to which Timothy had been called.

I want to remind you that yesterday we saw Paul in prison for the second time, awaiting trial and anticipating to be sentenced to death. In that situation it was essential for the Apostle Paul to make some arrangements for the preservation of the truth and for its accurate transmission to succeeding generations.

In verse 2 he envisaged four stages in the transmission. The first was that he himself had received the truth as a deposit from God. The second was that he now entrusted the deposit to Timothy. He had done so before many witnesses in his public teaching. Third, Timothy was to entrust it to faithful men. Presumably this meant ministers of the Word, Christian elders whose responsibility—like that of Jewish elders of the Old Testament—was to preserve the tradition. Fourth, these men were to be the sort of people who would be competent

to teach others also because of their ability to
teach, and because of their integrity and faithfulness.
    Now let me say, with all the emphasis at my
command, that this is the only kind of apostolic
succession which the apostles themselves envisaged.
It was a succession of apostolic tradition. It was
a transmission of apostolic doctrine handed down
unchanged from the apostles to the generations which
followed--from God to Paul, from Paul to Timothy,
from Timothy to faithful men, and from faithful
men to others also, which includes ourselves. This
was to be the succession, and the succession was
a transmission, not of authority by the laying on
of hands, but of the gospel, of the good deposit
of the apostolic faith of Scripture passed down
from the apostles from generation to generation
to generation, like the Olympic torch from hand
to hand. Now this, my friends, is our responsibility
in this generation. We have received the deposits.
How? From Scripture. This is where the apostolic
deposit is today--in Scripture. We receive it from
Scripture, and we pass it on to other people.

Qualities of a Christian Worker

    Now the Apostle Paul went on to illustrate
this, our fundamental task, in the rest of the
chapter by a number of illuminating metaphors:
three in the first part of the chapter, and three
in the second part of the chapter. Each of these
metaphors illustrates a different aspect of our
responsibility in the transmission of biblical
truth to our own generation, and the generation
that follows us.
    The first three metaphors are favorites--
the soldier, the athlete, and the farmer. We come
across them in several parts of Scripture. Let's
look at them one by one.

The Soldier

    First, the Christian worker is a dedicated

soldier (vv. 3-4). And the good soldier is so-called
in this passage because his dedication includes a
willingness to suffer, and a willingness to concentrate.
First Paul spoke of a willingness to suffer. (v. 3):
"Take your share of suffering as a good soldier
of Christ Jesus" (RSV). Soldiers on active service
do not expect a safe or easy time. They take
hardship, risk, and suffering as a matter of course.
These things are part and parcel of a soldier's
calling. So, too, is the Christian's calling. If
a Christian is loyal to the transmission of the
gospel, he must expect opposition, persecution,
and ridicule.

However, a soldier is not only dedicated
in his willingness to suffer but also in his
willingness to concentrate. (v. 4): "No soldier
on service gets entangled in civilian pursuits,
since his aim is to satisfy the one who enlisted
him" (RSV). He doesn't "get entangled in business,"
as J. B. Phillips puts it. On the contrary, he
frees himself from civilian affairs, in order to
give himself to soldiery, and so to "be wholly at
his commanding officer's disposal" (NEB). I remember
so often in World War II people would say to one
another, with a wry smile, "There's a war on."
It was a watchword, amply sufficient to justify
any austerity or self-denial, or abstention from
innocent activities, and it was necessary because
of the current emergency. So, too, the Christian
life is like this.

Now, don't misunderstand this. The Christian
is living in the world, and he cannot avoid his
ordinary, secular duties in the home, at his business,
on the campus, and in his academic work. And every
Christian should be known for his hard work and his
good degrees on the campus and in the wider community.
The Bible leaves us in no doubt that the Christian
is to be a good citizen. And in all things he
should be outstandingly conscientious. But what
is forbidden to the Christian soldier, the good
soldier of Jesus Christ, is not all secular
activities, but, rather, entanglements. Although

these may be perfectly innocent in themselves, they distract him from fighting Christ's battles. This should be especially true of the minister and the missionary who are set apart for the transmission and communication of the truth. But, in a secondary sense, it is true of every Christian who, through careful thought and prayer, must decide where he draws the line between what is essential as his Christian duty in secular activities, and what is an entanglement which he must set aside. Now then, every Christian worker is a soldier, even timid Timothy, because whatever our temperament, we cannot avoid conflict. And if we are to be good soldiers, we will be dedicated soldiers, committing ourselves to a life of hardship and suffering and renouncing the entanglements of the world.

The Athlete

Next, the second metaphor is a law-abiding athlete. Paul turns from the Roman soldier to the competitor in the Greek games. "An athlete is not crowned unless he competes according to the rules" (v. 5 RSV). In other words, in no athletic contest is the competitor giving a random show of strength or skill. Every sport has its rules and every event has its prize as well. In older days the prize was not a silver trophy but an evergreen wreath that was placed upon the head of the successful competitor. But no athlete, however brilliant, was ever crowned with this evergreen wreath unless he had competed according to the rules. "No rules, no wreath" was the order of the day. Now the Christian life is like a race, not in the sense that we are competing with one another, but in the sense that we have to keep the rules. We have to run the Christian race, to live the Christian life, lawfully. The Greek word is <u>nomimos</u> ("according to the law").

I want to say a word here about the new morality. The new moralists tell us that the

category of law has been altogether abolished in
the Christian life. They are talking sheer,
unadulterated rubbish. The Christian is under
obligation to live _nomimos_, according to the law.
He is to keep the rules. He is not under the
law for salvation or as a way of salvation. He
is under grace, not under the law. But he is under
the law as a guide to conduct. There is no crown
otherwise. Our law-abiding works can never justify
us. But without them, without obedience to the
law, we shall prove that we have never been justified.

The Farmer

The third metaphor is the hard-working farmer
(v. 6). It is the hard-working farmer who ought
to have the first share of the crops. If an athlete
must play fair, a farmer must work hard. He toils
at his work. Hard work is indispensable to good
farming, especially in underdeveloped countries
before mechanization arrives, where successful
farming depends as much on sweat as on skill.
However poor the soil, however inclement the weather,
however disinclined the farmer, he simply can't
afford to be a sluggard. He must keep at his work.
Having put his hand to the plow, he must not look
back. And the first share in the harvest will go
to the hard-working farmer. He deserves it. And
only if he has worked hard and persevered in his
work can he expect a good crop.

What's the application of that? Well, there
are several possible ones. I want to tell you first
that holiness is a harvest. It's the fruit of the
Spirit because the Holy Spirit is the chief farmer.
But we also have our part to play. We are told to
sow to the Spirit, to be disciplined in prayer and
in meditation in the Scripture, and to be in
attendance at other means of grace. There are many
Christians I meet who are surprised they are not
gaining the victory over temptation and that they
are not growing in Christian holiness. If someone
here is like that, I ask you, Is it because you

are a sluggard? Is it because you are not cultivating the field of your character? Why should you expect the fruit of holiness if you take no trouble in your Christian life? As Bishop Ryle, in his great book on holiness, says again and again, "There are no gains without pains in the Christian life." It is the hard-working farmer who has the first share in the crop.

If holiness is a harvest, the winning of souls is a harvest also. "The harvest is plentiful," Jesus said. Yes, and of course it is God who chiefly gives the growth. But again we have no liberty to be idle. Both the sowing of the good seed of God's Word and the reaping of the harvest are hard work. especially when the laborers are few. How we need to learn in our generation that the winning of souls is hard work. Souls are not won by the slick, automatic application of a formula Souls are won by tears and sweat and pain, especially in prayer, and in sacrificial personal friendship. Do you want to win a harvest on the campus? Remember, it is the hard-working farmer who has the first share in the crop. Soul winning is difficult, not easy.

Here, then, are three qualities of the wholehearted Christian worker who seeks to transmit the gospel that he has received from Scripture and pass it on to others: the dedication of a good soldier; the law-abiding obedience of a good athlete; and the painstaking labor of a good farmer. Without these, we simply cannot expect results.

Now verse 7 concludes that paragraph, "Think over what I say, for the Lord will grant you [the better manuscripts make it a promise rather than a prayer] understanding in everything" (RSV). I wish I had half an hour to preach to you on that verse. It is a very important verse of Scripture, and it combines two things which many evangelical Christians separate. "Think over what I say, for the Lord will grant you understanding in all things." There are some Christians who never get down to any serious Bible study. All they do is

skim through a passage of Scripture in a haphazard
and desultory way, like a butterfly flitting from
flower to flower. They hope and pray that the
Spirit may possibly show them what their readings
mean. But they do no hard work. There are other
Christians who are very diligent at their study.
They are hard-working farmers, as it were. They
use their minds, they grapple with the text of
Scripture, they compare the versions, they consult
the commentaries, they pore over the concordances.
But they forget thst it is only the Lord, ultimately,
who grants, (notice, it's a gift) understanding in
everything. So let's not divorce what God has
joined together. If you want to understand the
Scripture, then a balanced combination of thought
and prayer is essential. We must both give our
minds to the study of Scripture and look to the
Lord to give us understanding. "Consider what I
say and the Lord will give you understanding in
all things."

SUFFERING: THE CONDITION OF BLESSING

That brings us to verses 8 to 13. So far,
if you have followed me carefully, I think you will
agree that this has all been a variation upon one
theme: nothing that is worthwhile is ever easy.
No soldier, no athlete, no farmer ever expects
results without labor and suffering. In other
words, suffering is the condition of blessing.
Having illustrated this from the soldier, the athlete
and the farmer, Paul further enforced it from
experience: (a) the experience of Christ, (b) the
experience of the Apostle Paul himself, and (c)
the experience of every Christian believer (vv.
8-13). Let's look at this very briefly.

Christ's Suffering

First, the experience of Christ: "Remember
Jesus Christ, risen from the dead, descended from
David, as preached in my gospel" (v. 8 RSV). One

reason why Paul told Timothy to remember Jesus Christ is that Jesus Christ is the heart of the gospel. In these little phrases, "risen from the dead" and "descended from David," we really have the heart of the gospel. We have the divine-human Person and the saving work of Christ. "Of the seed of David" tells us that Jesus was human, born of the seed of David. But "risen from the dead" tells us that he was designated the Son of God with power, by the resurrection from the dead. "Risen from the dead," "descended from David," speaks of his humanity and his divinity. However, this verse speaks not only of his person but also of his work. "Risen from the dead" tells us that he died for our sins, and that he was raised from the dead to prove the efficacy of his sin-bearing sacrifice. "Of the seed of David" reminds us that he came to establish his kingdom as great David's greater Son. He was the king of David's line, he was the Savior who suffered and died and rose again, and he was the King who sits upon David's throne.

There was also another reason why Timothy had to remember Jesus Christ. Not only because Christ, risen from the dead and of the seed of David, is the essence of the gospel, but also because Christ's own experience illustrates the principle that death is the gateway to life, and suffering is the road to glory. He who rose again is he who died, and he who is reigning in glory upon David's throne was born in lowliness as David's seed. "Now Timothy, meditate on that," Paul was saying. "And when you get hold of that you will realize that you are called to suffering. You learn it from the experience of Christ. And if you are tempted to avoid pain and suffering in your ministry, Timothy, remember Jesus Christ, and think again."

Paul's Suffering

Then we turn from the experience of Christ to the experience of Paul: "The gospel for which

I am suffering and wearing fetters like a criminal.
But the word of God is not fettered. Therefore
I endure everything for the sake of the elect, that
they also may obtain the salvation which in Christ
Jesus goes with eternal glory" (vv. 9-10 RSV).
Paul was suffering for the gospel. Paul was
languishing in a Roman dungeon. Paul was enduring
the painful humiliation of wearing fetters or chains
upon his hands and feet, like a common criminal.
But although he was chained, the Word of God was
not chained. Even in prison, at his first defense
he was able to preach the gospel, and he could still
write letters expounding the gospel.

Now this is the point I want us to notice
very carefully: the relation between Paul's
sufferings and the effectiveness of the gospel was
not just one of contrast. "I am chained, the
gospel is not." It was actually one of cause and
effect.

The Christian's Suffering

Now look at this very carefully and note
verse 10: "Therefore I endure everything for the
sake of the elect, that they also may obtain the
salvation" (RSV). In some sense the elect were
to attain salvation through Paul's sufferings.
Now this seems to be an amazing truth, that somehow
the salvation of men and women in the world today
may be secured by our sufferings. Of course our
sufferings do not have any redemptive efficacy
like the sin-bearing suffering and death of Christ.
No, no. But the elect are saved through the
gospel which we must preach. And when we do preach,
we must suffer for the gospel. Any man or woman
who is faithful in preaching the gospel will suffer
for the gospel, and through that suffering will
bring salvation in the providence of God to the
elect. This is a profound truth on which to
meditate. Suffering is the experience of Christ,
the experience of Paul, and common Christian
experience.

This is described in verses 11 to 13 by a quotation from some common proverb, some "logos," as Paul called it, maybe some Christian hymn which he declared to be reliable. "The saying is sure" (v. 11 RSV). And this saying consists of two pairs of epigrams. The first pair is about those who remain true and endure. The second pair is about those who become false and faithless.

In the first pair, we see that the Christian life is a life of dying (v. 11) and enduring (v. 12a). It is dying with Christ. The thought here is not of the death to sin of which Romans 6 speaks, but of a death to self and a death to safety. Every Christian is called to die to himself as he takes up his cross and follows Christ. It is only if we die with him that we shall live with him, and it is only if we suffer with him and endure that we shall reign with him. The path to life is death, the path to reigning and glory is suffering. It is true of every Christian.

The second pair of epigrams concerns the dreadful possibility of our denying Jesus Christ (v. 12b) and proving faithless (v. 13). First, at the end of verse 12: "If we deny him, he also will deny us" (RSV). He said so. It is in the gospels. If we deny him, he will deny us. But if we are faithless, he remains faithful. Now probably, in this context, that doesn't mean that he is faithful to his promises (although he is), but, rather, that he is faithful to his threats. When he gives this terrible threat--if you deny me, I will deny you--he is faithful to his threat. Why? Because he cannot deny himself. And if he was not faithful to what he had said, he would deny himself. Rather than deny himself, he will deny us, if we deny him. Again, there is a great deal to think about here.

Now let us conclude the first part of the chapter, and see if we can restate the main theme that is expounded. From secular analogy: soldiers, farmers, and athletes; and from spiritual experience: Christ's, Paul's, and every believer's, we have learned one main lesson: that blessing comes through pain, fruit through toil, life through death, and glory through suffering. In other words, let us never expect the Christian life and Christian service to be easy. Why should we? The Bible gives us no such expectation. Rather, in the reverse, the Bible says again and again, No cross, no crown; no rules, no wreath; no pains, no gains. It is this principle that took Christ through lowly birth, and even lowlier death to his glorious resurrection and reign. It is this principle that brought Paul his chains, his fetters, and his prison cell, in order that he might obtain salvation for the elect. It is this principle that makes every soldier willing to endure hardship; the athlete, discipline; and the farmer, toil. I say again, never expect your Christian service to cost you nothing. Christian service is a costly thing. And that is why Paul began the chapter, "My son, be strong in the grace that is in Christ Jesus."

Now then, we come to the second part of the chapter in which we are given three more metaphors. In verse 15, a Christian worker is called "a workman who has no need to be ashamed." In verse 21, he is "a vessel for noble use." And in verse 24, he is "the Lord's servant" (RSV). So the active Christian is the Lord's workman, the Lord's vessel, and the Lord's servant. What is the characteristic that is expected of each?

THE LORD'S WORKMAN

First, the unashamed workman in verses 14 to 19. Now, let's look at verse 15: "Do your best to present yourself to God as one approved, a workman who has no need to be ashamed, rightly handling the Word of truth" (RSV). It is quite clear from this that the kind of work the Christian workman does is teaching. His work concerns the Word of truth. It is also clear that there are two kinds of workmen: one who is approved, tested and tried, and who passes the test; and one who is

not approved. One has no reason to be ashamed and
the other has every reason to be ashamed. It is
also clear that the difference between these two
kinds of workmen--approved, not approved; ashamed,
not ashamed--has to do with their handling or
treatment of the Word of truth. Paul puts these
two workmen in contrast to one another. Timothy
was to be a good workman, approved and not ashamed.
But in verse 17 we read of Hymenaeus and Philetus
who, on the other hand, were false teachers and
bad workmen. They forfeited God's approval and
had every reason to be ashamed.

Now please follow me carefully. The work
of these workmen in relation to the truth--Timothy,
the good workman; Hymenaeus and Philetus, the bad
workmen--is summed up in pregnant verbs. In verse
15, we are told that the good workman cuts straight
the Word of truth. According to the Greek word
"handling" means he cuts it straight. In verse 18,
we find that the bad workman swerves from the truth,
deviates from it. These two possibilities are in
contrast.

Let's look at the good workman. The Greek
verb in verse 15 is _orthotomeo_, and literally it
does not mean "to divide rightly," but "to cut
straight." It only comes three times in biblical
Greek--once here, and twice in the book of Proverbs.
In Proverbs 3:6 we are told that God will cut
straight our paths. So you see, the Word of truth,
which is the Scripture, is pictured as a road or
a path. And this road is to be cut straight,
straight as a freeway that goes right across the
countryside. The Arndt-Gingrich Greek lexicon
says that this means "to cut a path in a straight
direction, or to cut a road across the country,
a country that is forested or otherwise difficult
to pass through; to cut it in a straight direction
so that the traveler may go directly to his destination."
Or possibly the metaphor is taken not from road
building but from plowing, so that the New English
Bible translates it "driving a straight furrow, in
your proclamation of the truth."

Now what does that mean? I suggest to you
it can only mean one thing. In our exposition,
the Word of truth is the Scripture, the apostolic
faith of the New Testament, and to cut it straight,
or to make it as a straight path, is to be accurate
on the one hand and plain and simple on the other.
The good workman is true to Scripture. He does
not falsify it and he handles it with such care
that he stays on the path himself, keeping to the
highway, avoiding the byways. And he makes it
essy for people to follow. That is the good workman,
cutting it straight, expounding it accurately,
making it simple for people to follow and to
understand.

The second metaphor describes the bad
workman and it is a metaphor taken not from civil
engineering but from the sport of archery (v. 18).
Here the truth is likened not to a road that is
being built or to a furrow that is being plowed,
but to a target. The Greek word is <u>stochos</u>, meaning
"a target that is being shot at." And the Greek
verb <u>astocheo</u> here means "to miss the target."
You shoot at the target but you swerve from it and
miss it altogether. Are we clear that there are
two alternatives set before us in our handling of
the Word of truth? Every Christian teacher, if
he shoots at the truth, can either hit it or miss
it. And as he cuts the road, he can either make
it straight or he can make it tortuous and crooked.
As a result, other people are affected for better
or for worse. If we cut the road straight it will
be easy for other people to keep on the road and
to follow us. If we shoot at the target and miss
the mark, then the attention of other people is
distracted from the target, watching the arrow as
it goes astray.

Of this danger the Apostle Paul warned
Timothy. False teachers were denying the resurrection.
Paul referred to their word battles, their "godless
chatter." He said that their teaching spread like
gangrene and was very dangerous. They upset the
faith of their followers whereas God's firm foundation,

the true church, stood sure. And (in v. 19 RSV)
it had a double seal: the secret seal--"the Lord
knows those who are his"; and the visible seal--
"Let every one who names the name of the Lord
depart from evil."

THE LORD'S VESSEL

This reference to the need to depart from
evil brings us to the second metaphor, which is
the clean vessel (vv. 20-22). The picture here
is quite clear. In every house of every kind
there are vessels or utensils. And in a great
house these are many and varied. There are gold
and silver vessels for noble use, for the personal
service of the master of the house. And there are
wood and earthenware vessels for menial use in the
kitchen and in the scullery. So in God's house,
the church, there are true members and there are
counterfeit members. It's only the true members,
who prove their reality by their purity, who are
fit for the Master's use.

And, my brother and sister, is that not
your greatest desire? As I think of it, I may
humbly say it is my greatest desire to be a vessel
fit for noble use, ready for any good work, consecrated
and useful to the Lord Jesus, the Master of the house.
Can there be any greater privilege in the whole
world than to be a vessel in the hands of Jesus?

But there is a condition, and the essential
condition is that one purify himself from what is
ignoble. The Authorized Version says we must purify
ourselves "from these" and that is an exact
translation from the Greek phrase. "These" must
mean vessels for ignoble use.

But we must be cautious in our interpretation.
I know as well as you do that this verse is a
prooftext by which some justify separating from
all those in the visible church with whom they
don't agree. But I tell you that the context in
which the verse comes suggests a very different
application. For the verses are introduced by the

sentence, "Let every one that nameth the name of
Christ depart from evil," and the paragraph continues,
"Shun youthful passions, and aim at righteousness."
Timothy is to purify himself, not of all contact
with evil men, but of all evil in himself. He is
to separate himself only from evil associations
insofar as they exercise a corrupting influence
upon him. In a word, it is moral rather than
doctrinal purity that is in view here.

So the essential condition of usefulness
is to be clean. Paul went on to enlarge on what
he meant. Verse 23 gives positive and negative
counterparts. Verse 22 exhorts: "Shun youthful
passions and aim at righteousness" (RSV). Now,
let me spend just a moment or two on those two
verbs. "Shun" is the Greek word pheugo and it
literally means "to seek safety in flight" or "to
escape from danger." It is used literally in the
New Testament to indicate flight from physical
danger. Moses fled from Pharaoh into the Midian
Desert. The holy family fled from Herod's wrath
into Egypt. The hireling sees the wolf coming
and flees from its ravages. The apostles in
Gethsemane after the arrest of Jesus, forsook him
and fled. And the Judean Christians in A.D. 70,
when Jerusalem would be surrounded by Roman legions,
were to flee to the mountains. It is this verb
that is used for fleeing from spiritual danger.
Every man is told in Scripture to flee from the
wrath to come. That is the same Greek word.

Here the Christian is told to flee from
idolatry, to flee from immorality, to flee from
the spirit of materialism and the love of money,
and, in this verse, to flee all youthful passions.
This does not mean any sexual lust, but that of
sinful ambition, the spirit of materialism, and other
dominating passions that afflict the youth of the
world today. We are to flee. We are to recognize
sin as something dangerous to the soul. We are not
to negotiate with it; we are not to come to terms
with it. We are not to dillydally with it or to
linger in its presence. We are to get as far away

from it as possible, as quickly as possible. Like
Joseph when Potiphar's wife attempted to seduce
him, we are to take to our heels and run. Do you
do that with temptation? Do you want to be a
vessel unto honor, fit for the Master's use?

It is necessary to flee everything that is
sinful and then to follow after everything that
is good. "To follow after" comes from a very
strong word. It is used for pursuing or chasing
the enemy in war, or a quarry in hunting. The
Scripture tells us again and again that we are
to run away from spiritual danger and to run after
spiritual good. We are to flee from the one in
order to escape it, and to pursue the other in
order to attain it.

This is the consistent, reiterated teaching
of Scripture--to deny ourselves and to follow
Christ; to put off what belongs to the old man and
to put on what belongs to the new; to mortify our
members on earth and to seek and to set our minds
upon the things that are above; to crucify the
flesh and to walk in the Spirit. If only we
could learn this. There is no other way to become
holy. There is no other way to become a vessel
fit for noble use so the Master can use us. And
what a promise it is that if any man or woman in
this convention will purify himself from these
sins, he or she shall be a vessel unto honor.
It is a definite promise. Let us claim it.

THE LORD'S SERVANT

Now the third metaphor is the Lord's
servant (vv. 23-26). In verse 23 Paul referred
again to these wordy debates, this "godless chatter,"
these "stupid, senseless controversies" of false
teachers. In contrast to that, he said in verse
24, "The Lord's servant must not be quarrelsome
but kindly to every one, an apt teacher, forbearing,
correcting his opponents with gentleness" (RSV).
This is a demeanor fitting in the Lord's servants.
Jesus of Nazareth, the Lord's servant par excellence,

described himself as gentle (the same word) and lowly in heart. And so the Lord's servants today must also be kindly, forbearing, tolerant in spirit, (not tolerant of error or evil, but tolerant in spirit), and gentle. Then he will be a fit vessel in the Master's hand, if he adorns his Christian teaching with the Christian character and demeanor. And further (v. 25), if he is gentle in correcting his opponents, it may be that God will grant them repentance so that they may come to the knowledge of the truth, and (v. 26) that they may escape from the snare of the devil, who had taken them captive to do his will.

This whole chapter is a clarion call to Christian workers. We are to spread the good news, receiving the truth from Scripture and communicating it to others. We are to be good soldiers, athletes, and farmers, dedicated in our work. We are to be unashamed workmen, accurate and clear in our exposition. We are to be vessels for noble use, righteous in our character and conduct. And we are to be the Lord's servants, gentle in our manner.

We are to be committed in our laboring, clear in our teaching, clean in our living, and courteous in our speaking. Only so can we be of use. Only if we give ourselves without reserve to soldiering, farming, and running can we expect results. Only if we cut the truth straight and do not swerve from it shall we be approved unto God and have no need to be ashamed. Only if we purify ourselves from what is ignoble shall we be vessels for noble use and fit for the Master's service. Only if we are gentle and not quarrelsome will God grant to our opponents repentance and the knowledge of the truth.

Let us pray. "Lord Jesus, again and again your Word finds us out, humbles us and rebukes us. And we grieve that we fall so far short of the sublime standards that you have set for us. Enable every single member of our convention to seek to live according to Scripture and to obey these divine commands, that in your goodness we may become vessels unto honor, fit for you to use. For your great name's sake, amen."

3. God's Man: The Charge to Continue in the Gospel by John R. W. Stott

We open our Bibles again at the second letter of Paul to Timothy, chapter 3. We entitled chapter 1 "The Charge to Guard the Gospel," and chapter 2 "The Charge to Suffer for the Gospel." We shall entitle chapter 3 "The Charge to Continue in the Gospel."

INTRODUCTION

Let me read you the first verse and following: "But understand this, that in the last days there will come times of stress. For men will be . . ." (RSV).

Now there are three introductory points to notice about this verse which sets the context for us. First, they have to do with what are called "the last days." I want to assert that the last days are these days, the days in which we are living. It may seem natural, when you first look at this verse, to apply the phrase to a future epoch, to the days immediately preceding the end when Christ will come again. The biblical usage, however, will not allow us to do this. It is the conviction of the New Testament writers that the new age which was promised by the Old Testament arrived with Jesus Christ, and that with his coming the old age had begun to pass away and the last days had come. For example, the Apostle Peter on the Day

of Pentecost quoted a prophecy of Joel which said
that in the last days (the same expression) God
would pour out his Spirit upon all flesh. And
Peter went on to apply that prophecy to his own
day. This, he says, is what was spoken by the
Prophet Joel. So, in the conviction of the Apostle
Peter, the last days to which the prophecy of Joel
referred had come. They had come with Jesus. In
Hebrews 1:1 we're told that God who spoke in times
past through the prophets to the fathers, has in
these last days spoken unto us by his Son.

So the last days are these days. We are
living in the last days. The last days are the
period that extends from the first coming to the
second coming of Christ--the inter-Advent period,
the interim period in which you and I are living
between the two comings of Jesus. What follows,
therefore, in 2 Timothy 3 is a description of the
present and not of the future. It is a description
of the whole period elapsing between the comings
of Christ. Now this period may get worse as the
days pass, as he goes on to say, but already in
Timothy's day the last days had come. That's the
first point: the last days are these days.

Second, these last days are to include
perilous times--grievous times, times of stress.
What we ought to know and understand about the
last days is not that they are to be uniformly
and consistently perilous, but that they include
perilous seasons. Church history has amply
confirmed that truth. As the vessel of the
Christian church first put out to sea in the
early days, it did not expect a smooth and untroubled
passage, but, rather, storm and tempest and hurricane.

Let me delay for a few moments on the Greek
word that is used for perilous times. The Greek
word is chalepos, "hard" or "difficult" in one of
two senses--either hard to bear, and in this sense
it is used of any kind of pain, physical or mental,
that is hard to endure, or it can mean hard to
deal with and, therefore, dangerous or menacing.
It is used of the raging sea. It is used of wild

animals that are perilous or dangerous. The only
other New Testament occurrence of the word chalepos
is with regard to the two Gadarene demoniacs who,
like wild beasts, we are told, were so fierce that
no one could pass that way. And so the Christian
church in these last days in which we live is to
expect seasons or periods that are both painful
and perilous. Why?

That brings me to the third introductory
point, the beginning of verse 2: Because "men
will be . . ." (RSV). It's very important to grasp
that it is men who are responsible for the menacing
seasons which the church has to endure. They are
fallen men, evil men, men whose nature is perverted,
men who are self-centered and godless, men whose
minds are hostile to God and to his laws, and men
who spread evil, heresy, dead religion, and
persecution in the church.

Now let's recap what we have learned in the
first verse. First, we are living in the last
days; Christ ushered them in. Second, these last
days are to include perilous times. Third, these
perilous times are the result of the activities
of evil men. Paul said to Timothy: You are to
understand this. You are to know this quite clearly,
and, therefore, to be prepared for it when it comes.

MAN IN THE LAST DAYS

Now the rest of the first paragraph (vv. 2-9)
is devoted to a portrayal of these bad men who are
responsible for the perilous seasons through which
the church has to pass. The Apostle Paul described
(a) their conduct, (b) their religion--for these
bad men are religious, and (c) their beliefs.

a. Their Moral Conduct

In the three verses that immediately follow
(vv. 2-4), nineteen expressions are used. I think
it would be exceedingly tedious if I were to
attempt to analyze each of them separately. I

want rather to pick out various things in the
catalog and, in particular, to ask you to notice
the first and the last of these nineteen expressions.
The first, in verse 2, says that men will
be lovers of self, and the last, at the end of
verse 4, says that they will not be lovers of God.
That, in a few words, describes the conduct of
these men. They are lovers of self instead of
lovers of God. Indeed, four out of the nineteen
expressions are compounded with love, suggesting
that what is fundamentally wrong with these men
is that their love is misdirected. They're lovers
of self, lovers of money, lovers of pleasure, when
what they ought to be is lovers of God. In between
these expressions come fifteen others which are
almost entirely descriptive of a breakdown of
men's relationships with each other. The men who
are lovers of self and lovers of money are proud
and arrogant. As a result of their pride and
arrogance, they are abusive of other people. For
the higher our opinion is of ourselves, the more
shall we be contemptuous and abusive of other
people.
I don't want you to miss the next five
expressions which are grouped together, beginning
in the middle of verse 2. These seem to refer to
family life, and especially the attitude of young
people to their parents. In the Greek they're all
negative, seeming to stress the tragic absence of
qualities which nature alone would lead us to
expect. Let's look at these five. (1) Disobedient
to their parents--parents whom Scripture says the
children, during the years of their minority, are
to honor and obey. (2) They are ungrateful,
devoid of elementary gratitude. (3) They are
unholy. The Greek word is sometimes used in
classical Greek of a lack of filial respect. (4)
They are inhuman. They're utterly lacking in
normal human affections, as J. B. Phillips put
it. That is, they are heartless. It is part
of the natural created order that parents and
children should love one another. But in these

times of stress they don't; they're inhuman. (5)
They're implacable or irreconcilable. Young
people are so greatly in revolt against their
parents that they rebuff every attempt to
reconciliation. They're not even willing to come
to the conference table to negotiate. Therefore,
this relation of children to parents which the
Apostle Paul described is one that is marked by
disobedience, ingratitude, disrespect, lack of
affection, and unreasonableness. This is a mark
of perilous seasons.

The remaining seven expressions have wider
application than to the family; I will only mention
them. Men are slanderers, that is, backbiters or
scandalmongers, guilty of the sin of speaking evil
of others behind their back. They are profligate,
that is, people without any self-control. They
are fierce, savage, brutal, haters of good,
treacherous (a word that is used of the traitor
Judas), reckless--whether in word or deed--and
swollen with conceit. The list ended, as it began,
with pride. All this unsocial, antisocial behavior;
this disobedient, ungrateful, disrespectful, inhuman,
irreconcilable attitude to parents; this backbiting;
this absence of restraint, gentleness, loyalty,
and prudence is the inevitable consequence of a
godless self-centeredness.

God's order is that we should love him first,
our neighbor next, and ourself last. If we reverse
the order of the first and the third and put self
first and God last, then our neighbor in the middle
is bound to suffer. The root of the trouble in
perilous times is that men are lovers of self.
As J. B. Phillips said, "They are utterly self-
centered." Only the gospel has a radical solution
to this universal problem of self-centeredness.
Only the gospel promises a new birth, a new creation,
which involves being turned inside out, from self
to unself. The gospel brings a real reorientation
of mind and heart and life. It makes us fundamentally
God-centered when we have been fundamentally self-
centered. When God is at the center of our lives,

we are fundamentally godly people and can love
the world that he loves. Only when we seek to
give ourselves in sacrificial service to other
people is our attitude to our neighbor right,
for we have exchanged self-centeredness for
God-centeredness. This is the moral conduct of
these bad men.

b. Their Religious Observance

It may be a shock to discover that people
such as these who have been described--who lack
the common decencies of civilized society, let
alone God's laws--can be religious. But that is
the case. "They are holding the form of religion
but denying the power of it" (v. 5 RSV). In
the history of mankind, religion and morality
have been more often divorced than married. The
seventh and eighth century prophets B.C. fulminated
against Israel and Judah for this very reason:
they divorced religion from morality. Amos was
the first of these prophets. In his days there
was a boom in religion and a boom in injustice
at the same time. The Lord could say through
Isaiah, "Your new moons and your appointed festivals
my soul hates. They have become a burden to me,
I'm weary of bearing them. When you spread forth
your hands in religious diversion, I will hide my
eyes from you. Even though you make many prayers,
I will not listen, for your hands are full of
blood. Wash yourselves, make yourselves clean,
remove the evil of your doings from before my
eyes. Cease to do evil, learn to do good. Seek
justice, correct oppression, defend the fatherless,
plead for the widow." Jesus said the same thing
to the Pharisees, the religious people of his day,
who nevertheless lived in immorality and injustice.
Similarly, Paul said to Timothy that these people
have a form of religion, but they deny its power.
And there are many such in our own day who
have preserved the outward form of religion. They
put on their Sunday best to go to church. They

sing the hymns. They say the amen to the prayers.
They put money in the offering plate. They look
and they sound incredulously pious. But it is
form without power, outward show without inward
reality, piety without sincerity, religion without
morals, and faith without works. Such religion
is an abomination to God. True religion is a
combination of power and form--not power without
form, nor form without power. It is an inward
reality that expresses itself through the lips
and issues in moral conduct.

c. Their Intellectual Beliefs

It may be an astonishing thing that the
kind of people Paul described--those filled with
ungodly self-love and malice--should not only
profess religion but should include some who
actively exploit their sex. "Who make their way
into households and capture weak women, burdened
with sins and swayed by various impulses, who will
listen to anybody and can never arrive at a
knowledge of the truth" (vv. 6-7 RSV).

Now the proselytizing zeal of these people
is portrayed as a military operation. The Greek
word for "capture" (v. 6) means "to take prisoner
in war." But their method is not direct and open;
it is furtive, secretive, and cunning. They are
sneaks, using the back door rather than the front
These tradesmen of heresy insinuate themselves
into private homes, choosing a time when the menfolk
are out, presumably at work. They concentrate
their attention upon women. Their expediency,
especially their eloquent comments, are as old as
the fall of man. For, the serpent deceived Eve
first. This was the method employed by the Gnostics
in the second and third centuries, and it has been
used by many religious commercial travelers since,
including the Jehovah's Witnesses today. The
women who are worked upon are described in the
Greek as gunaikaria, the diminutive form which
expresses contempt, for these weak women have a

double weakness, moral and intellectual. Morally
weak, they are burdened with sins and swayed by
various impulses--laid down by a load of guilt
and carried away by strong temptations. The false
teachers worm their way into these households and
play upon these weak women's feelings of guilt
and of infirmity. But the women are not only
morally weak but intellectually weak (v. 7),
mentally unstable, credulous, gullible. Unable
to arrive at any settled convictions, they will
listen to anybody. Such women, weak in character
and in intellect, are an easy prey to door-to-door
religious salesmen.

As an example of such false teachers, the
apostle mentioned two men called Jannes and Jambres
(v. 8). The names, according to Jewish tradition,
were those of the two chief magicians in Pharaoh's
court at the time of the Exodus. They were wise
men and sorcerers with their secret arts. Notice
very carefully what the Apostle Paul said here.
He said that as Jannes and Jambres opposed Moses,
so these men, the false teachers, oppose the
truth that the Apostle Paul was teaching.

Now what is remarkable about the analogy
is not just that the Asian false teachers were
likened to Egyptian magicians, but that Paul
likened himself to Moses. Now Moses was the
greatest figure of the Old Testament. No prophet
arose in the Old Testament in Israel like Moses,
who the Lord knew face to face. See, said the
Lord, I shall make you, Moses, as God to Pharaoh,
and you shall speak all that I shall command you.
And for forty years Moses spoke with God's word
to the people. Now Paul likened himself to Moses.
As Jannes and Jambres opposed Moses, so the false
teachers opposed the truth that the Apostle Paul
taught. So whether it was Moses' law or Paul's
gospel, it was God's truth which men were rejecting.
Therefore, Paul rejected them as corrupt in their
mind and counterfeit as to the faith (v. 8). Paul
was confident that they would not get very far
(v. 9). False teaching may spread like gangrene,

but its success will be limited and temporary.
For, the folly of false teachers will be plain to
all, even as the folly of Jannes and Jambres became
evident.

Now let me pause a moment here. I think
that you and I sometimes become distressed, rightly
and understandably, by the many false teachers in
and out of the church who oppose the truth. And
we are especially distressed by the sly methods
of backdoor religious traitors. But I want to say
to you, we need have no fear. There is something
patently spurious about heresy, and there is something
self-evidently true about the truth. Error may
spread and become popular. It does. But it will
not get very far, for in the end it is bound to
be exposed, and God is going to vindicate his own
truth.

Now, let's look back at what we've learned
so far. I think it is plain what these dangerous
seasons are in the last days in which we live, and
also how they arrive. It is because in that part
of God's field, the world, in which God has sown
wheat, the devil has also sown tares. The devil
has his fifth column actually in the church.
Article 26 of the thirty-nine articles of the
Church of England says, "In the visible church the
evil is ever mingled with the good. And sometimes
the evil have chief authority in the ministration
of the Word and sacraments." Yes, in the church,
in the visible society of professing believers,
there are men of immoral character and conduct, of
purely external religiosity, and of corrupt mind
and counterfeit faith. They are lovers of self
and money and pleasure rather than lovers of God
and their neighbor. They retain a form of godliness,
but they deny its power. And they oppose the truth
and seek to win weak women to their pernicious views.
Morally, religiously, intellectually, they are
perverse. To my mind, it is a remarkably apt
portrayal of what in our own day we call the
permissive society, a society which genially tolerates
every conceivable deviation, even in the church,

from Christian standards of righteousness and truth.

That brings us to the second part of the chapter which begins with verse 10: "But you, Timothy" (J. B. Phillips), are to be different. I pray that God will write upon the heart of every man and woman here those two little words "But you" from verse 10. "Now you have observed my teaching, my conduct" (RSV). Not the ways of the world, but "my teaching." Again, "But as for you, continue in what you've learned" (v. 14 RSV). Timothy was not to catch the universal infection. Timothy was not to be carried away with the popular tide of the day. In contrast to these men all around him, in and out of the church, Timothy was to be different.

I tell you, my brethren, that every Christian ought to be different. We are not to be like reeds shaken with the wind, feebly bowing down before the wind of popular fashion and opinion from whatever direction the wind may blow. Certainly today the pressures that are put upon us to conform to the ways of the world are colossal--not only from the direct challenge to traditional views and Christian standards, but from this insidious, pervasive atmosphere of secularism in which all of us are called to live and work. Many people are giving in--sometimes not even realizing what they are doing. Again and again and again in the Word of God we are told not to be moved, not to be like reeds shaken with the wind, but to stand firm like a rock in a mountain torrent. Don't be conformed to the world.

Let's spend the rest of our time looking at these verses. In verse 10 Paul said, "You have observed my teaching." Here Paul reminded Timothy of his present and past positions. What Timothy had been doing and was still doing was following Paul's teaching. Then in verse 14 he said, "As for you, continue in what you have learned." He goes on to the future. So verses 10 to 13 describe Timothy's past and present loyalty to the Apostle

Paul, while verses 14 to 17 urge him to remain
loyal in the future. The two main verbs in verses
10 and 14 sum up the gist of the section. Maybe
you'd like to underline them in your Bibles. Verse
10 reads, "You have followed." The Revised Standard
Version uses the word "observed," but the Greek
means "to follow." It is used literally of one
man following another along the street, and is
used figuratively of one man following another
man's teaching, and taking another man's teaching
as his standard and his rule. So you have followed
me. That's the word that described what Timothy
has done in the past. The second verb is in verse
14, which reads, "But you continue." Continue in
what you've been doing. You have followed, now
continue.

TIMOTHY: PAST, PRESENT, AND FUTURE

Now we'll look into this a little more fully.
First, in verses 10 to 13, Paul said, Timothy, you
have followed my teaching. That means, in a word,
that Timothy had been a loyal disciple of the
apostle. He had taken pains to grasp the meaning
of the apostle's teaching, and had made it his
own. He had absorbed and digested it, and now he
was conforming his mind and his life to it. He
had observed and followed the apostle's manner of
life and teaching. So, in mind and conduct, he
had been and still was Paul's faithful follower.
Now, are we clear about the contrast between
these verses and the first paragraph? The men
portrayed in the first paragraph were also followers.
But what were they following? They were following
their own inclinations. They were lovers of self,
lovers of pleasure, lovers of money. But Timothy
was different. He was not following his own ideas,
his own inclinations. He was not a subjectivist.
He was following the teaching of the Apostle Paul.
He had an objective standard which he was following.
Then Paul went on to list his virtues and
his sufferings: "You've 'followed my teaching,

my conduct, my aim in life, my faith, my patience,
my love, my steadfastness' (v. 10 RSV). And you've
followed my persecutions and my sufferings." Now,
you may say, What a boaster Paul was! Fancy blowing
his own trumpet like that! Wasn't he a little more
than conceited in parading and listing his virtues
and his sufferings? It's all very well to have
said, "Timothy, you've followed my doctrine, my
teaching," but why did he go on to say, "You've
followed my virtuous life, my holy life, and my
sufferings"? I'll tell you the answer. It is
because holy living and suffering are two of the
chief proofs of a man's genuineness in what he
preaches. When a man is teaching something, but
is living an unholy life and is not prepared to
suffer for it, you may be sure that he does not
believe what he teaches and his teaching is not
true. But when a man not only teaches, but his
teaching issues in a holy life and he's so
convinced about it that he's prepared to suffer
and to die for it, then you may begin to be sure
that what he is teaching is true. Holiness and
suffering were the two things that authenticated
Paul's message.

Then Paul went on in verses 12 and 13 to
say that everybody who lives a godly life is going
to suffer persecution. So that's the position
of Timothy in the past and present. "You have
followed my doctrine. You have been a disciple
of mine. You have not been like the prevailing
world and following the popular notions of the
day. You have followed me." And Paul expected
that he was an apostle of Jesus Christ.

In the remaining verses, 14 to 17, we come
to the future. Again Paul said, "As for you."
These words are exactly the same in the Greek.
They're very emphatic. "You, Timothy, never mind
about these evil men of verse 13 who go on, who
advance--although it's a strange kind of advance,
because it's from bad to worse, and not from good
to better. In contrast to these men who are
advancing from bad to worse and are imposters,

deceiving and being deceived, as for you, Timothy,
continue." Now let's get hold of that. There is
a deliberate contrast between the evil men who
are advancing and Timothy who is to abide, to
continue. I long that everybody here will get
this message.

The church is full of innovators today,
men and women who pride themselves on being
progressive and advanced thinkers. They're not
content with the Scriptures; they want to go on
beyond them. They say, "We can't fossilize our
doctrines in the first century. We're advanced.
We have a new Christianity." There is a fortnightly
journal in England which is entitled "The New
Christian." They have a new Christianity. "We
have a new theology," they say. "We have a new
orthodoxy. We have a new morality. We have a
new reformation. We want to advance and produce
something new."

The Apostle Paul said, "Don't you go on.
You'll be like these evil men, the imposters, who
go on. Timothy, as for you, abide. Continue in
the things that you've learned and heard." As
for this new theology and morality, perhaps we
may be forgiven if--borrowing the words of Jesus--
we prefer to say that no one after drinking old
wine desires new, for Jesus said that the old is
better. So in verse 14 Paul reminded Timothy
that he had learned certain things from Paul and
that he had come firmly to believe them. Timothy
is to abide in what he had learned and believed.
He is not to let any man shift him from his ground.

Then Paul added two reasons for this abiding,
this stability in the truth. The first reason is
knowing from whom you learned them. I haven't
time to argue this, but it's my conviction that
the word "whom" referred here to the Apostle Paul
himself. He said, "One reason why you must abide
in the things you've heard and learned, Timothy,
is because you know from whom you've learned them.
That is, you know that I'm an authoritative apostle
of Jesus Christ who has dared (v. 8) to liken

myself to Moses, because I believe that God has
given me his Word to teach. And you've not only
followed my doctrine but you've seen my life and
my sufferings, and these things together
authenticate my gospel." And the gospel is still
authenticated to us by Paul's apostolic authority,
by his consistent godliness, and by his many sufferings
bravely borne. That's the first reason why we're to
abide. We know from whom we got the truth, namely,
the apostles of Jesus Christ.

The second reason for abiding is given in
verse 15: "And that from a child thou has known
the holy Scriptures." Timothy had been taught the
Old Testament Scriptures from childhood, doubtless
by his mother and grandmother. He was therefore
extremely familiar with the Scriptures. He believed
them to have been inspired by God, as Paul said in
verse 16. He was told to abide in what he had
learned from Paul not only because he knew about
Paul's apostolic authority, but because what Paul
taught was consistent with the Old Testament
Scriptures as well. Paul was no innovator. He
claimed before Agrippa that what he was teaching
(see Acts 26) was nothing but what the prophets
and Moses said would come to pass: that the Christ
must suffer, and that by being the first to rise
from the dead, he would proclaim light to both the
people and to the Gentiles.

Now let's get this clear. The two reasons
why Timothy should abide in what he'd heard and
firmly believed were (a) that it was apostolic,
taught by the Apostle Paul, and (b) that it was
prophetic, taught by the Old Testament Scriptures.
And these are the same two grounds today. The
gospel that you and I believe in is the biblical
gospel. It is the gospel of the Old Testament,
and it is the gospel of the New Testament. It is
vouched for by the prophets of God and the apostles
of Christ. And we intend, by the grace of God,
to abide in it for these reasons, and because of
this double authentication.

Now notice what we may learn about Scripture

in the remaining verses. Two fundamental truths
are taught us: First, its origin and nature--what
it is--and second, its purpose--what it's for.
First, its nature. "All Scripture is inspired by
God" (v. 16 RSV). This phrase "given by inspiration
of God," five words in the King James Version, is
one word in the Greek: theopmeustos, "God-breathed."
This does not mean that the Scripture or its human
authors were breathed into by God, but that the
text of Scripture was breathed out by God. In other
words, Scripture is God-breathed, issuing from his
mouth. Inspiration is a convenient term to use,
but "expirational spirantion" would be better,
because the Scripture is breathed out of the mouth
of God. The Scripture is God's Word because it
is God-breathed. It originated in his mind, it
issued from his mouth, although, of course, it was
spoken by human authors without destroying either
their individuality or its divine authority in the
process. But the authors of Scripture can say,
"Hear the Word of the Lord. I am speaking it, it's
coming from my mouth." But actually it is the
Word of the Lord, and the mouth of the Lord has
spoken it. So that is the nature of Scripture
according to the apostles of Jesus Christ, and
Jesus Christ himself. It is authoritative as the
Word of God because it is God-breathed.

    Now I want to say just a word about the
essential reasonableness of the Christian doctrine
of revelation. Its reasonableness is this: the
mind of God is unattainable by the mind of men in
and of themselves. In Isaiah 55 God said, "My
thoughts are not your thoughts, neither are your
ways my ways . . . . For as the heavens are higher
than the earth, so are my ways higher than your
ways, and my thoughts than your thoughts." There
is a vast gulf between the infinite mind of God,
and the finite mind of man. How then is my mind
ever to read the thoughts and the mind of God?
The answer is: it is impossible if I'm left to
myself. My little mind cannot climb up into the
infinite mind of God. There's no ladder by which

I can reach him. But if I'm ever to know what is
in the mind of God, he must reveal it.

How does anybody reveal what is in their
mind? Through their mouth; by speaking. If I
stood dumb on this platform, you would not have
the remotest idea of what was going on in my mind.
But at this moment I'm speaking. And because I'm
speaking you know what is in my mind, for I'm
clothing the thoughts of my mind in the words of
my mouth. And the words of my mouth are conveying
to you the thoughts of my mind. This is communication
from the mind through the word. This is what God
has done. He has spoken, and he has declared his
mind in speech. The Scripture is God-breathed,
spoken by the mouth of God through the mouths of
men.

We've seen that the nature of Scripture is
that it is God-breathed. What is the purpose of
Scripture? The answer is: it's profitable. Indeed
it is profitable for men only because it is inspired
by God. Only its divine origin secures and explains
its human value and profit. And what is its profit?
It can make us wise unto salvation (v. 15). The
Bible is a book of salvation and not a book of
science. The purpose of the Bible in the providence
of God is not to teach scientific facts which men
can discover by their own empirical investigations.
The purpose of the Bible is to teach moral and
spiritual truths which can be known only by divine
revelation, especially that man is a guilty sinner
under the judgment of God; that God loves him in
spite of his rebellion and sent his Son to die for
him and to rise again, and that the sinner can be
saved if he trusts in Jesus Christ.

Since the Bible is the handbook of salvation,
it is simply full of Jesus Christ. The Old Testament
foretold and foreshadowed him. The Gospels told
the story of his birth, life, death, resurrection,
and ascension. The book of Acts described how
Christ through his apostles continued to work to
preach the gospel of salvation and to found the
church. The Epistles displayed the full glory of

the divine-human person of Jesus and of his saving
work. The book of Revelation portrayed Christ
sharing the throne of God and promised us his
final victory. The Bible is full of Christ; it
depicts him supremely as Savior and invites us to
come to Christ. That is the whole purpose of the
Bible, to bear witness to Christ.

I want to say to you that evangelicals are
not bibliolators. We do not worship the Bible,
but rather the Christ of the Bible. Nor are
evangelicals like the Jews who supposed that
eternal life was to be found in the Scriptures.
No, eternal life is in Christ. The Scriptures
bear witness to Christ, and that's why we love
them. Just as a lover treasures the letters from
his sweetheart and her paragraphs, not for themselves
but because of the person of whom they speak and
because they speak to him of her, so we Christians
love the Bible, not for itself but because it speaks
to us of Christ.

The Bible is not only profitable to lead
us to salvation, but it's profitable for the
Christian life (v. 16), for teaching the truth
and correcting error, for training in righteousness,
and for reformation in manners. If you want to
overcome error and grow in the truth, if you want
to overcome evil and grow in holiness, it is to
the Bible that you must turn. For the Bible is
profitable for those things (v. 17) so that the
man of God may be mature. That is the purpose of
Scripture--to lead you to salvation and on into
maturity.

We live in times of stress, and very
distressing they are. Sometimes I wonder if the
world and the church have gone mad--so strange
are their views and so low their standards. Many
people are being swept from their moorings by the
flood tide of fashion today. Others feel that
going into hiding offers the only hope of survival
and the only alternative to surrender. Neither
of these is the Christian way. "Let these men
wallow in self-indulgence and propagate their lies,

but as for you--stand firm." How we need that message today. You've followed so far, now abide in it. You can become a man of God, a woman of God, if you abide in that which you have heard and come firmly to believe. You will grow into Christian maturity.

Let us pray. We confess to you Lord Jesus our great human weakness that every one of us by nature is a reed shaken by the wind. We find it so easy to conform to the popular fashions of the day. Grant us, we humbly pray, divine strength to stand firm and to continue in that which we have believed and been taught so that we may become men and women of God to serve our generation. For your great Name's sake we pray, amen.

4. God's Man: The Charge to Preach the Gospel
by John R. W. Stott

We come now to the fourth and last chapter
of the second epistle of Paul to Timothy. We
entitled chapter 1 "The Charge to Guard the Gospel";
chapter 2 "The Charge to Suffer for the Gospel";
chapter 3 "The Charge to Continue in the Gospel."
Chapter 4 is "The Charge to Preach the Gospel."

These words in 2 Timothy 4 that are before
us are some of the very last words written by the
Apostle Paul. Certainly they are the last of his
words which have survived. He wrote within weeks,
possibly within days, of his martyrdom. According
to ancient tradition, he was beheaded on the Ostian
Way outside Rome. For thirty years, without any
intermission, the Apostle Paul had been laboring
as an itinerant ambassador of Jesus Christ. Truly,
as he said in this chapter, he had fought a good
fight, he had finished his course, and he had kept
the faith. Now he awaited his coronation, the
award of the crown of righteousness which he said
was laid up for him.

THE APOSTOLIC CHARGE

These words that we shall study this morning
are, therefore, Paul's legacy to the church. I
think it is impossible to read them without being
profoundly stirred. They took the form of a solemn
charge: "I charge you in the presence of God and

of Christ Jesus" (v. 1 RSV). This was addressed
in the first instance to Timothy, Paul's apostolic
delegate, but it is equally applicable to every
man who is called to the ministry of the church
or to the mission field. Indeed, in a secondary
sense, it applies to every Christian witness, which
means every Christian person.

There are three aspects of the charge that
I bring you this morning. First, consider the
nature of this apostolic charge--what it is.
Second, we shall go on to see the basis of the
charge, the arguments upon which it was grounded.
Third, we shall see a personal illustration of it
from the example of Paul himself in Rome.

THE NATURE OF THE CHARGE

The nature of the charge is given in three
words at the beginning of verse 2: "Preach the
word." It would be very hard to find a better
motto for us as we prepare to leave this convention.
Every member of the church of Jesus Christ has
been entrusted with the message and charged to
proclaim it.

Our message is a word. It is, in fact, the
Word, God's Word which God has spoken. It's
equivalent to what is called in verse 3, the sound
teaching; in verse 4, the truth; and in verse 7,
the faith. This word consists of the Old Testament
Scriptures, God-breathed and profitable, and which
Timothy had known from childhood. It consists also
of the teaching of the apostles--what Timothy had
heard and received and learned from the Apostle
Paul, and which Paul had entrusted to him to
guard and to teach to others. The Word that we
are to preach is not our own invention. The message
that we are given to proclaim is the Word which
God has spoken and which is now committed to the
church as a sacred trust.

Our message is the Word, and our duty is
to preach it, to speak to others what God has
spoken to us and given us in the Scripture. Our

duty, then, is not just to hear the Word, nor just
to believe it and obey it. It is not just to
guard it from every falsification, nor even to
suffer for it and to continue in it. Our duty
is to preach it, to proclaim it, because it is
God's good news of salvation to sinners. We are
to proclaim it like heralds in the marketplace,
to lift up our voice without fear or favor and
boldly to make it known. Will you do that on
your campus this coming term? Preach the Word.
That is the commission, the charge that is given
to us all.

Now Paul goes into detail, and he tells
us how to preach the Word. Our proclamation has
four characteristics:

a. Our Preaching is to be Urgent

"Preach the word, be urgent in season and
out of season" (v. 2 RSV). J. B. Phillips:
"Never lose your sense of urgency." It's not
good proclaiming the Word or witnessing to a
friend in a listless and lackadaisical way. As
Richard Baxter writes in his classic book, The
Reformed Pastor,

> Whatever you do, let the people
> see that you are in good earnest.
> You cannot break men's hearts by
> jesting with them or telling them
> a smooth tale or patching up a
> gaudy oration. Men will not cast
> away their dearest pleasures upon
> a drowsy request of one that seems
> not to mean as he speaks, or to
> care much whether his request is
> granted. Let us, therefore, rouse
> up ourselves to the work of the
> Lord and speak to our people as
> for their lives, and save them by
> violence, pulling them out of the
> fire.

All true Christian preaching has a note of urgency.

The Christian herald knows that he is handling
matters of life and death--the sinner's plight
under the judgment of God, the love of God who
gave his Son to die for sinners, and the urgent
summons to repent and to believe.

Our preaching is to be urgent in season
and out of season. "Press it home on all occasions,
convenient or inconvenient" (NEB). Now what does
that mean? This is not to be taken as an excuse
for that insensitive brashness which has often
characterized our evangelism and brought it into
disrepute. We are not to barge unceremoniously
into other people's privacy and tread on everybody's
corns. We have no liberty to do such a thing.
No, the occasions are convenient or inconvenient
for the speaker, not for the hearer. And so the
New English Bible margin has it, "Be on duty at
all times, convenient or inconvenient." In other
words, what we're given here is not a biblical
warrant for rudeness, but a biblical appeal against
laziness. Be on duty at all times, whether it is
convenient for you or inconvenient.

Let us be urgent in our proclamation.
Charles Simeon, of Cambridge, used to preach with
great earnestness of voice and gesture, although
he was an Episcopal clergyman. On one occasion
a little girl who was hearing him for the first
time turned to her mother and said, "Oh, Mama,
what is the gentleman in a passion about?" He
was urgent in his preaching. Let us be, too.

b. Our Preaching is to be Relevant

"Preach the word, be urgent in season and
out of season, convince, rebuke, and exhort"
(v. 2 RSV). These are three possible ways of
preaching the word and of applying it. God's
Word is profitable for different ministries. It
speaks to men in different conditions, and it can
be applied in different ways. The preacher, the
witness, must remember this and be skillful in
applying the Word to the particular needs of the

listener.

"Use argument, reproof, and appeal" (NEB). That is to say, some people are full of doubts and need to be convinced by argument. Other people are full of sin and need to be rebuked or reproved. Other people are full of fear; they need to be exhorted and encouraged. God's Word does all this and more.

We must preach the Word relevantly. Don't be like that mayor of a certain Italian city of whom I read a year or two ago. He gave a learned discourse on economics to a delegation of economists (he thought) only to find when he finished that they were a football team. He had two speeches in his pocket, and he pulled out the wrong one. Our speaking is to be urgent, and it is to be relevant.

c. Our Preaching is to be Patient

"Unfailing in patience" (v. 2 AV). "With all longsuffering." That is, although we are to be urgent, longing for people's ready response to the message, we are to be patient in waiting for it. We are never to use human psychological pressures or attempt to force or contrive a decision. Our responsibility is to be faithful in the proclamation of the Word; the results are the responsibility of the Holy Spirit. Therefore, we can afford to be patient in waiting for people's response.

We're to be patient in manner as well. The servant of the Lord is to be gentle with all men. So however solemn our commission, however urgent our message, there is no excuse for a brusque or impatient manner.

d. Our Proclamation is to be Intelligent

"Unfailing in patience and in teaching" (v. 2 RSV). That is, we're not only to preach the Word; we are to teach it. Or, rather, we are to preach it with all teaching.

Many of you, I think, would be familiar
with the modern distinction of which theologians
are fond between the kerygma and the didache.
Kerygma is the proclamation to unbelievers of the
gospel, and didache is instruction given to
converts. Now for those who like that distinction--
and it is legitimate up to a point--this verse is
of importance. It shows that we must not
differentiate too rigidly between these two things.
The kerygma is to be proclaimed with all didache,
with all teaching. Our proclamation, whether we
are seeking to convince or to rebuke or to exhort,
must be a doctrinal proclamation.

The Christian ministry is essentially a
teaching ministry. According to Titus 1:9, the
candidate for the ministry of the church is to
"hold firm to the sure word as taught, so that
he may be able to give instruction in sound
doctrine and also to confute those who contradict
it" (RSV). And according to 1 Timothy 3:2, the
candidate for the ministry must be didacticos,
apt to teach.

There is a great need in every country in
the world, as the process of urbanization continues
and as the standards of education rise, for a
teaching ministry. You and I ought to have a far
greater burden for the intelligentsia of the
country. My own personal longing is that in our
own generation we shall see in every capital and
university city of the world an evangelical church
in which the gospel is faithfully, intelligently,
and thoughtfully expounded, in which the whole
counsel of God is taught. Paul said that he was
in debt, under obligation, not only to barbarians,
but to the Greeks; not only to the unwise and
foolish, but to the wise (Romans 1:14).

This, then, is our charge: to preach the
Word. And in our proclamation of this God-given
message we are to be urgent, relevant, patient,
and intelligent. Urgent in our application of
the Word, relevant in our bearing and manner,

patient in our presentation, and intelligent.
Would that we could take deeply into our hearts
and minds this apostolic charge to the church and
seek to obey it in our own lives. This is the
first thing, the nature of the charge.

THE BASIS OF THE CHARGE

We have already seen that Timothy was young
in years, weak in physique, timid in temperament;
and the times in which he lived were difficult and
dangerous. I think that as Timothy listened to
this apostolic charge to preach the Word, he must
have quailed. His knees must have trembled; he
must have been tempted to shrink from the task.
We, too, are called to this responsibility that
is far beyond our natural capacities. So Paul
did more than issue a charge. He added incentives.
He added a motivation. He bade Timothy look in
three directions: (a) at Jesus Christ, the coming
Judge and King; (b) at the contemporary scene;
and (c) at Paul, the aged prisoner approaching
martyrdom.

a. The Coming of Christ

"I charge you in the presence of God (he
did not issue this charge in his own name or in
his own authority, but in the conscious presence
of God) and of Christ Jesus who is to judge the
living and the dead" (v. 1 RSV). And I charge
you on the ground of "his appearing and his kingdom."
The charge was issued not only in the presence of
God, but in view of the coming of Christ. Notice
that Paul still believed in the epiphany of Jesus
Christ, that he is one day going to make a personal
and visible appearing. Paul wrote of this in his
earlier epistles and, although he knew he was
going to die before it took place, he still lived
in the light of it. He described Christians in
verse 8 as those who loved Christ's epiphany, his
appearing. Paul knows that Jesus Christ is going

to appear, personally and visibly, and that when
he appears he is going to judge the world and
consummate his kingdom. These things, although
future, were clear and certain realities in the
life of the Apostle Paul.

You and I need to live our Christian lives
and do our Christian work in the light of these
same realities. In particular, we are never to
forget that both we who preach and those who
listen are going to have to give an account to
Christ when he appears. So that is the first
motivation: the coming Christ.

b. The Contemporary Scene

"For (that is, because there's a reason
for my charge) the time is coming when people
will not endure sound teaching, but having itching
ears . . ." (v. 3 RSV). As at the beginning of
chapter 3, so the times described here were already
present. Timothy was to frame his ministry in
the light of the times in which he lived. It was
not just that bad times were coming and that
Timothy, therefore, must preach the Word before
they arrived, but that he was to go on preaching
the Word even when the bad times had arrived.

What were these bad times like? Paul
singled out just one characteristic. He stated
it negatively and positively and said it twice.
In brief, it was that men could not bear the truth.
Verse 3: They "will not endure sound teaching,"
but they "accumulate for themselves teachers to
suit their own likings" (RSV). Verse 4: They
"turn away from listening to the truth and wander
into myths" (RSV). They couldn't bear the truth,
and they wouldn't listen to it. They accumulated
teachers to suit their own likings.

You will note it all had to do with their
ears, which were mentioned twice. They had a
strange pathological condition called "itching
ears." The itching ear is full of curiosity. It
is listening for some spicy new teaching. Because

their ears were itching for novelty, they stopped
them against the old-fashioned gospel and opened
them to any teacher who would relieve their itch
by scratching it. What they were rejecting was
the firm, sound teaching of the truth. They
preferred their own likings. In other words,
they substituted their own preference for God's
revelation. The criterion by which they judged
teachers was not God's Word, as it ought to have
been, but their own subjective taste.

Now that's the same situation in which we
live today. People are ridiculing the gospel and
the evangelical faith, the message that is so
infintely precious to us. Instead, they have
itching ears for all these theological novelties
that are going about in the world and in the
church today. What, then, must be our reaction
to this situation? What was to be Timothy's
reaction?

In such a desperate situation in which
men and women were not going to listen to the
truth, but had itching ears for novelty, you might
think that Timothy would have been silenced.
Surely, he might have said that if people can't
bear the truth and if they won't listen to the
truth, then the prudent thing would be to shut
up shop and hold our peace.

But Paul reached the opposite conclusion.
"As for you . . ." (v. 5), Paul told Timothy for
the third time to be different. It is precisely
the same Greek expression in 3:10, 14. Timothy
was not to take his lead from the prevailing
theological fashions. He was to be different.
"As for you, always be steady, endure suffering,
do the work of an evangelist, fulfil your ministry"
(v. 5 RSV). In other words, the people around
Timothy were unstable, so he was to be stable and
to stand his ground. The people around him would
not endure sound doctrine, so he was to be willing
to endure suffering by continuing to preach sound
doctrine. The people around him were ignorant of
the evangel, so he was to do the work of an

evangelist. And the people around him were accumulating teachers to suit themselves, so Timothy was to be all the more conscientious in fulfilling the ministry God had given him.

Difficult times in which it is hard to gain a hearing for the gospel are not to discourage us. They are not to deter us from our ministry nor to induce us to trim our message to suit the fashions of the day. Still less are they to make us shut up and be silent. They are, rather, to spur us on to preach the more. Oh, my friends, the harder the times, the deafer the people and the more loud and clear must be our proclamation. That's the second motivation: the contemporary scene.

c. The Aged Apostle Paul

In writing to Philemon a few years previously, he called himself Paul, the aged. "For I am already on the point of being sacrificed" (v. 6 RSV) is another motivation for ministry. There's a clear contrast between verses 5 and 6. In verse 5, Timothy was to fulfill his ministry because Paul was on the point of closing his own. In verse 6, Paul said that he was on the point of being sacrificed, or, "already my life is being poured out on the altar" (NEB). Paul used sacrificial language. He likened his life to a libation, a drink offering. He believed his martyrdom to be so imminent that he spoke of the sacrifice as having already begun. "I am already on the point of being sacrificed; the time of my departure has come" (RSV). The Greek word for "departure" is a nautical word. It speaks of loosing a boat's moorings. It's as if the anchor is already weighed and the rings are slipped and the boat is about to set sail for another--and a heavenly--shore. "Now then, Timothy," Paul said, "I'm on the very point of being sacrificed. The fragile boat of my life is about to set sail for heaven. Now it is up to you to fulfill your ministry."

Verse 7: "I have fought the good fight (as a soldier), I have finished the race (as an athlete), I have kept the faith (as a treasure--I've guarded it; I've been a good steward)" (RSV). As soldier, athlete, and steward, Paul had been faithful to the calling that he had received from God. Then, in verse 8, Paul said, "There's nothing left for me. Henceforth there is laid up for me the crown of righteousness, which the Lord will give me when he appears. Even if Nero condemns me when I'm tried, even if his verdict is one of guilty. If he condemns me to death, then but a moment later Jesus Christ will reverse the verdict and give me a crown of vindication and righteousness. But, Timothy, my life is done. I've fought the good fight, I've finished the race, I've kept the faith. There's nothing left for me but the heavenly reward. Now, Timothy, it's up to you." That was Timothy's third spur to faithfulness.

And how you young people, just as young Timothy, need to get this message. Our God is the God of history. He is working his purpose out as year succeeds to year. He buries his workmen and he carries on his work. The torch of the gospel is handed down from one generation to the next. As the leaders of the former generation die, it is all the more urgent for the next generation to rise up, to step forward bravely, and to take their place.

I think Timothy's heart must have been deeply moved by this exhortation from Paul the aged, who had led him to Christ. Who led you to Christ? Is he beginning to grow old? The man who led me to Christ is now well into his seventies and is in semi-retirement. We cannot forever rest upon the leadership of the preceding generation. For the day comes when we must step into their shoes and assume the leadership ourselves. That day had come for Timothy and very soon, if not now, it may come to you.

In view of the coming of Christ to judgment, in view of the contemporary world's distaste for

the gospel, and in view of the imminent death of
the aged apostle, Paul's charge to Timothy had a
note of solemn urgency. Now it is up to Timothy
to preach the Word.

We've seen the nature of the charge and the
basis of the charge. Now in the rest of the
chapter we see an illustration of the charge from
the example of the Apostle Paul.

THE EXAMPLE OF PAUL

In verses 9 to 22, we learn that the Apostle
Paul preached the Word. He practiced what he
preached. He did exactly what he told Timothy to
do. He did it when he was on trial for his life
before Imperial Rome. But before we consider this,
look at the circumstances in which it took place.
I've fought a good fight, finished the course,
kept the faith (with a confident anticipation of
the future). Henceforth, there is laid up for me
a crown of righteousness. From this majestic
survey of the past, Paul returned in thought to
his present predicament in a dungeon in Rome.
We need to learn this. The Apostle Paul, great
and godly man that he was, was a man of flesh
and blood. He was a man of like passions with
us. Although he had finished his course and was
awaiting his crown, he was still a frail human
being with ordinary human needs. Let us look at
his plight as he described it in prison, and, in
particular, his loneliness.

Paul had been deserted by his friends. It's
quite true that he had friends overseas to whom he
sent greetings, especially Priscilla and Aquila in
Ephesus at that time, and the house of Onesiphorus
already mentioned. He also sent Timothy bits of
information about other friends, Erastus and
Trophimus. Then there were brethren in Rome--
Eubulus, Pudens, Linus, and Claudia--who must
have visited him sometimes. But Paul still felt
cut off and abandoned.

Paul was separated from the churches he

had founded and from the people in them whom he
had known and loved. A number of his own circle
of traveling companions had, for different reasons,
left him alone. He said in verse 10 that Demas
had deserted him; he had set his love on this
present world. Crescens had gone to Galatia; Titus
to Dalmatia; Tychicus to Ephesus. Only Luke, the
beloved physician, was with him. So for various
reasons, good and bad, Paul was alone except for
Luke, his doctor and companion for many years.

How did Paul react in this situation of
loneliness? Well, he wanted companions to cheer
him. He begged Timothy (v. 9) to do his best to
come soon while he was still alive. In any case,
"do your best to come before winter" (v. 22 RSV).
In winter it was impossible to navigate across
the sea. Have you ever thought of Paul like this?
Paul, who had set his love and his hope on the
coming of Jesus Christ, longing for the coming
of Timothy? Human friendship is the provision
of God for men. As wonderful as is the presence
of Jesus with us today, and the prospect of his
coming, there are no substitutes for human friends.
Paul wanted Timothy.

He also wanted a cloak to keep his body
warm (v. 13). This cloak was like a blanket, an
outer garment with a hole in the middle for the
head. He was cold in his dungeon. Then, he wanted
books and parchments to occupy his mind. We don't
know whether these were the Scriptures or some
other books on papyrus and parchment.

Now, have you got this lesson? Although
the Lord stood by him and strengthened him, and
although the Lord can stand by and strengthen us,
we are not to despise the use of means. When our
spirit is lonely, we need friends. When our body
is cold, we need clothing. When our mind is bored,
we need books. These things are not unspiritual.
They're human, the natural needs of an ordinary,
frail, and mortal man. Don't despise these things.
Don't become so super-spiritual that you say you're
above the need of human friendships. If you're

that super-spiritual, then you're super-scriptural.

There's a good example of this in William Tyndale, to whom we owe our Bible. In 1535, imprisoned in Belgium and not long before his fiery martyrdom, he wrote a letter in Latin to the Marquis of Bergen, the governor of the castle.

> I entreat your Lordship and that by
> the Lord Jesus, that if I must remain here
> in prison for the winter, you would beg
> the commissary to be so kind as to send
> me from the things of mine, which he has,
> a warmer cap. I feel the cold painfully
> in my head. Also a warmer cloak, for
> the cloak I have is very thin. He has
> a woolen shirt of mine, if he will send
> it. But most of all, my Hebrew Bible,
> grammar, and vocabulary, that I may
> spend my time in that pursuit.

Here is Paul, this frail human being, cold in his body, longing for his books, longing for his friends. On top of that, he was opposed by Alexander the coppersmith (vv. 14, 15).

He was not supported by anybody at his first trial (vv. 16 to 18). Plummer put it something like this:

> Among all the Christians in Rome,
> there was not one who would stand at
> his side in court, either to speak on
> his behalf, or to advise him in the
> conduct of his case, or to support him
> by demonstration of sympathy.

I daresay this moment was Paul's Gethsemane. Like his Master, he was alone in his great ordeal. In his greatest need, all his friends forsook him and fled.

Nevertheless, he was not alone. "But the Lord stood by me" (v. 16 RSV), he said. The Lord gave him inward strength. Inward strength to do what? To preach the gospel. Is this not a superb illustration? Paul was on trial for his life. All his earthly friends had left him in the lurch, or were unable to help him. Surely now, the apostle

would think of himself for a change . . . we would
see some trace of self-pity . . . he would rally
to his own defense and plead his own case. In this
time of grave, personal danger, his overmastering
concern surely would be for himself.

But no! His dominant concern and passion
is not to be a witness in his own defense, but to
be a witness to Jesus Christ. Not to plead his
own cause, but the cause of Jesus Christ. Paul
preached the Word before one of the highest tribunals
of the empire, before his judges, perhaps before
the Emperor himself, and no doubt with a large
cosmopolitan crowd present (the general public was
admitted to those trials either in a large basilica
or in the forum in the open air). If ever there
has been a Christian sermon preached out of season,
this was it. We do not know what he said, but
from verse 17 we know he fully preached the kerygma.
He took the opportunity to expound the gospel in
its fullness. It was mainly because of this that
he could say, "I have finished my course." That
was Timothy's model. In issuing a solemn charge
to Timothy to preach the Word and to do it urgently
in season and out of season, Paul had not evaded
the challenge himself.

Now let us look back over the whole epistle
and come to a conclusion. Underlying the epistle
of 2 Timothy is Paul's conviction, which I hope
you and I share, that God had spoken through the
prophets of the Old Testament, that he had revealed
himself through the apostles of the New Testament,
and that he had committed to the church a deposit,
a treasure, which is called the Word, the truth,
the faith, the sound teaching, the pattern of
sound words, the gospel.

But now the apostle, who for thirty years
had faithfully delivered to others what he himself
had received, was on his deathbed. His active
ministry was over; he was on the point of being
sacrificed. He seemed to have already caught a
glimpse of the gleaming steel of the executioner's
sword. So Paul burned with a passion of longing

that Timothy, his young but trusted lieutenant, will step into his shoes and carry on where he had left off in preaching the Word. Oh, he knew that Timothy would have problems to face, that Timothy was young and frail and shy, that the days were evil and difficult, and that the devil hates the gospel.

The devil seeks to stop the preaching of the gospel today by perverting it. He frightens those who preach the gospel into silence through persecution or ridicult. He persuades them to advance beyond the gospel instead of abiding in it. And he makes them so busy with other things—even with defending the gospel—that they have no time to proclaim it.

Paul knew the sacred deposit entrusted to him, he knew the imminence of his martyrdom, the natural weaknesses of Timothy, and the extreme subtlety of the devil. Knowing these things, he issued to Timothy this four-fold charge: Guard it—the gospel is a treasure; suffer for it—the gospel is an offense to the people; be willing to suffer for it—the gospel is profitable; continue in it—proclaim it, for the gospel is good news. Who is sufficient for these things?

I want to finish with two little phrases which I have so far omitted. They are Paul's very last words before he died and they seem to summarize so much of his message. First in verse 22, "The Lord be with your spirit. Grace be with you" (RSV). The Lord had been with Paul. He had stood by him and strengthened him. In the same way, Paul would have the Lord be with Timothy.

The other phrase is at the end of verse 18, "To him be the glory for ever and ever" (RSV). I can think of no better summary of Paul's life and ambition. In our heavy responsibilities to which God calls us, we need to receive grace from Christ, to be strong in the grace that is in Christ Jesus. And then we need to give glory to Christ. From him, grace; to him, glory. In all our Christian life and service we have no other philosophy than this.

Part II.   Four Panels

5. The Growing Church

ERIC FIFE: Introduction

We have been told that the church really
is not growing, that we are in the post-Christian
era, that the church is a has-been. Now it has
been my privilege while traveling in many, many
countries to find the church in unlikely places
and in very strange, to my Anglo-Saxon eyes,
manifestations. We have asked three men to give
us some information this morning about the fact
of the growth of the church. The first speaker
will be Dr. Donald McGavran. He served as a
missionary in India for thirty-one years and later
became the founder and president of the School
of Church Growth in Eugene, Oregon. Now he is
Dean of the School of World Mission and Institute
of Church Growth at Fuller Seminary. He is regarded
as the greatest scholar in the world on the matter
of the growth of the church. Immediately following
him, without any further announcement on my part,
we shall have Mr. Warren Webster, who has completed
fifteen years of service in Pakistan with the
Conservative Baptist Foreign Mission Society.
Pakistan is a difficult field, normally regarded
as being very unresponsive. He recently wrote a
superb article for the January <u>HIS</u> magazine. We
will ask these two men to speak on the issue of
the growing church.

DR. DONALD McGAVRAN: Church Growth

Many of you, perhaps most of you here this morning, have come asking yourself, How can I best invest my life? Where can I make my life tell most for God? I have good news for you. God is calling you to be his man in the time of greatest responsiveness to the gospel.

To put things in the proper perspective, let us remember that this Urbana missionary conference gathers under the biblical mandate to disciple the nations, to bring all people to faith in Jesus Christ the Lord. Whether for our classmates and other Americans, or for our peers in Asia, Africa, and Latin America, there is only one Savior, Jesus Christ. There is only one gospel—forgiveness and peace and power are available in Jesus Christ. Power to remake our lives. Power to remake our societies. The church proclaims this very good news and beseeches men saying, believe on him, be baptized in his name, be added to his church, feed on his Word, and go out to make your families, villages, cities, and nations more just, honest, peaceful, and brotherly places in which to live. The lure of investing our lives in this most rewarding enterprise attracts all of us gathered here. We are called to have a share in the Christian mission during its greatest days, when the church will surge forward as it never has before.

But before we know how to do the task, we must understand the world in which the task is to be done. The farmer going out to his fields needs to know whether it is sowing time or harvest, whether to take a plow or a combine. What kind of world faces us as we go out to make Jesus Christ known and loved and obeyed?

Before I give you my answer to that question, let me tell you why I have been invited to speak here. For twenty years I have made the study of church growth my chief business. For the last seven years as Dean of a School of World Mission

I have had the marvelous opportunity to have as
my students career missionaries and nationals from
scores of countries. We have dug out and plotted
the life histories of hundreds of denominations
in Hong Kong, Congo, Liberia, Brazil, the Philippines,
Japan, Korea, Ethiopia, India, Assam, Thailand,
Viet Nam, and many other places. I speak then
this morning as a special witness. I am not
indulging in rosy promotional pictures. I am
presenting hard facts based on scientific study
of many denominations from Lutherans to Pentecostals
in many nations from Mexico to Indonesia. Testifying
then as a special witness in the propagation of
the gospel, may I give you my considered opinion
that the world in which God calls you to invest
your life is most responsive to the gospel.

To be sure, there are still many resistant
people to whom the gospel must be proclaimed. Some
have set their faces like flint against the gospel.
You can preach and preach, teach and teach, heal
and heal, yet very few will believe on Jesus Christ
who died for them. But if you put all of the
resistant populations of earth here on my left
and all of the responsive here on my right, you
will find that there are so many responsive peoples
that the entire resources of missions could be
poured into them and still some responsive people
would be left waiting to hear the gospel. Far
greater willingness to hear and obey and believe
exists today than existed 1000 or 100 or even
twenty years ago.

Let me give you four examples. Consider
Korea--a small country which has been torn to
pieces by the Communists. The Communist armies
surged down the length of the peninsula, burning
and destroying. The South Korean army, assisted
by the Americans, surged back up the peninsula.
Then the Communists re-attacked, and halfway down
the land an uneasy peace and truce was established.
Can the gospel prosper, can the church grow, can
missionary work be carried out in a country like
that? The church did grow enormously there.

Between 1953 and 1963 the church grew more than
it had in the previous fifty years. Some well-
informed Christian leaders believe that Korea
will be the first mainland Asian nation to become
substantially Christian.

Again, consider Mexico--a somewhat larger
land. For many years the evangelical churches
in Mexico had very slow growth. The people were
suspicious of the Bible. They feared Protestants.
They stoned and burned churches. Very few became
evangelical Christians. But in the last twenty
years, tens of thousands have come to rest their
faith on Jesus Christ. And the total evangelical
community in Mexico now numbers over a quarter of
a million persons.

Again, consider Brazil--a still larger
land as big as the United States. Time would
fail me were I to tell of many small growing
denominations there, but let me mention four
large ones. The Presbyterians now number 160,000.
The Baptists have passed the 250,000 mark. The
Christian Congregation, and Italian movement to
biblical faith, numbers 400,000. The Pentecostal
Assemblies of God count more than a million
baptized believers. Most of this amazing movement
to personal faith in Jesus Christ has taken place
since World War II, has taken place since the
birth of most of you gathered here.

Again, consider Africa--south of the Sahara,
a land as large as the United States and vast
Canada put together. Stephen Neill, authority
on missions, says in his one-volume History of
Christian Missions,

> On the most sober estimate, the
> Christian is reasonably entitled to
> think that by the end of the twentieth
> century, Africa south of the Sahara
> will be in the main a Christian
> continent.

These four illustrations--and I could give
many more--show that we face not seed-sowing but
harvest, not May but September, and that we should

be going to the field not with plows but with harvesting combines.

Good reasons exist for this increased responsiveness. Today there are multitudes of Christians and younger churches in Asia, Africa, and Latin America. And populations are considered responsive because of them. There are at least twenty million evangelicals in Africa, fourteen million in India, and fifteen million in Latin America. True, even these numbers are small in comparison with the enormous populations of those lands. Nevertheless twenty million, fourteen million, and fifteen million are great companies of Christians. They need our help. They merit our help. They welcome us as allies.

In India I found that in sections of the country where few have become Christians, the baptism of a single man sometimes precipitates an anti-Christian riot. But in places where ten percent of the population has become Christian, the baptism of 1000 rouses no resentment. The Hindu neighbors have said as they have attended the baptismal service, "It is a good thing to become Christian. We have observed these people and their changed lives. The more people become Christians, the better it is for our beloved India."

In short, there are more "winnable" people today than there ever were before. In the United States there are far more than in the days of George Washington; in Asia, many more than in the days of William Carey. David Livingstone would never have dared dream of the numbers in Africa who today are abundantly "winnable," but they must be won. Men and women must volunteer. Missionaries must go. The gospel must be preached. New life must be demonstrated. And God calls for men and women to become his men and his women to preach it and demonstrate it.

The forty years ahead--the years of your usefulness and your service--are the most challenging and hopeful that the church has ever seen. Cardinal

Agaganian, an Armenian, head of Propoganda Fide
(the great Roman Catholic organization at Rome
to which all Roman Catholic missions report),
who knows more about missions than anybody else
on earth, wrote recently these significant words:

> All the missionary work done
> during the last three centuries
> of the evangelization of the non-
> Christian world is no more than
> an introduction, a preface to the
> true missionary work that must
> still come . . . . We have hardly
> dented the surface of the non-
> Christian world and have achieved
> apostolic success only among the
> primitive populations which have
> not yet entered the main streams
> of the social structure of non-
> Christian nations. Therefore the
> work waiting for us is, without
> a doubt, immensely larger than
> what has been done already.

God, you see, is calling us to Christian
missions in a day of unique openness to the gospel.

So far I have been speaking about winning
individuals and multiplying churches. What shall
we say concerning the desperate need both in the
United States and in every land on earth to
reconstruct society and make its framework more
honest and just and brotherly?

Responsiveness to the gospel has an enormous
meaning for the reconstruction of society. As new
and old nations face these revolutionary days,
they need reconstructed men. Their first need
is for men of integrity, unshakably righteous men.
Only reborn men in whose hearts Christ lives by
faith, who feed regularly on the Word of God, who
can meet the multitudinous needs of the nations
of the earth. East as well as west; and west,
believe me, as well as east.

This missionary convention is addressing
itself to the basic need of all revolutions and

reformations, all social advance and increase in peace and brotherhood and justice. Men who have been reconciled with God and live as God's men are absolutely necessary. The missionary carries the most needed medicine of all, the most needed food of all.

The life freely surrendered to Christ and then received back from him purified and empowered--this life is the ingredient each nation must have in abundance if the purposes of God for mankind are to be realized. If just, peaceful, and brotherly societies are to flourish everywhere, the gospel must be carried east and west, north and south, as it never has been before, into the most receptive populations that God has ever given his church opportunity to look upon.

WARREN WEBSTER: Where'er the Sun

King Solomon once said that "there is nothing new under the sun," and historians know that it is exceedingly difficult to speak of anything on the historic scene as being unmistakably new. Nevertheless, Dr. Stephen Neill in his recent History of Christian Missions points out:

> In the twentieth century one
> phenomenon has come into view which
> is incontestably new--for the first
> time there is in the world a universal
> religion, and that the Christian
> religion.

While the great ethnic religions--Hinduism, Buddhism and Islam--remain, for the most part, localized in the lands of their origin and early expansion, the Christian church alone has taken root in every continent and in practically every nation. In the modern world men have come to Christ from every race and religion, from every climate and culture, from every major linguistic grouping, and from every strata of society--both high and low. Today we live in a world where the sun never sets upon the church of Jesus Christ.

Two hundred fifty years ago in England,
Isaac Watts wrote a great hymn which is still often
sung:

>   Jesus shall reign where'er the sun
>   Does his successive journeys run;
>   His Kingdom stretch from shore to shore,
>   Till moons shall wax and wane no more.

I have often marveled that anyone could have written
a hymn like that back in 1718. At that time
Christian people in the world hardly numbered 150
million and there were great expanses where the
name of Christ had not so much as been heard.
Moreover, it was a time when the missionary vision
and concern of most churches in England, if not
in all of Europe, was at a lamentably low ebb.
It was written seventy-five years before the
entrance of the English-speaking world into the
modern missionary movement at the time of William
Carey, and it was nearly ninety years before the
beginning of the great Bible Society movement.
But what Isaac Watts foresaw by the eye of faith,
in the light of Psalm 72, has now become a reality
in the lives of men around the world.

Today it is possible to board an intercontinental
jet and to literally follow the sun in its journey
around the earth, but it is practically impossible
to find a land where there are no Christians. Dr.
Kenneth Scott Latourette, Professor Emeritus of
Missions and Oriental History at Yale University,
tells us that the church of Jesus Christ has never
been so widely planted, or so deeply rooted among
so many peoples as it is today. He says that as
far as we know,

>   In only one land which claims political
>   independence, the Mongolian People's
>   Republic, and possibly North Korea is
>   the church unrepresented.

Then he adds, most significantly,

>   Thirty years ago that could not have
>   been said.
>   Thirty years ago the church was unrepresented

in Saudi Arabia, Afghanistan, Tibet, and the Indian
borderland of Nepal, Bhutan and Sikkim. Today,
there are churches, or Christian believers, among
all of those peoples.

In Saudi Arabia today the church is represented
by Indian and Pakistani Christians, among others,
who are working in medicine, government service
and the oil industry.

In Afghanistan, where dedicated Christians
went in recent years as "tentmakers"--carrying on
their professions in the service of a developing
nation while living for the Lord and witnessing
to their faith when possible, there are now six
congregations of worshipping Christians. Granted,
that as yet most of their members are drawn from
foreign Christians employed there, nevertheless,
it may be said to the credit of the government and
people of that Central Asian land that the church
which is Christ's body is now present in their
midst.

In Nepal, Bhutan and Sikkim, once "closed
lands," the Bible Society recently reported the
distribution of 75,000 Scripture portions. Hindu
Nepal, despite a law technically prohibiting
change of religion, now has at least a dozen
communities of Christian believers meeting in
different places. In Sikkim where Christian people
enjoy equal civil rights with others and there is
no restriction on distribution of Scriptures and
Christian literature, scattered indigenous congregations
have taken root with their own local ministry. In
Bhutan where many Indian Christians have gone on
business, as settlers, or in government service,
local Christians are yet comparatively few in
number, but there is at least one Christian school
there and the church is at work today in Bhutan.

Tibet, long a "closed land," is no longer
an independent nation and hence, on one sense,
doubly closed--at least to ordinary penetration.
But in another sense Tibetan peoples are in closer
contact with the church than ever before. In
earlier days the gospel had entered Tibet by means

of scattered missionaries from China and India.
The Tibetan Bible, which was published in 1952,
has been carried across the border from India and
Pakistan by traders via yak-back. As a result,
there are Tibetan Christians today, though most
or all of them are in exile in India, where some
of their number are ordained ministers of Indian
congregations.

After the Communists forcibly took over
Tibet, reports began to come in of an increased
demand for Tibetan Bibles. Investigation revealed
that Chinese Communist officers had started reading
them, with the help of Chinese Bibles, in order
to learn Tibetan! It is also known that the
Tibetan Bible had reached highly-placed government
and religious leaders and was, in fact, being read
by the Dalai Lama, the so-called "god" of the
Tibetans. When he fled to India in 1959, leaving
everything behind, one of his requests was for
another Tibetan Bible with which to continue his
study of the Old Testament prophecies concerning
the coming of Christ. Now in North India along
the Tibetan border, refugees of the very tribe
from which the present Dalai Lama was chosen have
asked for Christian teachers and a school. And
they have indicated that if their children wish
to become Christians, they have no objection.
This is just one measure of the way in which God
is at work.

Even the Mongolian People's Republic, in
its mountain fastness, may not long retain its
dubious distinction as the only politically
independent nation in which the church is
unrepresented. It was recently reported that
there are Mongolian Christians in exile in Taiwan
and they, with the help of an elder missionary
statesman who once served in their land, are now
broadcasting the gospel back into Mongolia from
a radio station in South Korea, and it may well
be that some of the seed has already taken root
inside Mongolia itself! One more dimension in
which God is working in his world today.

Against this background, I am convinced that far too much has been made of a few relatively, or temporarily, "closed lands." We need to remember that in practically every country which is closed to foreign missionaries, the church of Jesus Christ is already represented behind that barrier, whatever it may be. From Russia and Eastern Europe come continuing reports of religious revival, even in the face of opposition. In Communist Rumania young people are reportedly coming to Christ in considerable numbers, partly because it is the "hard thing" to do.

In Burma, where the last Protestant missionaries had to withdraw in the face of a nationalization campaign of the government in 1966, a mature church with its own institutions and leadership continues to grow. On a recent visit there, I was told about three Burmese Christian young men from the Karen tribes of the mountain area who had gone to Russia on a scholarship to study music. Their parents and Christian friends were understandably concerned as to what might happen to their faith, but at last report the three young Burmese were in fellowship with Russian evangelical Christians and were witnessing to Communist students at the University of Moscow. God is simply not limited in the methods and means at his disposal for fulfilling his purposes in the world today.

In China and North Korea we have an admittedly different situation, an unhappy picture of a decimated and suffering church that is facing perhaps its most difficult days. But the truth remains that Christians are there behind the bamboo and barbed-wire curtains, and they merit our prayers.

Unquestionably, however, the fact of greatest significance on the world scene today is not the few lands which seem closed to outside Christian witness. Dr. McGavran is right when he says that there are more potentially responsive and "winnable" peoples now than ever before. This is true not only in Latin America (where the church is growing perhaps faster than in any place else in the world),

and in sub-Saharan Africa (which may be on its way
to becoming the next great nominally Christian
continent), but also in parts of Asia as well.

A striking example is Indonesia where
Christianity is demonstrating a vitality and rate
of growth that is reminiscent of the book of Acts.
In some parts of this great Muslim country, whole
villages have become Christian in recent months.
Particularly since the failure of the Communist
coup in 1965, reliably reported baptisms and
accessions to the church number at least 250,000
in the last 24 months, of which probably ten to
fifteen per cent--that is, some twenty to thirty
thousand--have come from Muslim backgrounds. Among
the animistic peoples of Timor, Kalimantan and
North Sumatra, baptismal services, at which 300,
500, and up to 1000 enter the church at one time,
are not uncommon. An evangelical pastor in Java
has reported personally baptizing more than 2000
converts in the last two years. One small village
church, in reporting 130 baptisms in the last
three months, said they have had to enlarge their
church building three times, and now they simply
have no room to make it any bigger.

The wonder and the glory of this spiritual
movement is that it is growing because lay people
are witnessing for Christ. Elders and teachers
in the church close down their shops and places
of business on Saturday and go out in the villages
or bazaars to witness. At the Christian University
in Salatiga, central Java, at least half a dozen
groups of Christian students take turns going every
day into the surrounding villages to "bring the
gospel." In the Indonesian Army, where a whole
battalion of 900 men reportedly became Christians,
20,000 Indonesian Bibles and 10,000 New Testaments
were purchased last year. And another 10,000 New
Testaments ordered by the Army could not be supplied
because the Indonesian Bible Society simply cannot
keep up with the demand for Scriptures. One more
area in which God is at work!

While we have been surveying particularly

the geographic dimension of the church's expansion
in the world, it should be remembered that the
gospel has not only spread geographically, but
also culturally and linguistically into almost
every corner of the world. In 1739 when Charles
Wesley wrote his majestic hymn, "Oh for a thousand
tongues," the Word of God had only been translated
into sixty-six different languages. Today the
Bible Societies tell us that the Scriptures, in
whole or in part, have been translated into more
than 1280 languages which are spoken by ninety-
seven percent of the world's peoples. This is
unquestionably the greatest achievement in language
communication which the world has ever known.
There may be places in the world where, measured
by sheer volume, the total mass of Communist
literature outweighs the quantity of Christian
Scriptures and literature available. But when
it comes to the number of languages and dialects
in which the Scriptures have been translated and
published, neither the Communists nor the United
Nations have come anywhere close to equaling the
record of the church of Jesus Christ. By way of
comparison the world's second largest religious
community--the religion of Islam, which claims to
be a universal faith for all mankind--has translated
its holy book, the Koran, into at most about 100
languages.

It is true that there are still some 2000
small language families and dialects into which
no part of the Word of God has been translated,
and this must be a matter of concern. But we need
to remember that all of these tribal peoples make
up less than three percent of the world's population.
Bbble translation has progressed to the point where,
for the most part, we are now working with language
populations under 10,000 speakers. Nevertheless,
these are people whom God loves and for whom Christ
died, and they have a right to hear the Word of
God in their mother tongue. Moreover, the task
is not impossible. Viewed against the background
of the church's achievements in penetrating languages

spoken by ninety-seven percent of the world's
people, we should be greatly encouraged to press
on and finish the job of Bible translation for
the remaining Bibleless groups. As a matter of
fact, today more than 3000 translators are at work
on more than 800 new Bible translations and revisions,
yet many more workers will be needed if we are to
complete the task for this generation.

When it has been said that the Bible is
potentially available, in whole or in part, for
ninety-seven percent of the earth's people, it
should not be uncritically assumed that ninety-
seven percent of the people on the globe have
heard the message of the Bible or been evangelized.
On the contrary, it has been estimated that in
Asia, where half of the people of the world live
between Karachi, Pakistan and Tokyo, Japan, only
about three percent of these people possess any
portion of Scripture. In such places the need
and potential for the distribution of Scriptures
and other Christian literature is immense.

At the same time we need to remember that
if a scripture portion could be put into the hands
of every man, woman, and child in a land like
Pakistan, fewer than twenty out of a hundred
could read it in any language. For that reason
the church continues to call for teachers and
specialists in literacy who, in conjunction with
government and Christian organizations, seek to
open men's eyes to the wonders that are in books
and preeminently to those which are in the Book
of books.

In the meantime, for the multitudes who
cannot read or do not have the Bible available to
them, God has raised up specialized ministries
like that of Gospel Recordings. According to
latest reports, the heart of the Christian message
has been recorded for distribution in more than
3508 languages and dialects--one more dimension
in which the gospel is being proclaimed throughout
the world!

Now what does all of this expansion and

accomplishment mean?

1. In the first place, it demonstrates that God is not dead, and his purposes in Christ are not about to be defeated.

2. Second, it underscores the words of our Lord who long ago commissioned his followers to "Go, disciple the nations," and then both promised and prophesied that the "gospel of the kingdom will be preached throughout the whole world, as a testimony to all nations; and then the end will come" (Matt. 24:14). What we have seen and heard to date reminds us that the "Omega point" of history has never been nearer than it is today.

3. This does not mean that the task of world evangelization is nearly finished so that Christians can begin to sit back and relax. Bishop Stephen Neill soberly estimates

> that one third of the people in the world have not so much as heard the name of Jesus Christ, and that another third have never heard the gospel presented in such a way as both to be intelligible and to make on them a demand for personal and existential decision. There is plenty still to be done.

4. It does mean that we are on the right track. God's purposes are being fulfilled; nations are being discipled; the message of repentance and forgiveness of sins in Christ's name is being proclaimed throughout the whole creation; and the church, which is his body, is being called out from every kindred, tongue, and nation into a Household of Faith which transcends all nations, cultures, and races. This is the great missionary fact of the twentieth century and the context in which the Living God invites the further investment and involvement of dedicated lives in every land for the glory of Christ.

ERIC FIFE

A little over a year ago I received an
invitation from Japan to take a week of missionary
meetings. In Japan? Now, I know that the Christian
population of Japan is perhaps approximately one-half
of one percent. Why would the Japanese be interested
in having missionary meetings to encourage Japanese
to become missionaries? It was all the more
impressive because the invitation was not contingent
upon American dollars; but the Japanese put up
Japanese yen to pay my fare out there. Arriving
in Japan I spent a week with Mr. Akira Hatori.
It's a tremendous privilege for me to welcome him
to this convention this week. I have asked him
to speak to you personally; I hope he does. He
has suffered for the cause of Christ, particularly
serving in the Japanese Army. Over all of Japan
I heard nothing but appreciation and praise for
his devotion to Jesus Christ and for his humility.
Again and again I heard him preach--very frustrating,
I could not understand a word he said--but again
I saw audiences moved as the Spirit of God used
his words. I have asked him to come today. You
have been given the world picture by Dr. McGavran
and Mr. Webster. I want that world picture to
be brought into personal focus by Mr. Hatori as
he tells you something of how he found Christ and
something of the missionary vision that God has
given to the Japanese Christians.

AKIRA HATORI

Standing before you, the cream of the young
people in America, the future hope of the nation,
I feel greatly honored to be invited to testify
to this great convention about the wonderful work
of missions in Asia, particularly in Japan.

First of all, as one from a younger church
in Asia, I thank you from the bottom of my heart
for your sending of missionaries over to Asia and
to Japan. I stand here as a proof of the Lord's

working through a missionary, a monument of the Lord's love built by a missionary, a trophy of the Lord's grace won by a missionary. It was suggested that I give my personal account with a missionary this morning, but before doing so, let me read from Mark 16:19-20. "So then after the Lord had spoken unto them, he was received up into heaven, and sat on the right hand of God. And they went forth and preached everywhere, the Lord working with them, and confirming the word with signs following."

Thirty some years ago I was a Buddhist boy. Being the first-born son of the family, my duty was to offer freshly-cooked rice and a glass of water every morning to our Buddhist altar and Shinto god-shelves. But I had no confidence in these religions because they did no good for our family. My parents used to fight with each other every day, day and night; there was no joy, no hope, no peace, no song. What was the purpose of life? In desperation I tried a few times to kill myself. What was the purpose of life? Could there be any purpose in living like this?

At that time I was going to a high school. One morning a teacher came to a classroom and asked, "Are there any Christians in this class? Raise your hand." Absolute silence. You see, Christianity is the enemy of Japan. I did not expect anyone to raise his hand, but one boy stood up and said, "Teacher, I believe in the Lord Jesus Christ who died for my sins." That brave testimony struck my heart, and I wanted to know the secret of his faith.

We became very close friends, and sure enough he took me to his church. There for the first time in my life I saw a missionary. She was an elderly lady missionary from England, and she led me to Christ. Then she said to me, "Now, son, when you go back to your house today, tell your father that you have accepted the Lord Jesus Christ as your Savior and Lord." It was a rainy

April night. Before I entered the house I knelt
down on the wet ground and prayed the first prayer
of my own. I said, "My God, how do you do. Please
take care of me." When I entered the house, I
told my father that I had accepted the Lord Jesus
Christ as my personal Savior and that when I opened
up my heart and accepted the Lord Jesus Christ,
the darkness went out. But my father got angry
at me and took me by the neck and pushed me down
in front of the Buddhist altar and Shinto god-shelf
and forced me to worship the idols in the house.
I said, "Father, I'll do anything for you, but I
cannot worship the idols anymore."

And you know, the missionary, Miss Burnett,
started to pray for me--not only for me but for
my whole family. She sent out letters overseas
to all of her friends asking them to pray for me
and for my family. And she tried hard to become
our friend. My stubborn father, my mother, my
sister came to know the Lord. My brother, who
was a Communist, now is preaching the Word of God
as an evangelist in Japan. Among my relatives
and family there are now more than twenty-five
ministers of the Lord, including one missionary
to Thailand.

When Miss Burnett went to be with the Lord,
she left not only my family but also twenty-five
churches--self-propagating, self-supporting,
self-governing. During the war time Miss Burnett
did not want to go home to her England. She
stayed right in Japan; so the government kept
her in a small Japanese house, guarded by many
policemen. Some of the policemen even became
seekers of the Lord secretly.

After my conversion I went to Tokyo to get
my education. I became a teacher, then later
was drafted. I had a hard time as a Christian
in Japanese military service, but it strengthened
my faith. When at last the war was over, I
resumed teaching business. Later when I was
teaching in a college in Tokyo, the Lord called
me into the full-time service. I resigned from

the college, took two suitcases with me and went back to Miss Burnett. I was afraid she would stop me, but to my astonishment she said to me, "My son, I knew that this day was coming. I have been praying for ten years without fail--every day, morning and night."

Miss Burnett took me in, and every morning she taught me the Bible. In the afternoon and evenings I went out to witness in home visitation, evangelistic meetings, street meetings, and tent meetings. I had very, very wonderful days of training. Miss Burnett wanted to teach me Greek, though she did not know the language. So she started to study Greek. One day she studied the portion, and the next day she taught me the same portion. Together we finished Machen's introductory text in two or three months.

Then she said to me, "Akira, I have taught you all that I can. Now you should go to America to get higher education." And she drew out all the money she had saved up and gave it to me so I could go to America. The day before my sailing I went to bid her farewell. And she had bought a new brown suit and a new pair of shoes for me. Those were very hard days, days when we could not get anything in Japan, right after the war. But somehow she had managed to buy a brand new pair of shoes for me. She asked me to put them on and to walk around her. I did. And with a big smile she looked me up and down. I saw big tears coming down on her cheek. And she said, "My son, now you go, but please don't forget to come back to Japan and to preach for me, to win souls for me, and to work."

She died; she went to be with the Lord one year after I came to America. I wept all night. I said to the Lord, "Why? Why?" But after several hours of agony, I suddenly felt a portion of her spirit come down on me. And I realized the Lord had picked me to preach the gospel, to testify, and to give my life to my own nation.

I started evangelizing among the Japanese

immigrants in California, and the Lord gave me soul after soul. I started radio evangelism in California, and the Lord blessed it. Then I went back to Japan, full of expectation, faith, and burden. Now when I stand before the microphone doing radio and television evangelism in Japan, I know I am actually speaking the Word of God to six million people. I also go out to preach the gospel, holding three-day campaigns all over the nation, averaging fifty to seventy campaigns a year. Each month we have been getting about 200 decisions for Christ.

I have never had a day pass without thinking about Miss Burnett, the dear English lady missionary. When she was twenty-six years of age, when the German submarines threatened the seven seas of the world, she came to Japan. She went forth to Japan to preach the gospel everywhere. The Lord was with her. Because she came to Japan, to us, and to me, I was saved. Because she trained me, loved me, and gave her life to me, I can stand before you today as a servant of the Lord. I want to give my life, too, not only to my own nation but to the whole world. Because Miss Burnett was obedient to the call, as she went forth and preached everywhere, the Lord went with her and confirmed her message with signs.

Miss Burnett not only trained me and made me a disciple of the Lord Jesus Christ, but she also gave me a missionary vision. I wanted to go out, but I could not. And so my secretary went out as a missionary. Two Japanese couples went out as missionaries to South America in my stead. And as Mr. Fife related to you before, I organized missionary conferences three years ago, and now there are missionary conferences all over Japan. Just about one month ago I spoke to a newly-organized missionary conference in Nagoya, the central city of Japan. The number of people who came was small, about 300. But when I gave out the word of challenge, out of that three hundred, 124 stood up and said, "I dedicate myself to go out to preach the gospel."

Japan is a poor country as far as the church

is concerned. And yet the Holy Spirit is moving in the nation, giving us a faith that we should go out to preach the gospel. We are so full of gratitude and thankfulness to the Lord who has sent so many missionaries to our own nation; I stand before you this morning with deep gratitude and appreciation for your sending of missionaries to Japan. And we do need more missionaries in Japan, but as a partnership. Will you help us become a missionary-sending nation in the near future? Thank you very much.

6. Who Needs Missionaries?

ERIC FIFE: Introduction

Our next three speakers are from overseas, and of course it's always a particular pleasure to welcome them. They do have two built-in problems. First, English is not their native tongue. And second, can they really speak frankly and honestly to us about whether they need American missionaries in their country? I have asked them to be as honest as they can. I know that they will be polite, but we don't want their courtesy to obscure their forthrightness. And I know you will take what they say in that spirit. Now I have no idea what they are going to say, but this is what we have asked them to do. First of all, Mr. Akira Hatori through whom the Lord spoke to us yesterday.

AKIRA HATORI: Asia

We need missionaries in Asia and Japan for at least three reasons. <u>First</u>, we have many people, many unevangelized people in Asia and Japan. And we need your help. If you come to Tokyo and try to get on the morning rush-hour train, you will know what I mean by many people. Japan's national labor company hires hundreds of thousands of people, young, strong people, just to push or pull people in or out of rush trains. My secretary is a

vocational missionary from America. When she
arrived at Haneda Airport in Tokyo, her first
remark was: "Are these all Japanese? Are we
going to evangelize them all?" Yes, we have to.
Among these multitudes of Japanese only one out
of every two hundred knows anything about Jesus
Christ. We have to evangelize them all.

Now, twenty years since the war ended,
we Japanese have almost everything--cars,
refrigerators, color television, bowling alleys,
go-go dancers, and even the Japanese version of
hippies--and spiritual barrenness.

The other day a news item shocked me very
much. One parent locked two of his own children
in one small room and left them without food
until they died of utter starvation. Not because
the parents didn't have any food, not because
they didn't have any money or clothing, but
because they had no love. No purpose of life.
No energy to live. What we need in Japan is the
gospel, the love of God, the forgiveness of sins,
purity of life, and purpose of life in the Lord
Jesus Christ.

Yes, we have Christians and Christian
workers in Japan, but look at these multitudes.
They are scattered like sheep without a shepherd.
They're fainting. Jesus said, "More laborers,
so few men." And I must cry the same cry to you.
In Japan, missionaries planted almost all the
churches that were opened after the war. Still
four-fifths of our 9,000 towns and villages have
no Christian witness at all. And I should say
that almost all of the farmers, fishermen, and
merchants are yet untouched people in Japan.
Missionaries have come from abroad with vision,
prayer backing, time, money, and ability. Most
of all, they have carried strangeness and
distinctiveness and holiness which attracted us
very much. So after the war, the missionaries
were the most effective Christian workers in Japan.
And now I must cry another Macedonian call to
you--we need more missionaries in Japan.

Second, we feel the urgency of concentrating on evangelism in Asia and Japan now. In the church history of Japan there have been two or three extraordinary chances for evangelism. But Japanese Christians missed them because of their lack of vision, lack of sound theology, the lack of training of lay Christians and witnesses, and the resulting lack of a simple and direct communication of the gospel.

Now I feel that we are facing another extraordinary opportunity for evangelism in Japan and in Asia. The Holy Spirit is moving over our nation. The Holy Spirit is working in our hearts. The other day after 9 P.M. one 73-year-old man came to see me. He said, "I want to know the Lord Jesus Christ. I want to be saved." And he got saved.

We had Billy Graham crusade two months ago in Tokyo. When Billy finished the first crusade meeting message which I was interpreting, one of the bodyguards, a policeman, came to me, ran to me, and said, "Teacher, be my counselor. I want to be saved." And he was saved. Of the fifteen thousand decisions made for Christ throughout these crusade meetings, the majority were from the nineteen to twenty-nine-year-old age group. In Japan not only the children but the young people, mature, deep-thinking youth are seeking for truth.

After we broadcast three television messages, fifteen thousand letters came in, and many pastors were awakened after 11 P.M. by seekers who had watched these programs. They wanted to be saved. So you know there is a hunger in the hearts of the people of Japan and Asia. This is the time to put every energy into evangelism so that we can cover the nation with the gospel, penetrate the nation with the preaching of the gospel of Jesus Christ.

Third, we know that Japanese and Asians themselves have great potential to become useful witnesses for the Lord Jesus Christ. In other words, we can become missionary-sending countries

in the near future if we have the right kind of
guidance. The Lord is giving Japan remarkable
natural and material blessings. Why? The Lord
wants to use Japan for his glory.

If Japan keeps her selfish way any longer,
I'm sure her days of prosperity are numbered. In
Japan there has been the tendency of isolationism;
the Japanese church--just for Japanese, by Japanese,
to Japanese. Instead of the "going out" structure,
the Japanese church has been built on the "come"
structure. We have to be going out to preach the
gospel. We have to be the witnesses of the Lord.
Going out--going forth anywhere and everywhere to
preach the gospel of Jesus Christ. And I feel
that the American missionaries can come to Japan
and give us the vision and the missionary training.
You can come and become our comrades in world
evangelization. Japanese young people are ready
to have your help, to have your companionship,
to have your comradeship.

Jesus said, "Many people, and few laborers."
He is looking for men, missionaries to send.
Before us there is the great missionary example
of the Lord Jesus Christ. He came down, and his
crown of thorns was exchanged for the crown of
glory. He bled and died on the cross in exchange
for the lives of many in the new world. So, you
can come to Japan and to Asia as your Missionary
Example did.

And also, you have the missionary right
because Jesus said, "All power is given to me in
heaven and on earth." Maybe some of the national
Japanese Christian leaders say, "No more American
missionaries; we want your money, but no missionaries."
And many of the Japanese young people, those who
are rioting and demonstrating and crying, "Yankee
go home," may say, "No more missionaries." But
you have the right to come because Jesus your
Sender said, "I have all power in heaven and on
earth." Regardless of what people may say, if
he has sent you, you have the right to come.

And before you there is a missionary might.

You can come with heavenly might because Jesus
said, "I have the power, all the power in heaven
and on earth, given to Me," and he said, "I will
go with you." You can come to Japan with the
power of love. You can come to Japan with the
power of direct and simple preaching of the Lord
Jesus Christ's gospel which is matchless, which
is transforming power. You can come to Japan
with humility which Jesus took when he came down
to this earth. Thank you.

ERIC FIFE

And now we welcome to the platform for
the first time, the Reverend Emilio Nunez. First
of all, he was born in El Salvador and later he
moved to Guatemala. He then came to take seminary
training in this country, and I am told that he
had very little knowledge of English. His main
method of study was to take the notes of his
classmates down to the basement of the seminary
at night and translate them with the aid of a
Spanish-English dictionary. Thus, eventually,
he got his degree in theology. He has been on
the staff of the Central American Mission Bible
Institute and Seminary in Guatemala and is presently
back taking graduate seminary work in Texas. Mr.
Nunez.

EMILIO NUNEZ: Latin America

One of the reasons why I am here as a
Christian in fellowship with you Christians is
that North Americans were willing to send missionaries
to my own country, and some North American Christians
were willing to go to announce the message of Jesus
Christ in that land. As a result of that work,
the evangelical church in Latin America has been
established, and now we have a number of leaders
who are preaching the gospel in those countries.
But some people here in North America have
asked me on many occasions, "In view of the fact

that you have so many Christian leaders in Latin
America--many of them very well-trained men who
preach a lot better than the North American
missionaries--do you still need missionaries in
Latin America?" To answer this question it is
necessary to realize that the missionary challenge
in Latin America is greater today than a hundred
years ago when the pioneer missionaries came to
preach the gospel among the Latin American people.
If our Christian mission is limited to evangelizing
a few souls and to starting an evangelical church
everywhere in the world, then we do not need any
more foreign missionaries in Latin America. But
if our missionary task is a dynamic one, and if
the development of the national church depends
on preaching the gospel to our generation, then
we need foreign missionaries in Latin America
today.

Relatively speaking, the work of Christian
missions is more complex today than when the
missionary pioneers came to our country. It is
said that the population in Latin America is growing
faster than in any place in our world. The very
existence of the Latin American church, our variety
of ministers in evangelism, Christian education,
and social work, demands the cooperation of a large
number of foreign missionaries in Latin America
at the present time. We need an army of evangelists,
educators, and specialists in different professions
to meet the challenge of the fastest growing
population in the world.

And we should remember that Latin America
is a mission field not only in the jungles in the
Amazonic region of Brazil. I believe that those
people who live in primitive conditions need the
gospel. And I have great respect and admiration
for the missionaries who are spending their lives
trying to preach the gospel to those tribes, but
Latin America is more than that. Latin America
is the working masses in the big cities. Latin
America is the professional people. Latin America
is the student population in the universities.

Guatemala City is small by American standards, only half a million people. But we have four universities in Dazeli, which indicates the increase of the student population in Latin America, and this is a mission field.

In many respects, the Latin American culture is in the process of change. It's a transitional culture. Many Latin Americans are striving to abandon their old customs, their old traditions, and trying to become adapted to a new way of life. The new attitude of the Roman Catholic Church is opening to us many doors of evangelism. I will say today that we have the greatest opportunity in the whole history of missions in Latin America.

This is an opportunity not only for the national leaders but for foreign missionaries from any country of the world, from any race in this world. Up to now, in missionary circles in the United States and in the national churches abroad, we have been emphasizing--overemphasizing perhaps-- the distinction between the national leader and the foreign missionary. I believe that the day has come when we should emphasize the universality and the unity of the church of Jesus Christ and our common task to preach the gospel to our generation.

My second reason why I believe that missionaries are still needed in Latin America is found in the missionary command of our Lord, "Go therefore and make disciples of all nations." This command is as valid today as it was more than nineteen hundred years ago. It is not just a suggestion to be considered. It is not just a theory to be expounded. It is a command to be obeyed.

We are to be on the march, moving forward, expanding our horizons in the Lord's war. We are not supposed to retreat in the name of the indigenous principle nor under the excuse of nationalism. I believe in the indigenous principle, but I believe that taking this principle to the extremes could paralyze, to a large extent, the lost who are around the world.

And I believe there is nationalism. I am

as nationalistic as you are as North Americans.
But I believe that exaggerating the problem of
nationalism may make an excuse for not preaching
the gospel everywhere in the world. The Roman
Catholic Church has been in Latin America for more
than four hundred years, but Roman Catholic
missionaries are still going to Latin America.
They are not thinking of retreating; they are
thinking of staying and expanding their work. I
don't need to apologize to my fellow citizens
because of the presence of American missionaries,
American Protestant missionaries, in my own country.
I have only to point to a large number of European
and Canadian priests--Roman Catholic priests--who
are working there.

The Peace Corps is going in the name of
democracy to help the people in the underdeveloped
areas in Latin America. Why shouldn't we go?
Jehovah's Witnesses, Mormons, and other religious
groups are going into Latin America. Why shouldn't
we go? Even the Communists are going to Latin
America to spread their atheistic and materialistic
philosophy. Why shouldn't we go with the message
of genuine freedom in Jesus Christ?

The third reason why I believe missionaries
are still needed in Latin America is that the Holy
Spirit is still calling missionaries to go to
Latin America. The Lord Jesus Christ is commanding
his church to go, and the Holy Spirit is calling
some people in a very specific way to go to Latin
America.

Let's suppose that we Christian leaders in
Latin America say we don't need more American
missionaries there. Who are we to question the
decision of the Holy Spirit? Who are we to question
his wise and sovereign purpose in sending missionaries
there? And who are we to say that the time for
foreign missions is gone if the Holy Spirit is still
leading Christian men and women to give their lives
for Christ in a foreign country?

The privilege and duty of the American
churches today is to follow the example of the

church at Antioch which sent out Paul and Barnabas
when the Holy Spirit said, "Set apart Barnabas and
Saul for the ministry to which I have called them."
And the privilege of those God calls to be
missionaries abroad should be to imitate Paul and
Barnabas in their willingness to go without delay,
following the leading of the Holy Spirit.

After all, the leading of the Holy Spirit
should be in any circumstance the primary
consideration for the Christian who is concerned
about the possibility of going into the mission
field. The main question is not, Where do I
think that I am needed the most? But it is, Where
does the Holy Spirit want me to go? It is not
even a question of which people in the world are
more interested in getting my help. The Holy
Spirit might send me to a people who are not as
conscious of their spiritual needs as I should
expect them to be. It is evident that the
Ninevites were not asking for missionaries. But
Jehovah sent Jonah to preach to them. The people
in the Roman Empire were not asking for missionaries
to the small Christian congregation in Antioch or
in Jerusalem, but the Holy Spirit sent Paul to
preach to them.

Instead of asking whether we need
missionaries in Latin America, I would prefer to
ask this morning, Does the Holy Spirit need
missionaries in that place? It is a fact that
he does, because he continues calling some men
and women to go there. I am praying that even
here in Urbana it might be the will of God for
him to call many of you to be ministers or foreign
missionaries. I confess that my joy will be greater
if the Holy Spirit calls some of you to go to Latin
America. I would like to be there to tell you,
"Mi norteamericano, apelo que el Senor le bendiga
en su mision." Welcome to Latin America; may the
Lord bless you in your ministry. Thank you.

ERIC FIFE

Today we shall continue the theme, Who needs missionaries? But I would remind you that tomorrow evening we are considering the theme, What are the qualifications of these missionaries? I'll ask our friends to be equally frank--a little more frank, rather--when they deal with that subject in order that maybe they'll hit more tender spots than what they have this morning. Next, I welcome on your behalf, Mr. Sandy Olutamayin, who is from Nigeria, who received much of his education in the Sudan Interior Mission schools there, and who is at present an engineering student in Princeton University, New Jersey. Mr. Olutamayin.

OLUGBEMI OLUTAMAYIN: Africa

Before we ask whether we need missionaries or not, I think it will help us if we find out what we mean when we say "missionary." To me a missionary is any child of God who is called to cross the religious or cultural or political frontier to take the message to some other people.

Now before I tell you whether we need missionaries in Africa, I wish you to bear with me while we look at what missionaries have done in the past and at their potential for the future. It is only on these grounds that we can clearly decide whether or not we need missionaries--if we can decide.

I am a product of a mission high school which was one of many educational institutions in my country. It is very obvious that Africa needs more than this one particular institution. You realize that there are many parts of Africa where development has not been quite as high as it has been in Nigeria, so the need for education is much greater now than it has ever been. Now, at this crucial point in our development, we need a lot more educational institutions of the nature of the one that I attended.

We need not only the establishment of such
institutions, but also their maintenance. Some
of our enthusiastic nationals, many of them well
meaning, agitated for missionaries to leave after
establishing these institutions. To the average
African in the street, missions seems to be only
a means to an end; to him the missionary movement
seems to be nothing more than a means of economic
advancement or capitalism without imperialism.
To him, of course, early departure of missionaries
is justifiable. If, however, the education is a
means to achieve another end--the spreading of the
gospel--this departure could not be justified.
Even if education were an end in itself, this
departure could not be justified. Likewise with
hospitals. Across the road from my school, there
is a perpetually overcrowded and understaffed
hospital; it is impossible to get enough Nigerians
who are capable of caring for these sick.

Insofar as education and health are ends
in themselves, we need staff who are academically
equipped to run and staff these institutions
efficiently. Insofar as our end is the spreading
of the gospel, we need men who are spiritually
equipped. Our taking over will have to be done
over two, three, four, or five decades. Rather
than supplant missionaries, we need to supplement
them as liberals under the same banner.

While we develop the necessary indigenous
manpower, we need outside help to try to keep up
with the competition of the secular sector of our
society. Most of the aid from governments from
the outside world--some is called propaganda, but
to us it is aid--has been to advance the secular
sector of our societies. However, we Christians
need to try to keep peace with the secular sector
of the world in communicating our message to people
of our day and in their language. So, as number
two, maybe we should "try harder."

There is another kind of missionary which
I want to tell you about this morning. It is the
kind that is standing before you this morning.

There are many of us who are not affiliated with
any mission, but who nevertheless have been called.
In this sense I consider myself a missionary to
the little university town of Princeton. I'm not
a very good missionary but, all the same, a
missionary. If we'd only lift up our eyes we
would see that many of us have been placed in a
particular position--a particular school--for a
time such as this. It is an enormous harvest field,
and while we fold our arms in indifference or
passive concern, our compatriots slide into eternal
damnation. We need American missionaries to reach
the young and the old, both in Africa and in America.

You are a missionary to your parents. You
may not believe this, but if you try to be, you
will find it is one of the most difficult kind of
missionaries to be. It is being a missionary because
you are crossing a cultural frontier, crossing from
the Pepsi generation to the Second World War veterans.

In this concern there are missionary societies
in Nigeria whose members are sent by Nigerians and
who are financed by Nigerian churches giving to
Nigerians. We want to avoid the tragedy that
happened in Israel where they had a vision on their
doorsteps, yet many of them ended up in eternal
damnation. This is the danger that faces our
society today.

We, the youth of today, constitute a presently
dormant but unique striking force. We need to
mobilize. I don't see why the flower children
should be more enthusiastic about their philosophy
than we who call ourselves God's children are about
Christianity. We have to start in our Jerusalems
and, as I said before, this is difficult and should
not be left to a chosen few who have been called
by God to be shepherds of our churches. Some of
us might not be called to Africa or to South America
or to Asia, but to Greenwich Village, or Las Vegas,
or Watts. We may seek to pacify our conscience and
to bribe God by paying for some few courageous men
and women of God to go overseas, but we cannot get
away with it if we neglect our home front. And

your DMZ and my DMZ might be much nearer home than
we have ever thought about, much more than we ever
like to think about.

The world needs missionaries today more
than ever. There is no doubt about it. The world
needs missionaries to penetrate the darkness of
ignorance in remote areas of Africa, to penetrate
the bamboo curtain, the iron curtain, and the
almighty dollar curtain.

We dare not close our eyes to this whitened
harvest field. We must go forth. How? The world
puts us to shame in creativity. In all the news
media and in the production of things and materials,
people are always coming up with new ideas, but
it seems that we Christians still rely sometimes
on outmoded methods. We must use our ingenuity
and creativity in the business of our most benevolent
Father. We each fit into the plan in a special
way, and if we honestly seek with an open heart
and a completely open mind and life, we shall find
our place in due time.

In passing I want to mention that there is
a kind of missionary that may do some harm. In
some measure they have brought the accusations
to God's cause by not putting their earthly and
heavenly citizenships in proper priority. This
kind of missionary we have never needed, we do
not need, and we shall never need. And I doubt
if God needs that kind of missionary either. To
bring this point home I'd like to quote for you
what a Nigerian friend of mine said to me once.
He said, "I am first a Christian and then a Nigerian,
and maybe a better Nigerian for that matter."

The world, even where there is economic
stability, is in abject spiritual poverty. We
see it daily, we live in the middle of it, we travel
through it, we see the need, we hear the need,
and we live in it. We need many more missionaries
today than ever before. God is calling both you
and me and, as soldiers of the cross, we should
be ready to pull ourselves together and take our
course. Some of us may not have the joy of serving

God in Africa, although there is a lot of need
there for doctors, and nurses, and lab technicians,
and teachers. However, some of us might be able
to serve God in IVCF, in summer camps, in Ecuador,
or in the Sahara, in Africa, in Miami, in Alberta,
or in our own homes.

There is an acute shortage of manpower in
the front line of the missionaries. That shortage
cannot be measured in terms of souls to be saved,
because I believe evangelism is not just the initial
introduction of the gospel of Christ; it is the
perpetual pounding in of the gospel. In this respect
we need more missionaries. But you and I both
realize that some missionaries in the past
contributed more to our country's economy than
to reaching the people with the gospel. So we
need more missionaries today. In the school I
come from there was always a shortage of staff
members. You find math teachers who have to chip
in on medieval history and things they never have
taught before. And, in this respect, we need a
lot more teachers. We need volunteers. We need
doctors, and we need nurses. But, much more than
these, we need young people who are ready to be
missionaries in their own Jerusalems, which is
always difficult, and in their own country--Africa
or America. May God help us to summon courage to
meet the world's need of missionaries, many
missionaries.

ERIC FIFE

When you passed through the registration
line, you received a book "You and God's Work
Overseas" by Michael Griffiths. I hope you read
that book. It has a great deal in it for missions
which is sane and is biblical.

Our closing speaker this morning is George
Verwer.

GEORGE VERWER: The World

Just for a moment let's unite our hearts
in a word of prayer: Father, we praise thee for
these three brothers from three different parts
of the world who have shown us an open door. We
thank thee, God, that thou hast given us the
greatest privilege of being ambassadors for Jesus
Christ. We ask in the name of the Lord Jesus
that the remaining moments of this morning together
may consolidate our thinking, and clearly show us,
O God, what You would have us do in the light of
the lost and dying world. Continue, God, to hide
this speaker behind the cross. Continue to over-
rule personality. And bring us into focus to our
blessed Jesus Christ, in whose name we pray, amen.

I wasn't privileged to be here in 1957.
I was only two years old and I couldn't make the
journey--I had only been converted in 1955. But
thanks to tape recordings, not long after that I
was able to sit down--I don't remember where--and
listen to the message that Billy Graham gave on
New Year's Eve, 1957. I'll never forget that
message. Since then I've listened to it more than
fifteen times because it shook me. It shook my
foundations, it shook my philosophy of life, it
shook my materialistic instincts, it shook my
social ideas. It shook me, and I've never recovered.

Wherever I've gone I've played that tape
recording, all over the United States, in dozens
of colleges and Bible schools. The tape has been
circulated until it could hardly be played at
times. For the last seven or eight years I've
lived outside of the United States. I've played
that tape in Spain, India, Oxford, and universities
throughout the British Isles. Everywhere we've
played that tape young men have responded. More
than anything else, at this conference I want to
say that what Billy Graham said in 1957, what
Stacey Woods has said, what Eric Fife has said--
what these men have said down through the years--
is absolute truth. And it works in the twentieth

century.

I believe many of us--perhaps a majority of us--will not really respond, will not really be revolutionized by what we're hearing in this convention. When one studies the statistics concerning those who attended the convention in 1957, and when one truly and realistically examines how many are literally living the life that Billy challenged people to live--if one is realistic, the statistic is not very bright.

I believe the explanation is that we in the evangelical church have fallen into a very dangerous situation. A dichotomy has been formed, and it exists here in this auditorium this morning. Everything I say will be worthless, everything our dear brothers have said will be worthless unless you are prepared to see this dichotomy broken down. This dichotomy is so serious in the ranks of the evangelical church that I think it could be analyzed as a spiritual schizophrenia. It almost made me an agnostic.

At the first college I went to after I was converted, no one pretended to believe the Bible. We had two to three hundred men preparing for the ministry; 90 percent of them denied the Bible to be the Word of God. The New Morality and all those things were the common philosophy of that day. When I think that these men are taking the so-called message to our churches in America today, I tremble. I tremble.

There are only a few evangelical Christians on that campus. A little group. I remember what I was told about them when I first got there. I was warned about a young man named Dale Rotan who has since pioneered evangelism and missionary work in Turkey. I was a freshman so green that I didn't even know what the word "fundamentalism" meant. I'd been converted one year and I thought that everybody who was born again was also on fire for Christ, living a Christian, holy life. You can say I was green. I was called a fundamentalist. I was warned about the prayer meetings, the fanatical, extremist, overpowered, unbalanced prayer meetings on the third floor. I was told that they prayed when the school dances went on.

I must confess I chose that school because they danced. I was sure that I had a verse from the Psalms that showed that dancing was completely compatible with Christianity. I loved rock and roll until it came out of my ears. If I couldn't find girls, I would dance with brooms (why Americans clap when you say you'll dance with a broom is something I haven't figured out). Anyway, I was warned about this young man. I was told that he was dangerous. I was told that he was a fanatic. I was told that he was baptizing people in the showers. And this was especially interesting because he was a Presbyterian.

I went to the prayer meeting, and I was shocked because I heard someone say "amen" in the meeting. It almost knocked me out. (No one ever made any noise in my church unless they fell asleep and snored.) Anyway, I discovered, as a young babe in Christ, real Christians. I met this young man, a Hungarian refugee, who was so much like Jesus Christ that I can't explain it.

I had so many typical American ideas I thought I was going to make an impact on that campus through basketball. And I loved basketball. I could eat and drink basketball. I thought that if we got a group of fundamentalists on a team together and if we won, this would be a tremendous testimony for Christ on this campus. Many of us have that idea. You become the most popular, the most well liked, and after that you tell them that you're a Christian. And all of a sudden they'll fall down and worship at your shrine. It doesn't work, but we think it does. Anyway, to make it short, I met real Christians.

God led me out of that school to an evangelical institution. There I met young men by the hundreds who had been reared on Bible verses, whose fathers were executives here, there and everywhere within the church. There I met young people similar, I believe, to many who are gathered here this morning.

During this time I was studying Marx and Lenin. I was a rebel, I must admit. I saw something in Marx. I saw something in Lenin. I saw something in humanism. I saw something in social revolution. There was something in each of these that attracted me. They were men who were ready, seemingly, to do anything--anything. And I'm sure that if I weren't a Christian today, I would be leading anti-Viet Nam riots and everything else that you could possibly think of.

At that school I met hundreds of young people who claimed to believe the Bible, who claimed to believe in world missions, who claimed to believe in this place of hell that I oouldn't understand. In fact, anyone in my former college who believed in hell was considered next to an imbecile. Yet, I saw young people who, in spite of believing all these things, had no reality in their lives, had no zeal, had no love, had no desire for reaching the world.

It was because a dichotomy had been formed: What we say we are and what we listen to and what we sing--the greatest hymnology in all the world-- is in an airtight compartment (psychology has proven that this is possible with the mind).

At this convention you and I can rededicate our lives, raise our hands, sing the hymns, agree with the speakers, and yet remain no different or become no different. You know and I know it's true. This isn't our first convention. I sat under the ministry of Alan Redpath in Chicago for two years. He broke me down, he tore me up, he killed everything that I thought was real, and sometimes I had to leave the meeting in tears. And yet I saw all around me hundreds of students who had been reared on Bible verses, hundreds of students who believed just as he was teaching, and they remained unmoved, unconcerned. I couldn't understand it. And I believe this is the greatest danger of this convention. Because this dichotomy has formed in our own lives, because this airtight compartment has been formed, what we say we believe, what we determine we believe, what we sing about, will not affect this other part of our life--our social life, our domestic life, our economic life--what we do with our time, our money, our energy, our everything.

Billy Graham said in one of his sermons, "You can tell a man's commitment by what he does with his money." I couldn't understand that, I always believed that it was your life that counts. But in that sermon Billy Graham went on to say that a man's money represents his life--time, talents, energy, education, everything--converted into currency. And what America is doing with her money, the way you and I spend our money, is a great representation of what we really believe and where we really stand.

Now I'll turn in these closing moments to describe the great unbelievable need around the world, with the prayer that as you see this need, the dichotomy will be broken and somehow you will be able to relate the two together. Let us quickly travel across the world. Let us mention some of the countries which have not been mentioned very much. I would love to have a chance to talk with Dr. McGavran; unfortunately, he has left. Semantics is a terrible problem, tremendous problem. And I'm just a . . . well, as one young man said at a meeting once, I'm just an intellectual neophyte when it comes to semantics. So if I confuse you with some of my terminology, write me; I love to get letters. And if everyone wrote me from here, I'd try, by the grace of God, in the next sixty years to answer you. But I know that this morning and tomorrow I'm going to say some things you don't like or you don't understand. I pray you'll write to me if you can't get to see me here.

Let us quickly go to Spain. What's the situation in Spain today? For years, we in America complained about a closed land. Now Spain is open. So what! The Jehovah's Witnesses go, and we remain watching. There aren't enough evangelical churches

in Spain to fill three pages in a notebook, if
you write small. Very few evangelical churches
in the entire nation. Most of them are located
in the area of Barcelona. The fastest growing
group in Spain today is the Jehovah's Witnesses,
mainly Americans who have discipled hundreds of
Spanish people and who are covering the nation
with their literature. Spain is probably 90
percent unevangelized and yet how many here speak
Spanish? Quantos aqui hablan Espanol? I believe
the time has come, and I say this to all my Latin
American friends, that we begin moving into Spain.
All the Latin American countries are 100 times
as evangelized as the land of Spain. I praise
God for Mexicans I know who are in Spain this
morning.

What about Italy? We've confused Christianty
with civilization. There are twenty million people
in just northern Italy alone. There are only a
few dozen evangelical churches in the entire area
north of Italy. I would love Stacey Woods to
speak about the student situation in Italy, where
all these years there have been two dear women
laboring with Inter-Varsity, practically alone,
among the hundreds of thousands of Italians in
the student population. And I praise God for
those who work among students in North America
and in Canada. I pray someone will one of these
days present the unbelievable need to go forth in
the barren, unevangelized universities in Europe--
universities with 100,000 students and not more
than twenty witnessing for Jesus Christ.

I could be here all morning talking about
the mission field of the world's universities.
It's incredible. In the city of Calcutta, India,
there are more than 100,000 students. I recently
spoke to the student union there and we had fifteen
out at the meeting. We cannot begin to grasp the
need.

I cannot even begin to explain to you the
need in Italy; the need among seven million people
in Austria where there is just a matter of a handful

trying to do the job; the need among nine million people in Belgium, one of the toughest countries in the world. We've been on university campuses where there is not one single known group meeting in the name of the Lord Jesus Christ. And what about France and so many other countries?

Can we jump a little farther to the land of Turkey? Turkey, thirty-three million people and less than fifty Turks know the Lord Jesus Christ. I hardly believe we can say that there is a church in that land when it is only an American air base church. There's that land challenging us this morning, calling for men. I praise God, I praise God for some Oxford men right now in Istanbul. I believe God is going to send even more from here to Turkey. Thirty-three million people and less than fifteen missionaries in the entire nation.

And then someone comes up to me and says, "But the need is so great in the United States." I want to tell you, and you can argue with me later on the forum, that there are more Christian witnesses in the United States than in all the countries in the world apart from South America. We are so blind to other countries. We are so egocentric as a nation. We are so selfish as a people that we think everything flows in and out of the United States.

All I can hear from people is the tremendous needs in the United States. I know that 90 percent of you will end up in the United States, while the Mormons send out 16,000. That's right. The Mormon male marching missionary population of Europe alone right now is 16,000. What are we going to do with our statistic? Are we going to let it fit neatly into the dichotomy? Or are we going to think and act upon it?

I could talk about Persia or Afghanistan. After the statistics from the panel yesterday, I went to a young man who lives in Afghanistan. I asked, "Where are those six congregations?" None of them are Afghans. I think that was made somewhat

clear anyway. You could probably find less than
ten declared Afghan believers among thirteen or
fourteen million people in Afghanistan.

And I could talk about Arabia. I've been in
all these countries in the past year. So many
times in missionary magazines we read about a
situation, but what is actually existing on the
fields is quite different. That's why I believe
you students, in this age of communication when
you can get to Europe for $125, need to get to
some of these places during your summers and see.
And you'll never be the same again.

Time doesn't permit me to talk about probably
the most unreached segment of the whole world, the
Communist world. We're always hearing about closed
countries. If we examine the world we realize
that about 50 percent of the world's population
is behind the doors of closed countries. But I
say this with all my heart--and, again, you can
ask questions--I don't believe in closed countries.
I've seen young men even from the United States
behind the iron curtain and I've seen them effective
for Jesus Christ. I've seen them in Poland,
Yugoslavia, Czechoslovakia. I've seen some of my
own books copied by hand and spread out in Communist
lands. 'I've stood in the streets of Moscow myself
and had the privilege of turning over gospel
literature to students in the University of Moscow.
I don't believe in closed countries. I do believe
we're being deceived. I believe we're looking for
excuses to sit still. Excuses for the status quo.
Excuses to maintain the dichotomy.

Young people, let us wake up in this convention
to the fact that 50 percent of the world has never
once heard of Jesus Christ. And I believe with
all my heart that it's our fault. It's my fault.
And the time has come to do something about it no
matter what the cost.

Praise God for the older generation, they
worked hard. They worked well. There needn't be
any competition. There need not be any arguments
over who has done the most. But let us pick up

the ball they will be leaving off. Or better
than that, let us pick it up with them. In our
generation, let us reach the world with the gospel
of Jesus Christ. Yes, the harvest is plenteous.
The laborers are few.

Billy closed his message with these words
that I will use for my closing. He said these
words found in the twenty-second chapter of Ezekiel
verse 30, "I sought for a man among them, that
should make up the hedge, and stand in the gap
before me for the land that I should not destroy
it." Billy said that it's the saddest verse in
the Bible: "But I found none." This morning God
is seeking men to stand in the gap. May you, may
I, be that man.

7. Some Current Issues

PAUL LITTLE: Introduction

We are not going to be able to deal with all the issues, and in our forums and panels we have not yet dealt with all of the issues you have raised. Remember there is one more forum when we can develop such questions as "What is the impact of Viet Nam on Missions?" "What is the impact of the racial problem, and how can we help to overcome it?" "What should be our responsibility as Christians as we face this very critical question of the race issue?" Our subject for this morning is Some Current Issues. The first speaker, who will speak immediately following opening prayer, is Mr. Michael Griffiths. He already has been introduced to us. He has just come to the United States to be with us here at the convention. He will speak on the issue of internationalism. Shall we pray just before he comes to us:

Eternal God, our heavenly father, we thank you for the peace which we have taken for granted in which we meet here today. We thank you that we are able to gather in this convention without fear, that there is no fear that a bomb will fall on us or that we will be interrupted by police action. We would, our Father, this morning be mindful of those around the world for whom this is not possible. We are reminded of the agonies

of warfare that are going on today in Viet Nam
and other places, and we pray that if it please
Thee, we may have peace in our time and that the
wrath of men ultimately shall be made to praise
Thee, but that peace may come by Thy grace.

And, our Father, as we have thought here
of missions and the possibility of some of us
going overseas, we remind ourselves that there
are some 42,000 missionaries not here but out on
the far flung corners of the earth. We remind
ourselves that it is already the Lord's day in
many parts of the world and many, many more thousands
of national pastors and Christians and laymen of
all nations are serving the Lord Jesus Christ.
And we pray for them in this hour even as we meet
to discuss these things, that the church may be
built, may be added to, may be sustained, and
may grow in this Lord's day that we ourselves
shall soon enter.

Our Father, we come to Thee now for this
hour asking Thy sustaining grace for each of those
who shall speak. We ask for alert minds and hearts
for those of us who listen that we may hear Thy
voice and learn what Thou dost want us to have
for this day this hour.

For Jesus Christ's sake, amen.

MICHAEL GRIFFITHS: Internationalism

As I stand before you, my knees knocking
a little, I'm encouraged that the organizers of
this convention apparently have decorated this
platform expressly that we might speak about
internationalism.

My mind goes back to the time of the Olympic
games in Tokyo. We were living in that city then,
and we watched the opening ceremony on a borrowed
TV set. The vast crowds in that huge stadium
gathered from all countries. Groups of athletes
marched behind their respective country's flag.
If your country begins with a U, it takes an
awful long time for your turn to come, and you

realize you're only one country among an awful
lot. Then comes that magnificent ceremony, so
beautifully organized, so superb, before the
Emperor of Japan. Though a foreigner, I was very
moved, even watching on TV, at this terrific
sight.

Then I realized that it was pale and
insignificant compared with the day that will
come, when a great multitude, which no one can
count (no turnstiles there) from every nation,
from all tribes and peoples and tongues, will
stand before the Throne and before the Lamb. It
will be the most wonderful international gathering.

If we're having international gatherings
in sports and art in the United Nations, we are
also, thank God, having them in missions. There
have been missionaries from countries other than
Western for many, many years. In the year 1912,
the Korean church organized its first general
assembly. They said, We must send missionaries
to Shantung in China. Who will go? The whole
general assembly stood to its feet. It was a
missionary church from its inception. Even before
the war the Japanese church was sending missionaries
to Manchuria. But I do not want to talk about
national missions--not even the fact that in Asia,
national missions are arising. I want to talk
to you about internationalism in missions.

I have to say a little bit about the
fellowship that I belong to, not because it is
the only international mission. It is not. You
can soon find that out by going around to all the
missionary display stalls outside this room. Nor
are we the only interracial mission. I apologize
for speaking of ourselves, but it is the situation
I know best. Three years ago--we had been
international for years--we suddenly realized that
we were not <u>interracial</u>. We were all Caucasian.
We included Europeans, German, Swiss, Dutch, New
Zealanders, Australians, Canadians, people from
these United States, from Britain, from Ireland,
but we were not interracial. We realized that it

was all wrong. There was nothing to boast about,
nothing to blow our trumpet about. Then we began
to realize we had to reorganize. We have now on
our Board of Directors Dr. Chu, a Singaporian
Chinese. We have home councils in Philadelphia,
London, Melburn, New Zealand, and Europe. We now
have them also in Japan, the Philippines, etc.
We have Filipino missionaries (not very many yet),
Korean missionaries, Chinese missionaries working
with us.

Now that sounds grand. But I confess that
when this decision was first made, one began to
think of all the problems--problems of language,
of education, of missionaries, problems of
integrating people from different countries, problems
of organization--and I had doubts. Is this just
some gimmick, just something that improves the
mission image? Perhaps our society was better
national than international.

Just around that time, shortly after
Christmas, I went to Hong Kong for a conference
sponsored by IFES for people who were engaged in
student work in different countries in Asia. I
was there from Japan. Mr. Chandapilla of India
was there, just back from the IVMC in Urbana in
that year. As we gathered together, we were
discussing this matter of internationalism in
missions. I remember Mr. Chandapilla saying,
"Don't you see, brother, haven't you read your
Bible? Look at Revelation 7:9. You're going to
have an international church in heaven. Are all
the missionaries to go home, are we just to be
left with a lot of national churches, and then
suddenly the last trumpet sounds and there's an
international church? Don't you see, brother?"

And there we began to see it in that very
exciting gathering. We all came from Asian
countries, but we began to realize how very
different we all were, and what a blessing and
challenge we were to each other: our Indian
brethren, very emotional, but very perceptive;
our Filipino brethren, delightfully happy-go-lucky

(they needed to be--they had not had any salaries
for six months!); our Chinese brethren, so cheerful,
so efficient (the conference was very well organized
by them); our Korean brethren, scholarly and yet
so warm and affectionate towards the rest of us.
All these nations are different.

There was with us one Vietnamese brother.
He could have gone back to Thailand to translate
the Vietnamese Bible, but--so quiet, so small, shy
but so determined--he said, "I must go back to my
people." And so you see how different we all were,
but how complementary, and what a blessing to each
other. We were different and yet what a wonderful
group we made together, and what wonderful fellowship
we had because we were all different. We began to
realize why God had made us different nations
and different people, although he has made of one blood
all nations of the earth to grow together.

This is an exciting day to live in. In my
thinking that conference was an exciting gathering.
What a saneness! God's blessings are not limited
to certain nationalities. I think of our overseas
student's group in Tokyo and the blessing brought
to us by an African brother there studying earthquake
engineering. He was a blessing to both Europeans
and Asians. God's blessing is not restricted.
In fact, if we want God's fullest blessing, we
are more likely to find it together. And this
surely is God's great plan that we see set before
us, that reaches its climax here in the book of
Revelation.

I want now to give you ten reasons for
internationalism in missions. Nobody has ever
said, There are these ten reasons, therefore we
must do this. Rather, it is something that is
happening, something that God is working out among
us in spite of our conservatism and our over-
organization and love for red tape and committees
and all the rest.

The _first_ reason is that it is biblical,
in accordance with Christ's command. The command
to go and make disciples of all nations is found

in all Bibles, in whatever language they may be
translated. In other words, the Bible teaches
that God's men are sent from all nations to all
nations.

Second, there is nothing new about it.
That is another reason why missions that have
become international and interracial should not
blow their trumpets about it or think they have
done anything. It is just that, in many cases,
they have missed something for about 1700 years.
If you look in Acts 20:4, you will see that Paul
was accompanied by Sopater of Berea, Aristarchus
and Secundus of the Thessalonians, Gaius of Derbe,
Timothy, and Tychicus and Trophimus of Asia.
There were three Europeans, Greeks, and four
Asians, together with Paul, who was a Jew--men
of different races, men of different nationalities,
in Acts 20, going together and taking the gospel
with them. So it is not only a biblical command,
it is a biblical practice.

Third, as I have tried to show you already,
this is something which heralds the coming of the
international church glorified in heaven.

Fourth--we now get to practical reasons--
this lifts missions above national politics. If
your country is in bad odor in the world for some
reason, and you are one mission among many, the
mission does not suffer because of the bad odor
of that particular nation and that particular time.

This works out in a wonderful way. For
instance, there was a time in Indonesia when we
were able to put in lots of British missionaries.
Then came a thing called confrontation, and some
of those had to leave, especially one who was
teaching Animal Farm as a textbook in a country
that was going Communist. He went. Suppose there
is a war. What then? This happened to us in
China, even then when we were only international
and not interracial. There was a war and those
who were the enemy nations of Japan had to go
into internment camp--but not the Germans. They
were of an allied nation, and so they were able

to carry on their missionary work. They were
able to bring food parcels to their "enemy"
brethren, if you can think of such a word, in
the prison camps. Internationalism lifts you
above these political problems. If, for example,
the English are no longer acceptable in Indonesia,
all right, let Germans and Dutch and Americans
go. If Westerners are not acceptable in Cambodia,
then let Asians go.

Fifth, you are international. You are not
identified with any one country. Certainly it
avoids a head-on collision between one national
foreign group and the local Christians if you have
differing viewpoints. But if you are international,
you have a whole row of viewpoints and they are
all complementary. There is no head-on collision,
and together you can come to a common mind because
of the mutual blessing that comes through our
different national temperaments .

Sixth, it will avoid chaos organizationally.
Now you just think about this. In the country
that I have been in--Japan--there are about 120
foreign mission boards, mostly derived from North
America with just a few European missions. Now
suppose all the Japanese denominations start
sending out missionaries to all the other countries.
And suppose the Koreans, Filipinos, Malaysians,
and so on, start sending missionaries from all
their denominations to all the other countries.
There would be chaos. And if all missions set
up home councils in other countries, look at all
the wasted administrative time of Christian men
and the nonsense that would go on. I personally
believe that there is both a minimum and maximum
size for effectiveness. We do not want great
monster missions. Deliver us!

I am sure that some nationalism is important,
and that we should work together where we can.
At our recent conference, we received a letter
from the Indian Evangelical Mission, the Indian
members of the Evangelical Fellowship of India.
They wrote, "May we send Indians to your part of

the world? We will examine the candidates and
send them out to work with you in Southeast Asia."
I expect somebody else working in Africa has had
a similar letter from them. This is the kind of
thing that is happening.

Seventh, it avoids the shame and scandal
of division and competition between all these
groups, living perhaps in different scales of
salaries. We need to be together as brethren.

Eighth, this is a day of scandal of racial
discrimination, of tribal wars in East and West
Africa, of racial problems not only in the West
but between Japanese and Korean, between North
Korean and South Korean. These things are
everywhere. Christians are all one in Christ
Jesus, and together we go on and on with the
gospel. That means something in today's world.
That is the kind of way we should do missionary
work.

Ninth, because it is right. Everything
in our bones cries: This is fitting. This is
proper. This is suitable to anything which calls
itself Christian. It is real. We go together,
from all nations to all nations.

Tenth, I believe this is for the glory of
God as in that day a great multitude which no
one can count from every nation and all tribes
and peoples and tongues will stand before the
throne and before the Lamb and worship him.

PAUL LITTLE

Our next speaker is Mr. Evan Adams. He
is the Assistant Missionary Director of IVCF with
primary responsibility for the Student Foreign
Missions Fellowship, which operates in the Christian
schools of the United States and Canada. He is
also one of the assistant Missionary Convention
Directors and has carried a major share of
rssponsibility for various phases of it, particularly
the prayer group and Bible study leadership,
recruitment and training, preliminary arrangements

for exhibits, displays, etc. Mr. Adams is going
to speak to the issue of youth and tradition.

EVAN ADAMS: Youth and Tradition

We're living in a world today where the
fact of internationalism lifts all problems out
of the range of provincialism. As we've just
heard from Mr. Griffiths, internationalism affects
missions. We live in a world today where every
factor is international. As we begin to deal
with the great factor in today's world of youth
and tradition, we're dealing not only with the
situation that you're facing as a student in
America or Canada, but we're talking about something
that all young people in the world are facing today.
Youth are struggling today, as you know
well, to find out from themselves and their adults,
What's real? To youth in the present generation,
we give either packages or institutions or quick
answers. But youth are still asking, "What's real?"
Somehow our world is full of the tensions of youth,
which you are experiencing, which the youth of
the world are experiencing today. You know as
well as I do that in the United States today some
of the youth are on pot, some are on sex, and
some of us are on Jesus Christ. All the world
is looking for something to be "on." And youth
have said they will not accept the old institutional
forms which no longer carry the reality that they're
seeking.
Somebody has described the world in which
we're living today as something like a cosmic insane
asylum in which the inmates are in charge. As
we begin to look at youth and the problems that
they're facing, we have to agree that somehow we
have left them a world in which the question is,
What's real? And who is really in charge?
No doubt many of you have read <u>Mere
Christianity</u>, by C. S. Lewis, in which he discusses
his own approach to faith. As he looked at the
reality offered by the world and the reality of

the Christian faith, he said, "I had to be convinced it was true because no one could have concocted this farce." And so C. S. Lewis, in a sense, says to us that the reality of the world today, if it exists, does so in our Christian faith and in Jesus Christ. We who are the children of God through Jesus Christ, whether youth or adult talking to each other across a certain span of time, are facing the reality of the world together, and we must recognize that this is the world in which we must be responsible.

If you consider all of reality today, if you can somehow comprehend the totality of the world, the population, the problems, where we come from and where we're going, the only word that describes it is fantastic. This is the world which God has given you as the youth of this generation to take over and to do something about.

Stop and consider that, according to the Scriptures, approximately 9,000 of us here today have been destined to be in the image of Jesus Christ. That is fantastic, when you consider who you are and who I am. But that's the future that you and I are involved in. As I consider this convention, I realize how fantastic it is. If you had been behind the scenes, as some of us have been for many months, you would realize this. But the fact that we're here from so many places with so much information, with so much purpose, is in itself a fantastic fact. (Sometimes I feel like a computer that is choked to death on data.) Yet, while we were here, two young men in Indiana kidnapped a young woman, stole her car, took her as far as Utah, and were captured there. This makes national headlines. Here 9,000 students are gathered to represent the forward movement of Jesus Christ in this generation. In a sense you are students coming to grips with God at this point in history, but I doubt that we're getting front-page national coverage. So we really have the privilege of asking, "What is real?" Is the world in which we find ourselves real?

There's the danger that even youth get

caught in tradition just as some of us older
people do. There is, of course, the danger that
even Urbana may become a tradition. Of course,
if Urbana gets caught in tradition, it will pass
like all other institutional forms which God has
not necessarily ordained.

My own experience in the Urbana convention
began very interestingly in 1961. When I was a
student a number of years ago in the university
there were not yet such great gatherings of students
for missions. But just as I had completed about
10 years' work among a primitive tribe of people,
some friends who were involved in the Urbana
Convention said, "By the way, would you like to
chaperone a train-load of students to the Urbana
convention in Illinois?" Well, they were to pay
my train fare, and I was looking for a little time
of relaxation, so I took the offer. And as I got
on this train with 200 students--culture shock!
I had been out of the university fifteen years,
and suddenly the students were one generation
and I was another.

I'd just been on the train a few minutes,
and we were pulling out of the station when a very
handsome fellow came up and looked at me and said,
"How about trading seats?" Well, I didn't
understand exactly until I suddenly realized that
I was sitting beside a very beautiful young woman.
But I was alert enough to say yes, get up, and
give the man the seat. He apparently thought I
was a grad student. He didn't know I was the
chaperone of the train. This young man, by the
way, is married to that young woman; they have a
happy family in California today. I get a Christmas
card from them every year, thanking me for the
trip to Urbana. And so my first real shock from
the student generation came when I stepped from
the Navajo reservation to a crowded train of
university students headed for Urbana. Ever since
then I have been going through the process again
of coming to know what it means, to understand what
it is that you young people are trying to face.

I recall first going out into university student work after the Urbana convention. (IVCF had asked if I would be on the staff. I wasn't sure what I could do, but I was willing to try.) One of the first things a young woman said to me after I arrived on a campus was, "What do you think of existentialism?" I wasn't even sure I could spell it. I didn't know if it was a capital E or small e. I recall another time a young woman asked me, "What do you think of John Stuart Mills' concepts of freedom?" I didn't know that I had ever met him. I thought George Washington was the authority on freedom. But, anyway, this is the way I entered the student world, and before long I was aware of how much I was out of it. Within the first year I began to read every book I could get my hands on, with the hope that God would update me and make me a part of this generation. So through the process, primarily of Inter-Varsity Press, I have become aware of some of the things youth are thinking.

The great factor of our time is the emergence of youth as a great social block in history. I'm sure you're aware of it from your own experience. In the past, youth have always existed. But youth exist today in a more unique way. Youth are more numerous today. They're more visible, as well as vocal. Very few of us older people were prepared to realize that suddenly history would turn and the majority of the population would be young people, that they would be in charge, and that we had made many great mistakes in what we gave them. I think as a result we, the passing generation, must realize youth are, therefore, more important than at any time in the past--to the church, to missions, to the future of everything. We're thankful for you, and I can say personally that under God I trust you with the future.

Now another great factor, which is related to that of the youth of our time, is that the world is passing through a situation we could call the disappearance of traditional society. I think the great transition, which we might call "from the tribes to the cities," is taking place today. We're moving from the past to the future. It's as if the world that was at one time focused in one direction has now pivoted and everybody is going in another direction. The past is put back and everybody asks, Where is the future? So the young people in a sense are saying, Since the old people don't understand the future, we must take charge. This is true in many of the institutions of our time.

You will recall that in the Apostle Paul's ministry he went to the cities to find the alert and the elite and to send them to the tribes across the world. In your lifetime the world will be detribalized. And in your lifetime the tribal people will be sent back to the cities as missionaries--the whole process of history in reverse.

Now what is the role of youth in this whole thing? If you are reading youth magazines and papers, I'm sure you're aware that youth are making themselves heard all around the world. Latin American students could tell us about their universities, about what's taking place in terms of leadership. We're all aware of the Red Guard movement in China, where the youth of China have said, We're going to paste over the past with wall-to-wall posters. We'll only go toward the future; total revolution aimed toward a total future that we will have in our control. In Indonesia the students, the Maki, Mapi student groups, toppled Sukarno from his throne after twenty-two years as the father of the country. In India, after just twenty years of leadership, the great Congress party is pushed aside by the youth of the nation, because the party had lost its contact with the younger generation. By the way, The Chicago Tribune recently polled a certain number of British students. As of the devaluation period, 43 percent said they would be glad to emigrate. So there is this kind of movement going

on among students. They're not satisfied with
the status quo.

Youth are the leaders of our history. You're
part of American history. You know more about it
than I do. You should be here talking about it.
But Toynbee in his recent article on America said,
"Young people are consciously and openly in a
large-scale revolt against the Middle Age." And
that's me. Society is being restructured. No
longer is it coming my way; it is now your way.
As young people you're taking your cues from your
peers. You're not sure you can trust the older
people. The question is whether you can trust
their values, their goals, their institutions.

From my position as parent, as student
worker, and as human being, I've noticed that
there are three factors in this problem. I've
called them credibility gap, communications gap,
and confidence gap.

First of all, the credibility gap. The
youth of America are asking, Can we really believe
what adults are saying? Do they really know what
they're talking about? Second, the youth are
asking us basically, Are you really hearing us?
Communications gap.

Third, the confidence gap. I think they're
saying, Can we really trust them? They live by
double standards.

Why are there these problems? It's the
passing of the historical types of societies of
the world. In the past the world societies
controlled their youth by various means. There
was the supernaturalism which one could refer to
as the control in life. But we're now living in
an age when supernaturalism is past, and with it,
control. The old concepts of authority are gone.
Those of you who are aware of what it means to
be in tribal life are also aware that the old
rites of passage--by which a young man was capitulated
overnight into total adulthood by going through a
certain ceremony--are gone. Today, rural youth
are moving toward the cities, they're disengaging

from the old society, and they are now looking
for what is real and where authority lies.

What is the rite of passage for our American
youth today? It's the driver's license when a
boy gets to 16. From then on he has the freedom
of an automobile. He's come of age and can pretty
well make his own decisions. So this is a picture
of the world that we're in today.

Now the danger of the alienation of youth
from adults and parents is a breakdown in the
important institutions of life. For instance,
if war is changed, it will be youth who change
it, because youth are the resources of war. We
hope you can change war. I doubt if you will.
If the church changes, it will be primarily the
result of youth. Let me just give you an example
of how I have seen youth look upon adults in terms
of the institution of the church. A group of West
Coast college students recently said, "We no
longer find opportunity in our church fellowship
for worship." And so they started their own Sunday
afternoon worship service. They said, "All we're
getting is propaganda. We want to worship Jesus
Christ." They got an exciting worship group going.

I have a 15-year-old daughter who is now,
we can say, in the youth pattern of life. She
came home one evening from a baby-sitting job,
and she was really disillusioned. She was baby-
sitting for a leading elder in a church, and she
was shocked to find out that Playboy magazine was
one of his favorites. This was her moment of
disillusionment as far as the church was concerned.

I was recently at a very outstanding missionary
church, of which many of us would be glad to be a
member, and a guest speaker was invited in on a
Sunday evening. I was there visiting a friend.
The topic assigned for the speaker was "Viet Nam
in Prophecy." Viet Nam in prophecy? How about
Viet Nam in history? Aren't we facing Viet Nam
today? In the balcony behind the speaker were
about fifty college and high school students. Here
were students who wanted to know about Viet Nam,

students who might have to register with the Draft
Board next week. And the speaker was speaking
about Viet Nam in prophecy. He was having quite
a job finding Viet Nam in the Old Testament.

So today youth are questioning our institutions.
They're asking us if we can prove, if we can pass
on, and if we can grant to them the privileges of
the future. I'm convinced that the future lies in
youth; it always has. And we give it to you in
this convention.

PAUL LITTLE

Our next speaker I think you have met. He
is my friend and colleague, Eric Stanley Fife.
As you will have gathered, he was not born in
America. He served in North Africa during the
war, became interested in Muslim missions, and
served as one of the home staff of the North Africa
Mission in 1957 at the Urbana Convention. He
became Missionary Director of the Inter-Varsity
Christian Fellowship, and has served in that
capacity ever since. Eric, of course, is the
Director of this convention. Eric speaks to us
on the issue of the biblical and the cultural.

ERIC FIFE: The Biblical and the Cultural

Speaking of the biblical and the cultural,
I would like to draw your attention to one book
that is on the book stand, Hudson Taylor and Maria.
I think it's partly through my emphasis that this
is now being reproduced economically in paperback
at $1.95. It explains in great measure the attempts
that one man made to adapt to the culture where
God sent him. And he made that adaptation over
100 years ago.

Francis Steele told us that everybody is
a witness. This is true. Everybody is not necessarily
a missionary. At least not if we take to be true
the statement in the Urbana brochure, that a
missionary is one who crosses a political or

cultural frontier in the service of Jesus Christ,
whether that frontier be an urban ghetto or wealthy
suburb or a jungle tribe, a Japanese working in
Indonesia, an American evangelizing in Britain,
an African witnessing to students in the U.S.A.

The church in every land needs the church
from every other land . England needs the ministry
of Billy Graham. America evidently can profit
from the ministry of John Stott and John Guest.
This is the fact of the missionary enterprise:
crossing barriers that are cultural and barriers
that are political.

The Apostle Paul had something to say about
crossing barriers. He said, "I have become all
things to all men that I might by all means save
some." He was eager to identify himself with the
Greeks, with the Romans, with the Jews. I don't
have time to expound the lengths to which he
went to make himself acceptable that he might
gain a hearing from these people.

A serious missionary is one who takes
cultural barriers very seriously. In many ways
I find that it is very easy to talk about this
subject by making jokes and telling funny stories
of failures of missionaries who have gone overseas.
I want to avoid that by majoring on my own mistakes.

My experience was very similar in some ways
to that of George Verwer. I was brought to Christ
at about age sixteen from what I suppose you would
call a street gang, although it was not a gang
that specialized in violence. I came from a pagan
home, and evidently, unlike George, I came from
a slum home. Immediately I began to witness to
Jesus Christ. This was tough to some extent, but
at least I understood these people. There was no
particular cultural barrier to cross.

I faced my first cultural barrier when I
found it necessary to be identified with a church.
I went to church, and I was disgusted by the people.
They were smug, they were overdressed, they were
complacent. They gave a lot to missions but did
nothing to evangelize their own people. I was

nauseated. So what was my reaction? They wore
black coats and vests and striped trousers. So
I would preach to them; I went to church wearing
blue jeans. After a few weeks of this treatment,
I got my first audience. A dear old lady came to
me and gently rebuked me for coming to church
dressed like this. I said to her, "Madam, I'm
aware of the scripture that commands us to worship
the Lord in Spirit and in truth. If you can show
me the scripture that tells me to worship the Lord
in a black coat and vest and striped trousers,
I'll do that." And I walked away feeling how
smart I had been, what a success. It was months
before God began to get to me and to say, Don't
you understand that the people in striped trousers
need what you have to say? And they'll listen
to you far more fully if you wear striped trousers.
If this is conformity, I became at that stage all
things to all men in London to win some.

I soon found that it was not only the
cockneys of London that needed the gospel message,
but people in other classes. I had to fight a
greater barrier which only my British friends
will be aware of--the barrier of trying to cultivate
an accent that would be reasonably acceptable in
other circles. All things to all men--I have
found that Christ has been making me become this.

In a sense, he put me in the Armed Forces,
and there I found immense cultural barriers to
cross. I can say before God that when I was sixteen
to twenty there was no air raid shelter that I was
not prepared to preach in, no street corner that
I was not prepared to preach on. But, oh, I found
that there were some barriers that were extremely
hard to cross, and again and again I made a dismal
failure at crossing them. These failures militated
against the effectiveness of my presenting the
gospel of Jesus Christ.

I came to America and found a totally
different culture. A friend of mine had been
over here eighteen months and had written back
saying that he was desperately unhappy. But I

said to my wife, "We're going to enjoy America because this is where God has put us. We're going to love it and admire it." It wasn't always easy. And I haven't succeeded very well. But I have tried to understand the American mind and American history. I should point out that I am a neophyte in American history, but I find I know more American history than some Americans.

Then I found that I had to cross the cultural barrier of the academic world. I was invited to come over here thirteen years ago by the North Africa Mission. One of the missionaries in that mission who is now working among students in Algeria said, "Eric, God is going to give you a mission to students." I said, "I flatly refuse to speak to students. I do not have any Greek." I arrived and found that Frances Steele had booked me to speak at Penn State University. My first meeting was in a fraternity. And I was so naive that I thought a fraternity--we don't have fraternities in England--was another name for an Inter-Varsity group. I learned the hard way.

A serious missionary makes an attempt to understand the people to whom God sends him, to empathize with them. It is doubtful if he will ever completely lose his accent, although Mike Griffiths and John Stott probably think I have. But it is doubtful that I can ever lose my English accent. That is true of most missionaries going overseas. It is certainly true that we cannot change the color of our skin. But we can at least make an attempt to show that we understand and that we empathize with the problems that are being faced by those to whom God sends us.

Now let me say that for sensitive people this very frequently involves an enormous emotional strain. I find, for instance, that to speak to the students in Atlanta is quite different from speaking to the students in northern California. I could go on enlarging on the fact that to try to understand and to preach to each of their needs is an exhausting business. It may well be that

the tension and the pace of modern life will shorten
the life ministry of some men today. If so, so
be it.

It is, of course, a basic fact of anthropology
that religion is always conservative. If a church
were to move from the stone age to the steel age,
the religious people would be the last ones to take
to steel knives. We define ourselves not merely
as religious people, but as conservative evangelicals.
We are in a strangely dangerous position. I got
through one conference where many of the people
did not share my theology. One girl said to me,
"You're the weirdest mixture I've ever met in my
life." I said, "I can understand that, but just
in what particular degree is the mixture so weird?"
She said she had never thought that it was possible
to be conservative in theology and so progressive
in every other area.

And I am convinced that this is precisely
what God needs today. Men who will be true to
the Word of God, who will have absolute standards,
and yet will try to recognize that there are
peripheral things that are not basic to the truth
that they preach. We have much light from anthropology
that can help us here. (You should read some
anthropology and sociology.) This subject becomes
more and more important as people travel so much
more and see so many more TV programs.

I got to the West Indies to speak to the
students there. One student said to me, "If I'm
a Christian, is it necessary for me to be married
in a church?" I said, "Well, in John chapter 2
it does say that Jesus went to the marriage at
Cana." I knew that was not a very good answer,
because Jesus went to a funeral, too, and I don't
suppose it means he approved of that. I had to
say to the student eventually, "No, I know no
scriptural reason why you should be married in a
church. I think it is reasonable to gather your
Christian friends around you to rejoice with you
and pray with you." In honesty I had to say to
her that most weddings that I attend--incidentally,

I attend as few as I can--do not come in that category. To me, they consist of a spectacle at the front of the church to which a large number of people are the spectators, and that does not seem specifically Christian.

This past summer some students from Denmark laughed with me about a visit I had paid to their university a year before. I had been speaking to this group of students--all English speaking--about how they could win their fellow students to Jesus Christ. They laughed at me because they said they knew that deep down I was so shocked, because right through the meeting five of the girls in the chapter were smoking pipes. But they went on to tell me that that particular visit had changed the ministry of that chapter throughout the entire academic year. I was glad I had not made an issue of their smoking pipes.

Then this past summer, German students were joking with me about the particular view of evangelicals in America on the matter of rock and roll. But let me say this, I want to be sensitive to the spirit of the age, not to write off rock and roll as being wrong without giving any thought to why it originated. To me it is a narrow-minded intolerance that cannot be justified from the Scriptures. I've told my children that I'll defend their right to listen to it just so long as they don't make me listen to it.

Thus far I've given the impression that everything is relative. I become all things to all men. Does this mean I become a chameleon? I blend in with the landscape? There is nothing I stand for? Was that true of Paul? There were things that he would fight for. There were undergirdings for what he believed. I want to do all I can to be sensitive to issues that are cultural. But I will, to my dying day I trust, demand that I be loyal to the biblical.

And there are biblical absolutes. I think that what the Bible says about polygamy is often misunderstood. But the Bible is very clear about

fornication and about adultery, and I'll preach
it clearly and strongly.

It seems that the church today is largely
divided into two extremes. One extreme has become
fossilized and the young people on the whole are
utterly disgusted with it. Dare I ask you to be
more understanding and sympathetic with that group
than I was? They need help too. The other extreme
says that we're out of date and we must change.
"Let's listen to the anthropologists. Let's listen
to the psychologists. Let's listen to the sociologists.
Let's listen to the management consultants." And
we do have much to learn from all of them.

But in closing, allow me to remind you the
acid test is, Where is your authority? Is it the
anthropologists? Is it the psychologists? Or
is it the Word of God? Even a lot of Christian
anthropologists think in terms of anthropology
rather than of the Scripture, and would rather
try to find scripture to fit their anthropological
principles than vice versa. For that I can see no
justification in Scripture at all. The Scripture
has a great deal to say about leadership and
management. Let us be sure we're aware of it.

But let us by no means throw overboard
the heritage that is ours in the Scripture. Young
people, if you rebel as I rebelled, remember that
the Bible has something to say about respect to
elders and to those in the church who have oversight
of you. Let us, as John Stott has said, be living
in obedience to the Scripture, getting our answers
from the Scripture. It is hard. It is much easier
to give as an answer what your mission board says,
or what your culture says. But it is more spiritual
and much harder work to give the answer in terms of
what the Bible says.

8. My Life to Give

ERIC FIFE: Introduction

The platform speakers have not hesitated to lay upon you demands, in the name of Christ, that are really totalitarian. They affect every area of your life. It thrills us to hear about so many of you--I wish we had time to tell you what we know has been going on in the lives of some of you people, and in the lives of some of us. But the question naturally arises, "Why should I do all this for Christ? Why should I give myself so unreservedly to Christ?" This morning three men who have been introduced before will speak to the issue of motivation. First David Howard, second Warren Webster, third Arthur Glasser.

DAVID HOWARD/Motivation: The Need

The topic which has been assigned to me is one which, from one standpoint, I would prefer not to deal with--the need of men as a motive for missions. The reason I say I would prefer not to deal with it is simply this: I disagree wholeheartedly with the idea, which I used to hear proclaimed rather vociferously when I was a student, that the need constitutes the call. If this were true, why am I not a missionary in India?

I know there are needs in India. Or to bring it
closer to home--five weeks ago today I stood on
the streets of Lima, Peru, and watched the final
parade of Evangelism in Depth in that great city.
I saw poverty, such as I have seldom seen anywhere,
in the terrible slums of Lima, some of the worst
slums I have seen in any part of Latin America.
I see a tremendous need in Lima, Peru. But I am
not a missionary in Lima, Peru. The need cannot,
by itself, constitute the call. The need must
be supplemented by the things which will be dealt
with by the other men on this panel.

But look at it from another angle. Any
other motive is insufficient unless a man can
see a need. You are not going to go somewhere
to serve the Lord unless you are convinced that
there is a need there. The need must enter in,
but it cannot be the only basis. In fact it is
not the final basis. The other men are dealing
with much more fundamental issues. But we cannot
leave out need.

When we think about need and motivation,
what do we mean by motivation? The simplest
definition I have found in the dictionary is,
"A motive is something within a person, as need,
idea, organic state or emotion, that incites him
to action." Something within a person that incites
him to action. We are dealing today with things
which we trust will be used of God to incite us
to action. This will be our motivation.

What are the kinds of need that mankind
faces? There are physical needs, intellectual
needs, emotional needs, spiritual needs. Every
one of these is a legitimate need. I believe
that the character in Scripture who combines
these needs, upon whom all these needs converge
at the same time, is Job. Job was a man who
suffered simultaneously under every one of these
needs--physical, intellectual, emotional, and
spiritual. Let us look briefly this morning at
Job as an illustration of the need of man.

First of all Job suffered tremendous physical

<u>need</u>. He lost everything he had materially--his
houses, his cattle, his sheep, his oxen, and even
his children. Nothing left. Then God gave Satan
permission to touch even his body. Covered with
sores from the top of his head to the bottom of
his feet, Job sat down in sackcloth and ashes and
scratched himself miserably with a potsherd. You
know, there is an amazing thing in the book of Job.
We find no indication that anybody did anything
to help him physically. Isn't that strange? Three
men came along and sat down silently by him for
seven days to commiserate with him; then they began
to argue with him for days on end. But there is
no record that anybody tried to help him relieve
the physical suffering. What a terrible thing.

When I look back in my life, some terrible
memories come to mind from time to time. I find
miserable failures in my life. One memory just
tears at my heart every time I think of it. When
I was a student in college, I used to go to Skid
Row in Chicago on Saturday nights with a group of
fellows to witness to the down-and-outers there.
We would try to talk to these men, lying literally
in the gutter, about their souls. I remember one
cold, wintry night, about twenty years ago now,
I stood under a street lamp and talked to a
shivering man. I tried to tell him of his need
of Jesus Christ.

He turned to me and said, "Friend, would
you buy me a bowl of soup?"

I said, "No, I've got something better for
you. I want to tell you about Jesus Christ."

The man turned away and stood there and
listened apathetically as I continued to try to
tell him of his need for Christ.

He turned a second time and said, "Look
buddy, can't you buy me a bowl of soup?" I had
been conditioned not to give anything to these men
because they would spend it all on liquor. But
he wasn't asking me for money. He wasn't asking
me for liquor. He was a cold, shivering, hungry
man asking me for soup.

I said, "No, I've got something better for
you--Jesus Christ." Do you think that helped him?
I wish I could live that day over; I would buy him
ten bowls of soup.

The physical needs of man cannot be denied.
This question of social action versus the preaching
of the gospel is not an either/or situation. It
is both/and. True preaching of the gospel must
be followed and accompanied directly by a ministration
to the physical needs of men. Men with hungry
stomachs and cold bodies are in no condition to
grasp the demands of Jesus Christ. You and I have
a responsibility before us to help meet the needs
of these men.

I know of no more heart-rending sight than
one that I see periodically because my work takes
me to Bogota, the capital of Colombia. Little
street urchins run by the hundreds and thousands
on the streets of Bogota. I have never seen another
city like it. They are in every city, but Bogota
is jammed with filthy-faced little street urchins
who never saw a cake of soap in their lives. They
live in the shivering cold of that high mountain
city, just grubbing in the gutters during the day.
As nightime falls, they shiver and huddle in a
doorway. The physical need of men cries out to us.

But this was not Job's greatest need. Those
physical sufferings were really incidental to the
deeper need that Job suffered. Job had intellectual
needs that tore his heart. He was struggling with
cosmic problems. The idea that the book of Job
deals only with physical suffering is a misunderstanding
of the depths of this book. The book of Job deals
with some of the most deep and cosmic problems of
all time. How can a man know God? This is what
Job was dealing with. You are students--you know
something of intellectual problems and how they
tear at your mind and heart.

I talked yesterday to a girl at this
convention (Don't try to guess who she is. There
are 9,000 of you here and 8,950 of you never met
her, so there is no sense in trying to guess who

she is.), a Christian girl from a Christian
background who has known Christianity all her
life. She told me that the day before a fellow
had asked her, "Are you a Christian?" This girl
is going through some real problems at the
present time, some intellectual struggles. She
is struggling with cosmic problems and honestly
so. When this fellow asked, "Are you a Christian?"
do you know what she answered? She said, "Hell,
I don't know." I sympathized with her when she
told me that. I could see that she was in the
midst of problems that were deep and vast. It
would do me no good to sit like Job's miserable
comforters and answer back the way they answered
Job.

Job cried out in the midst of his suffering,
"I'm full of confusion" (Job 10:15).

You know what miserable Eliphaz answered
a few chapters farther on? He said, "Are you the
first man that was born? Or were you brought
forth before the hills? Have you listened in
the council of God? . . . What do you know that
we do not know? What do you understand that is
not clear to us?" (15:7-9 RSV).

What a way to deal with a man who is suffering
the depths of agony and intellectual problems!
The intellectual needs of today cry out to you
and me. We must be motivated somehow by this.

But Job had even a deeper problem. He
had emotional trouble. Job was a lonely man.
There should have been one person in all the
world to whom he could turn and pour out these
problems and share them. When those three comforters
sat there to commiserate with him and then did
nothing but argue with him day after day, he should
have been able to turn to his wife.

I thank God for a godly wife. I come home
feeling sometimes the pressure of the work, seeing
problems around me, and feeling utterly crushed
by the magnitude of the job and the depths of
the problems that surround the church of Jesus
Christ in Latin America. Sometimes I lie awake

in bed at night and think through these things
and struggle with them. Then I turn to my wife
and just pour them out to her. I thank God for
a godly, loving, patient wife who listens and is
a comforter.

Job turned to his wife, and what did she
say? "Job, curse God and die. Forget the whole
thing. Give it up, Job. What's the use?" (See
Job 2:9.) That's a big help, isn't it, for a man
who is in the midst of emotional need?

Beside loneliness, Job knew something of
fear. He speaks of fear and says, "Amid thoughts
from visions of the night, when deep sleep falls
on men, dread came upon me, and trembling, which
made all my bones shake" (Job 4:13-14 RSV). Have
you ever been scared to death?

Every time I come back to the University
of Illinois, I remember with a certain amount of
amusement the time I was most scared to death.
It happened right here on this campus.

I was a freshman in college. By some
strange quirk, fate, or luck, I was about the
only man in the college who went out for a
particular weight class on the wrestling team.
I made the varsity team because there was not
much opposition. Our first inter-collegiate match
happened to be against the University of Illinois,
who were Big Ten champions that year. We came
down here on a Friday night and I made the mistake
of reading the newspaper. I found out that my
opponent the next day was a conference champion.

It was the first match I had ever had. I
went into one of these big gymnasiums here (When
you get out on the wrestling mat you don't have
ten other men to lose the game with you, as you
do on a football field. You lose, and you're
lost, buddy. You're the only one.) I stood out
on the edge of what looked to me like a gigantic
mat in the midst of a huge gymnasium. My opponent
was a stocky, square-built, little Japanese. (My
apologies to Mr. Hatori.) This fellow--I thought
he probably knew all the jujitsu in the book--was

going to tear my head off. When that referee said,
"Ready, wrestle," I had never been so scared in
my life. That little Japanese charged across the
mat at me.

I thought I knew something of fear then; I
look back at it now and laugh. But it was real
at the time. (You know who won the match? Never
mind.)

You are living in fear sometimes too, aren't
you? And Job was. He had emotional needs. These
things are deep and they mean something to us.
It does not help a bit, in the depths of emotional
need, if somebody treats us the way Job's wife
treated him. Men and women who are living in the
depths of loneliness and fear cry out and look for
help. You and I ought to be motivated by their
emotional need.

Job had one more need--the deepest of all
the needs--his <u>spiritual need</u>. Job was groping
after God in the midst of all this. This tremendous
need builds up throughout the book. In chapter
23 Job is crying out in desperation, "Oh, that I
knew where I might find him" (I can't even find
God), that I might come even to his seat! . . .
Behold, I go forward, but he is not there; and
backward, but I cannot perceive him; on the left
hand I seek him, but I cannot behold him; I turn
to the right hand, but I cannot see him" (vv. 3,
8, 9 RSV).

Did you ever feel like that in your own
life? Oh, that I knew where I might find him.
I've gone every direction, forward and backward,
left and right. I don't find God. I'm lost.
Every man on the earth without Christ is like this,
because Jesus Christ said, "No one comes to the
Father, but by me" (John 14:6 RSV). There is no
way to find God except through Jesus Christ. This
is the message that he has given to us. "I am
the way." The way, not one of many ways. "No
one comes to the Father, but by me." Men grope
in darkness and cry out, "Oh, that I knew where
I might find him."

Job found at least one thing. He said in the next verse, "But he knows the way that I take" (Job 23:10 RSV). Thank God for that. Job recognized this at least: I don't know where he is but, thank God, he knows where I am. He is seeking me. "I sought the Lord, and afterward I knew he moved my soul to seek him, seeking me." This is what ought to motivate us.

How did needs motivate Jesus Christ? We read in the Gospels that when he saw the multitudes, he was moved with compassion because they were harrassed and helpless and wandered as sheep without a shepherd (Matt. 9:36). What did he do? He did something for them. He healed their physical needs. He taught them, showed them the way. He preached to them, proclaimed the good news of God in Jesus Christ.

We must see the needs of men and women. We must do something to meet their needs. That hymn we sang last night, "The Vision of a Dying World," captures some of these thoughts in the second verse. "The savage hugs his god of stone and fears descent of night (the fear); the city dweller cringes lone amid the garrish light (loneliness): Lord Jesus Christ, arouse thy church to see their mute distress! Lord Jesus Christ, equip thy church with love and tenderness."

WARREN WEBSTER/ Motivation: The Mandate

If you want to understand the meaning and motivation of the Christian message today, I advise you to not turn to the newspaper or even to mission magazines, but to return to a profound study of your Bible. Such a turning to the Bible has been at the root of every great missionary movement in history. The Bible itself is missionary literature from beginning to end. In Genesis we read of the God who made all things. In Revelation we read of the consummation, when all things are made new. And in between we read of the divine concern for the redemption of a world of sinful men.

Since the Bible is itself a missionary textbook, we should not expect to find either the basis or the motivation for missions in a single verse of scripture, but, rather, in the tenor and teaching of the Bible as a whole. Nevertheless, we can turn to certain passages that help bring into focus the global image of divine concern. One of these familiar passages is found at the end of Matthew's Gospel, where we find our Lord on a hillside in Galilee, surrounded by a small band of rather insignificant disciples. We count them and find eleven rather ordinary men. But they are men who have just been given an extraordinary commission to go out and conquer the world and to lay it at the Master's feet.

Other men have tried to conquer the world. We remember the names of Alexander, Caesar, Charlemagne, and Napoleon. But only Jesus Christ will ultimately succeed, because the authority to do so has been given by God to him alone. No other commander, either before or since, has given such a command to a group of eleven men. It is all the more audacious when you realize that the commander had no money or political influence and very little status or prestige to back up his command. Perhaps it is even more astounding that those eleven men believed what he said. And they went out and did it, because they had the promise of their leader to be with them always. In that perspective we see that eleven men, plus the Holy Spirit, are not such a small minority as we might have thought. I suggest to you that back there two thousand years ago, before the terms were ever coined, we find real commitment and real involvement. Within thirty-five years these men had planted churches in all the major cities of the Roman Empire apart from Gaul.

The Great Commission as we find it recorded in the first Gospel (Matt. 28:18-20), outlines for us the universal, all-inclusive scope of the missionary mandate in four dimensions: our mandate

is based upon all authority, it reaches to all
nations, it includes all teaching, and it extends
validly to all time.

Jesus said, "All authority in heaven and
on earth has been given to me. Go therefore"
(Matt. 28:18 RSV). This authority roots in the
sovereign God of the universe, who created men
and by whose power alone men can be recreated.
It is an authority that was given by the Father
to the Son, and which, in turn, he imparts to his
disciples as an authorization for missions. He
imparts the authority through the Holy Spirit who
is given to those who obey him. There is no
adequate motivation for missions apart from this
inner mandate or authorization that comes from
the Spirit of God himself. The history of missions,
not only in the book of Acts but throughout succeeding
ages, is predominantly a history of the Holy Spirit's
work in the hearts of men. For this reason, I would
caution you against basing the motive for your
missionary involvement simply on the tremendous
need of men.

The need of the world is immense and staggering.
As a result it has sometimes been suggested by
enthusiasts that if you have no clear call to
minister at home, the need itself is all the call
that you require to go abroad. Frankly I doubt
that very much. The needs of the world are so
tremendous that they will crush you. It is the
inner, divine authorization alone which can sustain
you.

David Bentley-Taylor, who served the Lord
faithfully in the land of Indonesia, reminded us
in his little booklet on the call of God to the
foreign mission field that Paul and Barnabas did
not go to the uplands of Asia Minor just because
they had no call to stay in Antioch. They were
sent by the Holy Spirit. Then he pointed out that
God's call to individuals is communicated in a
different way to almost every person. There simply
are no stated laws for what constitutes a missionary
call. That is why we have not stated them for you.

The way God calls one person may differ as much
from another person's call as your conversion in
a mass meeting differs from the conversion of
another person in the quietness of his room.   David
Bentley-Taylor suggests that in all of these divine
leadings there is a common denominator: the
continual sense that a certain course is God's
will for me, that I must do this and not anything
else.   This conviction is common to missionary
calls throughout history, and comes from the
divine inner authorization, that divine inner
mandate.

Now, the Holy Spirit does lead people in
terms of needs, also in terms of their ability to
meet particular needs around the world.   But let
no mission ever be undertaken without the additional
inner mandate of God's Holy Spirit, who alone
empowers the work of missions.   Recently a very
stimulating book in missionology appeared with
the title Pentecost and Missions.   It points out
that the missionary movement in the century and
a half that has elapsed since William Carey
appeared on the scene has been pre-eminently a
Great Commission-oriented era.   Obedience to the
Great Commission has been the dominant theme and
the dominant motive for missionary conferences
and missionary sending.   But by contrast, the
author finds that in the New Testament missionary
expansion was motivated and directed primarily
by the continuing experience of Pentecost in the
life of the church.

It is perhaps instructive for us to note
that following Pentecost there is no restatement
of the Great Commission, either in the book of
Acts or in any of the Epistles.   We have church
growth and missions on every side, but they continued
without any urging or exhorting or laboring of
obedience to the Great Commission as the primary
motive for witness.   Rather, we find in the church
then, as today, that wherever men are filled and
motivated by the Spirit of God, urging and
exhorting them to witness is quite unnecessary.

And wherever men are not motivated by the Spirit of God, seemingly no amount of urging to missions is very effective.

Missions, in the last one hundred and fifty years, has put a great emphasis on going in an age when historical and technological factors have made extensive going more practical and more possible than ever before. Nevertheless, you and I should be aware that in these verses called the Great Commission only one of the four Greek verbs is in the imperative, and it is not the verb "to go." The main Greek verb and the only one grammatically structured as an imperative is "to make disciples" of all nations. The command is to <u>disciple nations</u>. All the other action words here are expressed by participles in a subordinate relationship to the main verb. They tell us what is involved in making disciples. That is, we make disciples of men and nations by going, by baptizing, and by teaching.

Going is necessarily involved; but the goal of missions is discipling, not merely going. A literal translation from the Greek might read, "Having gone, or by means of going, make disciples."

I am reminded of the comment of a mountain preacher who was trying to get this text across to his young people. He said that what Jesus is saying here is, "Bein's as how you're goin', be sure to make some disciples while you're about it." Now I doubt very much if that mountain pastor knew any Greek, and you might think that his paraphrase was overly casual, but he came surprisingly close to capturing the import of the original text. It really means wherever you go as Christians, wherever you live, wherever God sends you, your main job is to make disciples.

Some find here a case for what might be called migration evangelism. It reminds church historians that much of the most effective and extensive growth of the church throughout the world, past and present, has taken place when members of the body of Christ moved about in the normal course of seeking their livelihood, taking their faith

with them. This is happening today in South
America and Indonesia and many other places. When
the honest emphasis of the Great Commission is
placed where it belongs, putting the imperative
on the command to disciple, you may get a new
picture of missions. I leave you with a whole
lifetime to work out its fascinating implications
for yourself.

Now before you go back to your campuses
and communities to get completely involved in
discipling just the people who are around you, I
would remind you that the command is to disciple
all nations. That means that some of you will,
and some of you must, go to the nations. Those
of you whom God clears to live and to minister in
the land of your birth will nonetheless be involved
in reaching all nations through prayerful intercession,
sacrificial giving, and concern for peoples of the
world who come to you here. All of Christ's
disciples are in this great world mission together.

We have seen that we not only have all
authority to go, but we are to go to all nations.
And we are to teach them to observe all that he
has commanded us. Communication involves more
than just going or speaking. It is possible to
speak and yet not to communicate. In fact, someone
has said that the most difficult aspect of
communicating the gospel of Jesus Christ is not
slogging through the jungles of the Amazon or
Central Africa. It is not going to live in the
desert of Pakistan halfway around the world, ten
thousand miles away. The most difficult, the
most crucial aspect of communicating the gospel
is in getting across the last eighteen inches
after you arrive. If you and I fail to communicate
Jesus Christ in face-to-face situations where we
confront men and women who are lost, then we might
as well have stayed at home. Our going, however
difficult, is rendered useless and ineffective.

Jesus said, "Go and tell. Go and communicate
all that I have commanded you." What is the "all"?
It would take a long time to list all the commandments

of Jesus; however, they are very conveniently
summarized in I John 3:23. There we read, "And
this is his commandment, that we should believe
on the name of his Son Jesus Christ"--yes--"and
love one another" (RSV). Now we find a strange
phenomenon: There are some individuals, churches,
missions who put a great emphasis upon the heart
of the gospel, the sinfulness of man and his need
for redemption through Christ; and they stop
there. They have little to say about love for
one another or the social implications of the
gospel. There are other groups who have little,
if any, gospel message, and so they major almost
entirely on the love aspect and the social part.
I declare to you that both of these single-emphasis
presentations are inadequate representations. If
we only preach half the gospel, we should not be
surprised if we are getting less than half the
expected results. The wonderful thing is that
when the gospel is preached and proclaimed in its
two-pronged fullness, we see lives transformed
and societies changed even today.

The divine mandate is both _intensive_ and
extensive. We are to go, but we must stay long
enough to teach. That is why we will never fulfill
the Great Commission by simply running into a
village, hooking up a loudspeaker or phonograph,
distributing a bit of literature, checking off
one more village, and running on. This may
contribute something to the extensive outreach
of the gospel, but it hardly meets the intensive
requirements. We must stay long enough to teach
them "all that I have commanded you."

Finally, we note that the promise of Christ's
living presence is with his people for all time
even "to the close of the age." The word here for
time does not depict endless time, but rather the
period of time preceding the end. The Great
Commission looks to the great consummation. It
is because of this promise of his presence always
that we know that the mandate for mission was
given to the church in all ages, not just to those

first apostles, as some have erroneously thought.

Jesus here implies what he clearly taught
elsewhere, that the proclamation of the gospel as
a witness to all nations is itself a sign of the
end. The coming of Christ in his kingdom does not
depend on the ultimate success of missions, but
primarily on the fact of this world-wide proclamation,
which has never been more evident and widespread
than it is today. Nevertheless, only God himself
can say at what point obedience to both the extensive
and the intensive aspects of the Great Commission
have been fulfilled so that his purposes are
completed and Christ may return. In the meantime,
the existential question for you and for me is,
How are we going to give and live our lives for
the cause of Jesus Christ?

Let me talk to you personally in conclusion.
When I was a student like you, though a Christian,
I had no serious anticipation of serving Christ
abroad. But I remember when the Spirit of God
brought to bear upon my life the words of a man
who had lived a long and fruitful existence. When
he came to the end of it, he said,

If I had my life to live over again,
I would live it to change men, because
you haven't changed anything until
you've changed men.

I began at that point to change my university major
and to prepare specifically for a life of changing
men.

Subsequently I went to seminary, but with
no thought of serving God abroad. As late as my
senior year in seminary, I expected to remain in
this country. But I had to come to a moment of
truth. I realized that I could not stand in a
pulpit in America and challenge young people to
go out and do a job I was not willing to do. Nor
could I minister in the same way in a university.
When I squarely faced this fact, the implications
of the Great Commission were brought to bear and
I offered myself for God's service. He progressively
opened the doors and said, Come ahead. I have been

an ambassador abroad ever since.

I know that many of you are in this same position. I respect your realism and your sincerity. You have already said (some of you last night), "I am willing, under God, to go where he wants me to go." But for many of you this is a passive sort of dedication. Today I want to challenge you to go on to the next step: Begin today to pray positively for the privilege of being a missionary. But I warn you, don't pray it unless you mean it. You may be surprised at how quickly he opens the door and says, "Come along. This is what I've been expecting you to do all the time." And for those of you to whom God says, "No, I have another privilege," you have cleared yourself, before him, to remain in the land of your birth without any sense of guilt or complex whatsoever. He will help you to work out a lifelong ministry in your land, working to change lives to the glory of God, and to have your impact felt abroad.

I close with this story. During the last world war, on the Gold Coast of Africa, there lived an elderly African man who had honorably served his Majesty's government and had been given a small pension. With it he retired to the hills to farm. One day while he was working with his hoe, he heard a message come by drumbeat across the jungle forest. He stopped to listen and to translate it for himself. He learned that a great war had begun and that his Majesty's government was in great need of help. About a week later at the little ramshackle post office down on the coast, the postmaster processed a grimy little post card on which this eloquent message was written: "Your Majesty, I am coming." May God hear that from hundreds of hearts today: Here am I, send me.

ARTHUR GLASSER/ Motivation: The Lord's Return

Help must come to man in his need from outside. It is the command of Jesus Christ. Disregard for what Christ has commanded is evidence

of disloyalty to Jesus Christ. And now the coming
of the Lord--living for the glory of God.

When the Apostle Paul entered the city of
Athens, that great intellectual center (Acts 17:
16-34), he found the place filled with idols.
Athenians were worshipping, but not the God who
was their creator, the Lord who loved them. God
was being robbed of his glory. Paul exploded.
Filled with exasperation, he spoke of Jesus Christ.
He was concerned for the glory of God and aware
of the appearing of Jesus Christ.

The book of Acts, chapter one, begins
with the record of the resurrection of Jesus
Christ--Jesus Christ the truth of God. The truth.
Someone has said that truth did not forever stay
on the scaffold. Truth came down from the scaffold.
Truth walked out of the tomb. Truth ate boiled
fish. Christ, resurrected, demonstrated the
reality of his victory by confronting his apostles
with many irresistible proofs. He also spoke to
them about the kingdom of God and the consummation
of God's rule. We read:

> "So when they had come together, they
> asked him, Lord, will you at this time
> restore the kingdom to Israel? He
> said to them, It is not for you to
> know times or seasons which the
> Father has fixed by his own authority.
> But you shall receive power when the
> Holy Spirit has come upon you; and
> you shall be my witnesses in Jerusalem
> and in all Judea and Samaria and to
> the end of the earth" (Acts 1:6-8 RSV).

It is fixed, prophesied--"to the end of the earth."
These are the last words of Jesus Christ.

> "And when he had said this, as they were
> looking on, he was lifted up, and a
> cloud took him out of their sight.
> And while they were gazing into
> heaven as he went, behold, two men
> stood by them in white robes, and
> said, 'Men of Galilee, why do you

> stand looking into heaven? This
> Jesus, who was taken up from you
> into heaven, will come in the same
> way as you saw him go into heaven'"
> (vv. 9-11 RSV).

When Jesus Christ bade his friends good-by, as he
was taken from them, as he was extending his last
blessing (as Luke tells it), the word was "I
will come again."

I once bade my friends good-by, but I couldn't
say, "I will return." It was in southwest China--
8,500-foot elevation, great pine forests, stone
mountains, bitter cold, snow, the midst of winter.
I was saying farewell to the Nasu church. It had
been my privilege to labor there. We had a training
school for evangelists. There were 27,000 Christians,
scores of churches, disciplined evangelistic
activity. We had over fifty teams of men out week
after week during the summer of 1949. Now we had
to say good-by. The Communists were going to take
over the next day, and we missionaries had to
leave.

That night there was a knock on the door.
My wife went to the door and then she said, "They
want you outside." I went out into the darkness.
Six men. We walked to a little grove. Great trees,
snow, darkness. We stood in a circle, silent.

Then one of them said, "K'o mu-shih, ch'ing
wei wo-men t'ao-kao. (Pastor K'o, please pray for
us.) I said, "I can't pray." Then I turned to
leave.

"You are our leader; you lead us." These
were men with whom I had traveled and preached
in villages above 10,000 feet and down in valleys
at 4,000 and 5,000 feet. I couldn't pray.

Then another was asked if he would pray.
"No." We stood in a circle, silent.

Then dear brother John, another evangelist,
said, "I'll pray." He folded his hands and stepped
into the center; then started that wonderful prayer,
"Our Father, who art in heaven." We joined in,
"Hallowed be thy name. Thy kingdom come; thy

will be done, on earth as it is in heaven." I
remember the words slowly spoken in Chinese, the
falling snow, the circle, my brothers in Christ.

They said, "We will glorify God by our
obedience. We will continue by his grace to
preach the gospel. We are going to proclaim his
name. We will pray that his kingdom will come.
We will labor for his church. We will meet again,
but it will not be on this earth. It will be
only when he returns."

There were tears that night. Then they
slipped into the darkness and I went back to the
house. The next morning the Communists moved in,
but before they came we already had left on the
road. The glory of God: the coming of Jesus
Christ.

A friend in Philadelphia said, "You're
going to talk to today's students with this theme
for motivation? They're not going to buy that.
Jesus Christ coming back to this world? Why,
even the churches aren't preaching it today."

It seems incredible, fantastic, absurd.
In no place is the Bible more dated, more incredible,
than where it insists that Jesus Christ is going
to come back to this world. It is utterly incredible
to modern man.

Here we are on this campus of thirty thousand
students. It has the largest faculty for a university
of this size and type in all America. How many
believe that Jesus Christ is coming back to this
world?

Bultmann said that it is no longer possible
for anyone seriously to hold the New Testament view
of the world. We can no longer look for the return
of the Son of Man in the clouds of heaven or hope
that the faithful will meet him in the air. And
yet the idea keeps popping up.

Were you listening to Eric Severide on
October 3rd? He was sort of exploding because
Stalin's daughter, Svetlana, was being criticized.

He said,
        I've got to defend her. She's no

> literary figure to be pulled apart
> by critics. She's a fresh breath
> of humanity. She's a small miracle
> direct from the power politics of
> her father's iron-distant era.

And then he added these words,

> Svetlana is not the second coming,
> but she's the nearest thing to it
> that mortals can expect for some
> time to come.

The second coming--incredible. And yet, tremendous! Ask yourself what we mean, what you mean, what the Scriptures mean by the second coming. The text we read indicated that it is something personal--this Jesus. It is something visible, his visible presence. Jesus of Nazareth is coming back to this world. The Bible leaves us no doubt on these things.

Christ's return will be in marked contrast to his first coming on Christmas Day, in weakness and humility, silently, almost secretly--except for a handful of witnesses. But his second coming will be visible, dramatic, glorious. "Every eye shall see him and they also which pierced him: and all kindreds of the earth shall wail because of him" (Rev. 1:7). There will be no need for a telstar radio communications satellite to flash the news from Jerusalem to America to Asia. Oh no, Suddenly this world shall see the sovereignty of Jesus Christ demonstrated. With great power, the Bible says, he will come; with great glory he will come (Mark 13:26). Christians have always believed this. How does the Creed put it?

> He ascended into heaven and sitteth
> on the right hand of God the Father
> Almighty. From thence he shall come
> to judge the quick and the dead.

"He has fixed a day," Paul told the Athenian intelligentsia, "on which he will judge the world in righteousness by a man whom he has appointed, and of this he has given assurance to all men by raising him from the dead" (Acts 17:30-31 RSV).

You know, the whole of world history is like a
complex game of chess. A critical move has been
made: Christ came forth from the grave. All
subsequent moves in the chess game are determined
by this move. The game goes on, but it has only
one end. As C. S. Lewis says,

> The curtain is going to be rung
> down at any moment.

The return of Jesus Christ is inevitable;
but more, it is imperative. We have heard of the
hopelessness of man, the tragedy of his existence.
Twenty-one major civilizations have risen, flourished,
and fallen, and man is still unable to solve his
basic problems. He is unable to live at peace with
his neighbors. In the last sixty years, 100 million
people have been killed through war. Man fails
to find satisfaction in life--pleasure, drugs,
alcohol, sex outside of marriage--and he cannot
resist the glittering lure of power.

Our day is characterized by the disappearance
of hope. Who is optimistic about the future? But
if you step into the world of the Bible, you find
the writers speaking of hope. Paul uses the noun
or verb form of hope forty-nine separate times.
And yet the Bible speaks so plainly of sin, so
truthfully of the fact that man cannot perfect
human society.

The Bible says that Christ shall return.
The world will then be finally and totally purged
of evil. Don't you yearn for Christ's return?
Oh, you yearn for Christ's victory in your own
life, as I do. But also, in this troubled, tragic,
and weary world, don't you yearn to see God glorified
in the universe? Don't you want to see his victory
finally revealed? It is not enough that Jesus
Christ died on the cross. Apart from the second
coming of Christ, there is no final deliverance
from evil; his return is necessary to God's victory
in history.

How can a Christian refrain from crying
to the Lord in prayer, "Come quickly, Lord Jesus."
The Bible commands us to look for his coming, yearn

for his coming, wait his coming with desire and patience and holiness. But Scripture says more. What were the Apostle Peter's last words? In 2 Peter 3 he described the fact that people will mock this matter of Christ's return and dismiss it as fantastic, absurd. But Peter says the day of the Lord will come. And then he makes this startling application: we should not only look for it, but we should hasten it.

Hasten the coming of Christ? Someone said this means causing the day of the Lord to come more quickly by helping to fulfill those conditions without which it cannot come. The day of God's final triumph in history is not so inexorably fixed, so irrevocably decreed, that the church is unable, by its obedience, to hasten it.

How do you hasten it? What has the priority? Turn to that passage that has been quoted again and again in this conference, that tremendous statement in Matthew 24:14: "This gospel of the kingdom will be preached throughout the whole world, as a testimony to all nations; and then the end will come" (RSV). Mark 13:10: "The gospel must first be preached to all nations" (RSV). Must--that is imperative. You believe the text (John 3:7) a man must be born again. If people are not born again, they will someday wish that they had never been born at all. "You must be born again," Jesus said.

This is another imperative: the gospel must first be published among all nations, the unreached. This is the priority--God glorified by proclamation, announcing the fact that God is and that he has done something wonderful for men to make them fit for his presence and his friendship.

We were all heartened this morning by the exposition of 2 Timothy 4, where Paul pleaded with Timothy to love Christ's appearing because by this he would gain the crown of righteousness. Then followed the description of Paul at that great trial--Paul in chains, facing the Tribune

on the ivory throne. In that vast assembly were
representatives of every segment of the world as
he knew it, the Roman world surrounding the
Mediterranean basin. Here was the world in
representation. And because Paul loved the
appearing of Jesus Christ, he cried to the Lord
for strength. He recorded his experience: "All
men forsook me . . . . Notwithstanding the Lord
stood with me, and strengthened me; that by me
the preaching might be fully known, and that all
the Gentiles might hear" (2 Timothy 4:16-17)--
the peoples of every tribe and tongue and nation.
You cannot love the appearing of Jesus Christ and
be indifferent to the task of evangelizing this
world.

Now let me confront you with another figure,
Elijah in the Old Testament. He watched the people
of God slip down that awful road to complete
apostasy. They had been sucked in by Baal worship,
the fertility cult worship of the ancient world,
sex worship; playboyism was all about them. And
what did he, one man, do? He stood athwart the
path of Israel. He said, "No. For God's sake,
no. God must be glorified among his people."
One man facing the priests alone. You remember
the prayer he offered on Mt. Carmel, "O Lord, God
of Abraham, Isaac, and Israel, let it be known
this day that thou art God in Israel, and that I
am thy servant, and that I have done all these
things at thy word" (I Kings 18:36). No one
followed him, but he glorified God, and God won
a smashing victory.

There is coming a day unlike all previous
days in human history. It will begin like every
other day, but it will not end as every other
day has ended. There will be the sound of the
trumpet, then the invasion from outer space of
the God of creation. Jesus Christ shall return.
In that day you shall thank God for the privilege
of having lived in subjection to Scripture, having
lived for the glory of God, having spoken of God
and his salvation to a needy world. May we not,

at that late hour, discover that our concern for
God and his glory was so small that we allowed
ourselves to be defiled by the rot of the times
and we failed to glorify God in our lives and by
our lips.

Part III.   Missionary Introduction

9. Special Opportunities in Missions

ERIC FIFE: Introduction

The following four people will speak in order: Robert H. Bowman, the General Director of the Far East Broadcasting Company; Mr. George Cowan, the President of Wycliffe Bible Translators; Dr. Robert Foster, who has done very good work in medicine in the Africa Evangelical Fellowship; Jim Kraakevik, who is on the faculty of Wheaton, but has spent several years in education in Africa, and is, I believe, going back. These four men will speak about their specialities. They have the whole of six minutes to tell you all about things like education. So first of all, Mr. Bowman.

ROBERT BOWMAN: Radio in Missions

In the first thirty-seven chapters of the book of Job an earnest discussion was held between Job and his comforters: What is the reason for the deplorable situation in which Job finds himself? In the thirty-eighth chapter God asked Job penetrating questions and demanded some answers. In the thirty-fifth verse he asked, "Can you send forth lightnings, that they may go and say to you, 'Here we are'?" (RSV). A puzzling question indeed. I went to the old familiar commentaries--those by Matthew Henry, and Jamieson, Fausset, and Brown, among others.

Most of the commentaries skip that verse and go
on to the next. Suddenly a thought struck me.
Why, how could these men of old have commented
apart from a supernatural revelation of God? They
lived before the day of radio. What is lightning?
It is an electrical impulse. What is radio? It
is an electrical impulse transformed into radio
frequency. In a day when many countries are closed
to the gospel by governmental decree, God still
comes to them on the lightning wave and says,
"Here we are. What will you do with my Son who
is called the Christ?"

There is no such thing as a closed-to-the-
gospel area in our world today. Closed to a bodily
presence, yes; to the gospel, no. For example,
in China, the largest nation on earth, the body
of Christ meets here and there by two's and three's.
Every church building closed; not a missionary in
the land. Has the church died as was intended?
A recent authoritative survey shows that the church
is growing numerically and spiritually. From
Scotsman George Paterson's Communication Challenge,
we learn

> The significant factor that has come
> out of recent surveys is that the
> voice of radio is adequately keeping
> the faithful in China.

More than seventeen hours daily of Chinese
programing is beamed by both medium and short wave
to China. God will never leave himself without
a witness concerning his beloved Son.

This generation has more than 500 million
radio receivers. Place six and one-third persons
around each radio in the world and you have the
total population. The largest number of receivers
are presently found in the cities, but this picture
is changing rapidly. It is more and more common
to see an old head-hunter walking a jungle trail
wearing only a G-string, a spear in one hand and
a transistor radio in the other. Or an oriental
farmer plowing in the rice paddies with a transistor
tied to the horns of his carabao.

The world's darkest regions are becoming
aware of the existence of instantaneous world
communication. They now know that their tribal
boundary is not the end of the world, and they
want to know about the millions beyond who have
their same hopes and fears. So they are turning
to the little transistors. But how are they
obtaining these? God bless the Japanese who are
building transistor radios by the millions and
are selling them in most parts of the world.
How do tribal areas buy them? I know of one
head-hunter tribe in Borneo that receives transistor
radios in payment for the raw rubber they extract
from the trees.

Now we know that radio is not the entire
answer to the world evangelization problem. But
working side by side with the church visible and
its many aspects of gospel outreach, radio,
because of its very nature, can perhaps help
close the deplorable gap which exists between
the reached and the unreached in our world of
exploding populations.

Forty-seven years ago the sound of the
human voice first traveled on the lightning wave.
It was made possible by the discovery of the
vacuum tube rectifier by Dr. Lee DeForest of
Stanford. Eleven years later the pioneer missionary
station, HCJB, was founded in Quito, Ecuador.
Sixteen years passed before the second missionary
station, TIFC, of the Latin America Mission, was
air-borne in Costa Rica. Three weeks later (in
1948) on the opposite side of the world, the Far
East Broadcasting Company placed its first
transmitting station on the air in Manila, in
the Philippines. Under God's direction, the
vision of radio as a powerful instrument for
world evangelization began to grow rapidly.

Today there are fifty-six international
missionary broadcasting organizations with more
than seventy-five transmitters located in Latin
America, Asia, Africa, Europe, and one operating
from the United States. They are proclaiming

the gospel in approximately 150 major languages
and dialects, several hundred hours each day.
Approximately 600,000 letters are received annually
from practically every country on earth. If one
letter represents 200 listeners (the official
statistic of Conservative Radio, Australia), then
missionary radio is reaching upwards of sixty
million people annually.

Three decades ago it was possible to
effectively operate missionary radio stations with
on-the-job trainees, but in today's sophisticated
world, missionary radio needs more qualified
personnel. Interested students can prepare for
God's call to international missionary radio by
majoring in (1) radio program operations under
which come journalism, radio writing, studio
production, dramatic production, music, radio
announcing, radio speaking, news writing and
reporting, and news analysis; or (2) the engineering
field under which come transmitter engineering,
studio engineering, propagation engineering,
antenna engineering--all specialized fields. An
engineering physics major gets a highly qualified
background for electronics. (3) In missionary
radio today there is also an increasing effort to
use program evaluation research techniques. For
example, FEBC has recently established a mass
communications research center in Hong Kong for
study of all far eastern nations. The research
department of Stanford University has given
invaluable assistance in the initial stages. (4)
Missionary mass communications seeks those majoring
in anthropology, sociology, political science,
interpretative journalism, church growth, mass
communications, and computer engineering.

The harvest is white. The grain stalk is
tough; qualified laborers are few. I appeal to
you, the young people of this generation. Today's
electronic sowing and reaping instrument calls
for new pioneers, chosen of God and willing to
match brain and dedication to the task of effectively
communicating the gospel to today's sophisticated world.

GEORGE COWAN: Missionary Linguistics and Translation

Dr. William Wilmers of UCLA on one occasion said that if you took one speaker from each language of Africa and put them all in the same room, you would have in that room over one thousand people, not one of whom could speak to a single other person in the room. This is to highlight the great diversity of languages on one continent. And this is only one continent--one that in many respects has been more missionized than others.

Yet of these Africans only about 400 have anything of the scriptures available in their own language; less than 100 have the whole Bible. Competent authorities tell us that there are between 3000 and 5000 different languages spoken in our world today. Of the 1280 languages into which something of the scriptures has been given (as reported this morning), only about 900 are actually still in use with scriptures available today. So it is no exaggeration to say that there are at least 2000 languages, which represent populations ranging from two million down to a few hundred speakers, with nothing of the scriptures in their language.

Progress is being made, however. Every three weeks a new language receives something of the Word of God for the first time, and we expect this to speed up as the experience and advantages of modern technology are applied to the task. One of the acute needs is churches without Bibles, no Scripture in the language of either the pastor or the people. There are scores of such churches around the world. One pastor, responsible for thirty-eight churches in eastern Nigeria, tried to reduce his language to writing and to translate the scriptures for his people. He found it was beyond his ability and came begging for help-- for someone to help him reduce his own language to writing and to do the translation. Many such people in the world today are meeting without the advantage of the written Word of God in the language of the pulpit or the pew.

In addition there are 600 to 700 different languages which already have something of the scriptures, but need more. They only have part of it.

Language is one of the most powerful--in fact, I think we can say it is the most powerful--communicative medium that God has given to man. All other media use it as one of their tools. The mother tongue is the most efficient of all the languages that will reach man's heart and enable him to communicate with others that which touches him most deeply.

Therefore, the missionary, as linguist, does not bemoan, decry, avoid, or try to escape the responsibility of the different languages. Rather, he seeks to use language as a powerful medium, the most powerful medium, to reach man with the gospel of the Lord Jesus Christ. He analyzes and studies the language to exploit its fullest resources of grammar and vocabulary to make the gospel intelligible, idiomatic, and powerful, reaching the inmost parts of a man's being. He reduces the language to writing, if it is not already written, so that the gospel may benefit by the written page--be disseminated more widely, be studied more thoroughly, and be preserved both for the individual and for posterity in its use. He produces primers and bilingual materials to bring the newly literate into the world of Christian literature in other languages as well as his own. Finally, he publishes his linguistic findings as his contribution to the general knowledge and scientific knowledge of our day. Governments and educators often respect his contribution and many times allow his gospel, spiritual ministry to go on where they might otherwise prohibit missionaries as such.

The missionary as translator knows that ultimately the whole work of God must be soundly and thoroughly based upon the written Word of God in the language of the people--the sooner, the

better. So he translates to provide a tool for
both his own and the national believers' evangelism.
He translates in order that the gospel may be a
basic reader for the literate, so that among the
things he reads the literate may have access to
the Word of God. He translates so that the authority
and the assurance of the written Word of God may
stand behind each newborn believer, so that this
man may have the strength and the conviction to
stand under fire and persecution. The missionary
as translator wants to provide food to help the
new convert grow and come to maturity in his faith
in Christ. When the missionary translates, he provides
a thousand messages for the preachers; he also provides
the charter for the church in its doctrine, discipline,
and conduct. No church is truly indigenous if it
still has to worship with a foreign-language Bible;
that is a contradiction of terms.

Finally, there is the mandate for missions,
the missionary demand upon every child of God and
every part of the church of Jesus Christ to give
the gospel to others. One of our men met some
believers in the Philippines one day and asked
them where they were going. They said they were
going to such and such a place to tell the people
about Christ. And he said, "Who sent you?" "Who
sent us?" they asked. "Does someone have to send
us? Doesn't God's Word say 'Go into all the world
and preach the gospel'?" They had their mandate
for missions and evangelism.

Who should do this task? Who can do it?
Any Christian who is born again by faith in Christ,
who is convinced that the Bible is an inestimable
treasure and the authoritative Word of the living
God, and who has a disciplined mind can be trained
to do this task.

How many are needed? An average of three
or four people are needed for every new language
entered today. This number includes supporting
personnel as well as those who do the actual
translation work. Training facilities are available.
Over 600 young men and women are trained every

summer. The total is more than that each year;
in ten years 6000 to 8000 more can have the
training which will equip them to do this
linguistic and translation work.

How long does it take? Fifteen years after
a person begins he can have a whole New Testament,
a lasting contribution of the Word of God, in
the language of the people.

ROBERT FOSTER, M.D.: Missionary Medicine

During the past seventeen years it has
been my privilege to serve the Lord in a country
in Central Africa called Zambia with the Africa
Evangelical Fellowship.

Ever since the Lord Jesus Christ sent out
his disciples and said to them, "As ye go, preach,
Heal the sick, cleanse the lepers" (Matt. 10:7,8),
there has been an integral mixing of medicine and
the preaching of that gospel. Sometimes there
seems to be a tension between these two things.
However, there is no tension in my mind; these
two are integrally related since we are seeking
to reach the whole man--body, soul, and spirit.
Medicine has a very significant part to play in
reaching that man for God.

Traditionally it has been felt that medical
work is a sort of ice cracker--something of an
ice breaker that will give an opportunity for
others to come and preach the gospel. Through
medicine we make contacts; through medicine we
open new areas; and this is very true. I am very
thankful to the Lord for the many wonderful
opportunities that have come to me as I have
sought to use medicine as a tool to contact men
and women for Jesus Christ. Medicine is only a
tool. Sometimes we think it is an end in itself,
but it is not, and we need to realize that our
calling as a Christian supercedes our calling in
our profession, whatever it may be. In this sense
every one of us has an opportunity to use whatever
tools God has given us as a means to reach man in

his totality. But to me medicine, as a profession, is the best tool by which I can reach other men and women.

However in this day and age, medicine not only affords the opportunity to be the ice breaker, but it also affords us opportunities to strengthen the church and play a very significant part in the establishing of indigenous churches. I do not think that this latter opportunity has been felt to be true in the past. But during these years that I have been in Zambia, it has been my privilege to establish two mission hospitals, and out of this we have seen a tremendous amount of good results in the establishing of the indigenous church and in the strengthening of believers.

I would like to mention two or three ways in which medicine has a significant place not only in evangelism, but in the strengthening of the church and the establishing of it in this day in which we live.

It is my conviction that for a hospital to be most effective, it must result from the request of national Christians. Now I do not have time today to go into all the why's and the wherefore's, but I would say this: it is only when you have their participation and when the hospital is set up at their request that the national Christians feel that a hospital or any institution belongs to them; otherwise it is a foreign institution which is run by foreigners. When the national Christians request and are willing to participate in making the institution a reality, then a board to run that institution is formed of local people. This takes it out of the hands of foreigners and makes it an institution in which local people can become enthusiastic and see value. This is particularly true in the opportunities that face us in the church. As we have sought to dovetail the ministry of the church and the hospital and to get a local board of local people together to supervise and to run the hospital, the church has seen in this a tremendous opportunity

for lay evangelism. We have had the opportunity
to train men to come into the hospital to do
personal visitation and to use the opportunities
that the hospital affords for lay people in the
church to work for God. As the church has seen
that this is their hospital and their opportunity,
they have assumed the responsibility for all the
spiritual ministry that goes on in the hospital.
Time and time again I have heard Africans say,
"This is our hospital," because they felt that
through it they are reaching their fellow men for
Jesus Christ. During these last few years at
Luampa, where I have been in Zambia, about ninety
percent of those added to the church have come as
a result of the ministry in our mission hospital.

In addition to this privilege of using
the hospital and encouraging the Africans to use
it for evangelism, there is also the tremendous
opportunity that comes to us today in training
African nurses, hospital assistants, lab technicians,
and so on. Here we have an opportunity not only
to train them in technical skills and professions,
but also to disciple them for God. In their
instruction we include study of the Word of God,
day by day seeking to teach them the Word and
living it out before them as we work together.
It has been a tremendous thrill to see how God
has blessed in this work.

Today there are opportunities for men and
women to reach out for God in every realm in
medicine. We want you to join with us in seeking
to advance the cause of Jesus Christ.

JAMES KRAAKEVIK: Education in Missions

Education is not optional to missionary
work; it is mandatory. It is not peripheral, but
central. Our Lord said, "Go therefore and make
disciples of all nations . . . teaching them to
observe all that I have commanded you" (Matt.
28:19,20 RSV). The scope of educational activity
ranges from literacy classes to the university

level, from a basic understanding of the gospel
to a deep draught of the Berean Springs of God's
revelation to man. In 2 Timothy 2:2 we have the
familiar exhortation of Paul to Timothy, ". . .
what you have heard from me . . . entrust to
faithful men who will be able to teach others
also" (RSV). It must be a progressive, portractive,
reproductive process, not a single exposure. We
must infiltrate and penetrate society for Christ
intensively, extensively, geographically, vocationally.
And what more natural method is there to accomplish
this than through education? However, the command
of Christ is not sufficient motive as Rolland Allen
points out in his missionary principles. The real
motivation for any missionary work anywhere is the
presence and power of the Holy Spirit within, doing
God's work through individuals. What a day in
which to be alive! What challenges face this
generation! It is a good thing that young people
today are idealistic and vigorous, for the
opportunities and demands have never been greater.

What, really, are the objectives of educational
work? Primarily, education ultimately must be
directed toward evangelism and church building or
it ceases to be a necessary part of missionary
work. Particularly, it provides the opportunity
to confront students with the person and work and
claims of Christ on a continuing basis. It provides
a biblical foundation for their total education.
It is the means for developing Christian leadership
and, in the spirit of 2 Timothy 2:2, it is meant
to produce national replacements for missionaries,
who can then move on to other areas of service.
Thus today missionaries not only work alongside
nationals, but often serve under them in this
cooperative educational enterprise. We must
remember that a necessary condition for spiritual
leadership is discipline and discipleship. Obedience
precedes authority and responsibility, and missionary
education provides unique settings for such lessons.

What are the present opportunities for
educational work? There is scarcely any field in

educational work throughout the world that cannot
be used in God's service.

First there are Bible schools, which range
from basic instruction in vernacular languages
to a thoroughgoing curricula in English, French,
or Spanish at post-primary levels.

Then there are seminaries, which are usually
post-secondary and provide serious study in
biblical languages, theology, and related subjects.
The products of these institutions are already
moving into positions of leadership in the national
church. An A.B. plus a B.D. degree is generally
appropriate for this area.

For the indirect area of Christian education
there are primary schools, teachers colleges,
secondary schools, and colleges. Here the need
for teachers has been moving steadily to the
higher levels. In Africa where over twenty-five
percent of the personnel of one mission are directly
involved in educational work, thirty-five more
teachers are needed for 1968. In another mission,
ninety teachers are needed in a rapidly expanding
program in all areas of the arts and sciences.
There is a ten percent annual increase in educational
input in Nigeria. In Christianity and African
Education by R. P. Beaver, it is estimated that
developing countries will continue to need
educational assistance for ten or twenty years.

Further opportunities exist at the university
level. However these are primarily available
through the United States government, host countries,
and the universities involved (through direct hire).

Additional opportunities are available in
the teaching of missionary children. This teaching
taps a vast reservoir of future missionary potential.

Another unique ministry is in the teaching
of Bible in government schools. In many countries,
particularly in the British Commonwealth, religious
education is required in the schools. And this is
often in environments that are nominally under
other religious systems.

In addition to regular terms of service

(usually four years), missions now provide short-term service for those so directed. Young people at the beginning, or older people at the end, of a teaching career can contribute a short term abroad and be permanently effective for missions. The academic preparation for secondary college or teacher training is generally the same as in the United States. The spiritual preparation is a living Christian faith, practical knowledge of the Bible, and a burden to evangelize and disciple. Personal preparation requires independence with submission; adaptability, but with a definite plan; cooperation with creative initiative.

And what are the results? You heard one this morning from Dr. Hatori. You will hear from others on the platform later. You will meet still more products of missionary education in dormitory and dining halls. And not only the direct leadership in the national churches (which is an obvious result), but also the lay movement of Acts 1:8 with its concentric responsibilities outward is being duplicated in the developing countries of the world. What a challenge to be involved in this aspect of the missionary enterprise today--claiming for Christ the minds and energies of young people throughout the world.

ERIC FIFE

I have been unusually privileged in being able to see most of these forms of service undertaken in various countries. Our next speaker will talk to us about the opportunities for business. I find the Christian public seems quite willing to regard a preacher as having a missionary vocation but somewhat loathe to recognize that an accountant or a secretary may have a role to play. Following is Olan Hendrix, the Home Secretary of the Far Eastern Gospel Crusade. Next will be the Rev. Phil Hogan, who is the Vice-President of the Assemblies of God. I am a city boy, born and bred; it does not make me like the city any more,

but I know the city. I have never seen any work
in the city more effective than that done by the
Assemblies of God. Following him we shall have
Charles Mellis speak to us about missionary aviation.
And finally, George Verwer will speak to us about
literature.

OLAN HENDRIX: Business in Missions

I want to talk to you about the opportunities
for business in missionary service today. The
president of the American Management Association
was in Detroit some time ago for some talks, and
in an effort to describe the rapidity with which
change is taking place in our world, he referred
to the rate of change of change.

And this rate of change is hitting the
missionary enterprise hard. For example, in the
early days of the missionary enterprise, as we
understand it and know it from history, missions
was a fairly uncomplicated, simple operation.
Men knew God and they went overseas and told of
him; people came to God and the church wss built.
Now that is quite an over-simplification, of course.

But today we have become almost infinitely
more complex and sophisticated because (if for
no other reason) of the number of people involved
in the missionary enterprise. This in itself
demands such things as automation, automatic
bookkeeping systems, electronic devices, and what
have you. So today people with skills previously
not even considered in missionary service are
absolutely essential. Not only highly-skilled
women to work with computers and this sort of
thing, but particularly men with business and
managerial skills are necessary.

In the last few years several men and
organizations have been sponsoring and teaching
so-called management seminars and management
courses for Christian workers. I think some of
you might be surprised at the tremendous level
of interest in this subject. Why? Because it

is displacing the Holy Spirit? Because we are
bankrupt spiritually and have to resort to these
techniques and these skills? Not at all! It is
because we have become more complicated and more
sophisticated. The demands of government are
greater, the numbers of people involved are
greater, and the needs are more diverse: therefore,
administrative skills, managerial skills, and
business skills are more essential than ever in
the missionary enterprise.

This means simply that your course in
business administration is not necessarily wasted.
This means that if you have the inborn gift of
problem-solving and problem-identification, if
you enjoy planning and executing, you may well
have a strategic role to play in foreign missions.
Not only this. It also means, in our complicated
day, that if your basic orientation is that of
preaching, you want to preach; if you are a teacher,
you do not want to be bothered with administration,
management, and all of this--you just want to
teach. I hope you will never make secondary things
primary, but I hope that you will recognize that
in this complicated day some of these skills are
absolutely essential.

J. PHILIP HOGAN: Missions in Urban Areas

For the past one hundred years or more,
some evangelical foreign missions effort has seemed
to produce an image much like that of the Old West.
The image lives on only in fancy; the actual,
current situation is sometimes very far removed
from the image being projected.

In earlier days missions tended to concentrate
on going to the more remote, the difficult of access,
the mountain or the jungle people. There seemed
to be a feverish push to get into areas where, and
I hope there were better reasons, it seemed the
only motive would be the emotional value to the
folks back home who were supporting the cause.
If the situation were modern, if it had sanitation,

194

if it had a roof that didn't leak, if there were
no rats or crawling pests, if there were no witch
doctors with feathers, and if it could be reached
by anything more utilitarian than a jeep or a mule,
it just couldn't be foreign missions. The trademark
of this enterprise was the pith helmet and the
bush jacket. This image dies very slowly.
Unfortunately it is kept alive by a considerable
segment of the church of Jesus Christ that is not
really aware of the real frontier of modern
missionary endeavor. Could I surprise you and
even shock you by saying that the mission field
of greatest opportunity and challenge today is
not necessarily the bush? It is probably the
boulevard.

If we would divide the world into city and
rural, the smallest and weakest concentration of
evangelical missionaries, apart from a few exceptions,
would be found in the largest city centers. Yet
by every argument conceivable the city is where
the witness needs to be made. Look at from the
standpoint of the scriptural precept. It seems
clear from both the Old and New Testaments that
God's major missionary strategy throughout the
ages has been to attempt to reach the nations
through their heart--their great cities.

When God wanted to reach Assyria, a major
world empire of mid-Old Testament times, he called
the prophet to its capital city Ninevah. At least
three times he added very pointedly, "That great
city, Jonah, is where I want you to establish a
strategic beachhead."

When the gospel witness was fully established
in Jerusalem, God moved Paul to plant churches in
the great cities of the Roman empire. Paul's
work was so successful that Rolland Allen, in
<u>Missionary Methods--St. Paul's or Ours</u> said:

> In less than ten years, Paul
> established the church in four
> provinces in the Roman empire:
> Galatia, Macedonia, Achaia, and
> Asia. From 47 A.D. to 57 A.D.

this work was done, until the
Apostle Paul could speak as if
it were finished.
Indeed a study of Paul's labors would indicate
that these cities were chosen strategically. In
every city where he worked at least four distinct
features were present: It was a center of Roman
administration, Greek civilization, and Jewish
influence, and above all, it was established on
the crossroads of the major commercial trade
routes of that time.
There is now, of course, and there always
will be, an important place for rural, out-of-the-
way missions. It has been the glory of the
Christian church that she has gone to the regions
where no one else has dared or desired to go.
That God continues to call men and women to this
arduous pioneer work no one would want to deny.
Yet if we take any lead from the Scripture, (and
the Apostle Paul is the pacesetter of this strategy),
then we must not neglect the teeming, seemingly
impenetrable metropolises from which the truth
of the gospel can radiate into all the corners
of the nations.
Let these statistics bring their momentary
impact upon your minds. In this great revolutionary
time there are at least five concurrent major
revolutions. One of these is the demographic
revolution (sometimes called the population
explosion). Within this revolution is another--
the growth of the urban community of our world--
just as important as the population explosion,
and perhaps more strategic and challenging to
Christian statesmanship.
In 1900 only 11 cities in the world had
over one million population. In 1925 this number
had grown to 56; by 1955 there were 83, and now
there are over 100. These cities invariably
become the centers of government and education,
and have the largest concentration of college

and university students in a comparatively small area. And the city is often the place for the questing mind and the spiritual vacuum.

Since on an average the majority of the people in large city populations now are under twenty-one years of age and are rapidly becoming literate, they offer the greatest challenge for the use of mass media.

This current swelling in the urban centers is comparatively new. There are still a great many mobile social tides moving in these cities. Many of the young people are detribalized. They have forsaken the old culture of the villages; they have escaped the control of the elders. The sights, the sounds, the solicitation of the cities are all new. The stratified social and religious customs of the centuries are broken up; minds and souls are like open fields welcoming any wind that blows and any seed that falls. Such is the posture of the twentiety century's greatest open door--the cities of the world.

The immediate question before us it: Who can reach the cities and by what means? I would like to detail for you briefly my picture of an ideal urban missionary. The Apostle Paul facing the colossus of Rome exclaimed his willingness to go and preach there and said triumphantly, "For I am not ashamed." Many modern translators put it, "For I have every confidence in the gospel of Christ." Paul was like a salesman entering a new territory for the first time and comforting himself with the fact that in his briefcase were samples that would meet any competition. He believed in the simple, profound adequacy of the gospel.

The missionary, facing the cities of today's world, must believe that the Word of God is truly the incorruptible seed and that when faithfully sown and watered by the Holy Spirit it will spring up and produce life. None of the overburden that the modern, complex world has added to bury deeper that intrinsic hunger in the human heart can really

suppress the power of the gospel in the cities.
The city missionary must have a simple reliance
upon the Holy Spirit and faith enough to start
somewhere, depending upon the Holy Spirit to
guide further. He must quickly recognize the
significance and the importance of the rank and
file Christian. He must toss this torch on to
multitudes, the quicker the better, because there
never will be enough American dollars or missionaries
to reach the cities of the world.

CHARLES MELLIS: Missionary Aviation and Radio

Radio communication networks is in contrast
to radio broadcasting: it is the "Bell Telephone
system" of the mission field. Eric Fife has
defined a missionary as one who crosses a political
or cultural frontier in the service of Jesus Christ.
If this is true, then aviation and radio communication
may be two tools that will help the missionary to
cross these frontiers and the barriers associated
with them and thus accomplish his mission.

Historically we have been concerned chiefly
with topographical barriers--jungles, mountains,
swamps, etc. As the modern missionary movement
hit its full stride in the first third of this
century, there was always the frustration of
effectively reaching inaccessible areas to which
many tribal peoples had retreated. Usually living
in relatively small, scattered groups beyond
rugged land barriers, these people were a challenge
to the already overworked missionary. But he
needed better transportation, preferably barrier-
hurdling transportation; then when he got to
these people, he needed some form of communication
with home base.

In many roadless areas aviation and radio
networks have provided effective solutions.
Probably the most dramatic result and solution
has been the penetration of West New Guinea, where
the combination of airplane and radio transceiver
actually spelled out the difference between entrance

and nonentrance to the land-locked highland valleys
of the deep interior. Al Lewis, the pilot for
the Christian and Missionary Alliance, landed the
first missionaries in a valley in West New Guinea
less than fourteen years ago. Today this area,
just out of a Stone Age Culture, has one of the
fastest growing churches in the world.

The penetration of the Amazon Basin, the
great jungle heart of South America, has been
only slightly less dramatic and considerably more
extensive. As the Wycliffe Bible Translators,
for example, have cracked the linguistic barrier
in tribe after tribe, they have relied on the men
of their jungle aviation and radio service first
to give them access and then to support them in
their remote tribal locations.

More recently, during the past eight years,
aircraft and communication networks have also
helped to bridge barriers created by political
factors. Several years ago a church was barely
planted among the Miao tribespeople of northern
Laos when the missionaries had to leave as they
fled before the path of Pathet Lao. Eventually
the interior towns were secured against this
military action, but the guerillas still controlled
the trails (even to this day). Missionary aircraft
began to carry Bible teachers to these politically
isolated villages, and in this case they were not
carrying American missionaries so much as Miao
tribesmen who had been trained in the interim.
In Congo, which once had a fairly good system of
roads, the bridges and ferries have been mostly
destroyed in each recurrent rebellion that has
beset that country; this has made transportation
more and more dependent on aerial highways.

Aircraft and radio communications also
make good teammates for medicine, relief work,
and other "cups of cold water" which the missionaries
carry to people in need. Congo presented a unique
need for relief work back in 1960. A mere forty-
five missionary doctors wanted to do what they
could to cover for the seven hundred Belgian doctors

who were forced to flee. Missionary aircraft
shuttled them from hospital to hospital where
they supplemented the valiant work still being
carried on by the African medical assistants.
The same aircraft carried food supplies to refugees
in remote areas and then later brought in baby
chicks and other stock for a longer-range solution
to the problems these displaced people faced.

These physical services are important in
themselves if we are to adequately represent Jesus
Christ; but they serve the additional function of
bridging barriers of prejudice. In Central America,
airborne dental clinics have opened villages for
gospel preaching--villages where evangelists had
previously been refused entrance and even threatened
with stoning. In several areas permission for
missionaries to enter the area has been primarily
due to, even contingent upon, the accompanying
air service.

Most of these activities in missionary
aviation and radio are carried on today by specialists
who are technically trained and professionally
proficient. In the case of pilots or aviation
personnel, that means an emphasis on operational
skills. For pilots it means commercial licensing,
and practical skills beyond that. For radio
personnel, both practical and theoretical knowledge
is important because we are using and anticipate
using to a greater extent very sophisticated
devices and techniques.

But these men must also be academically
and spiritually trained to take their place alongside
the church leaders, missionaries, and linguists
whom they serve. Although the majority of their
time is spent in technical services, their
effectiveness is dependent primarily on their
ability to relate to people--people of another
culture as well as those of their own.

GEORGE VERWER: Literature in Missions

I would like all of you to take your Bibles

and hold them up in the air. (I was taught this
in India.) Hold your Bible up. Praise God. I
don't know how many of you have seen 9,000 Bibles.
I asked you to do that because I want to remind
you this afternoon that seventy-five percent of
the world could not do what you have just done.
Seventy-five percent of the world could not hold
up a Bible because they have never seen one.

Missionary conferences are my weak spot.
In my first year at college I did not know such
an affair existed. I had been converted through
reading a Gospel of John, through picking up a
secular magazine about Billy Graham on the newsstand,
and through going to Billy Graham's meeting in
Madison Square Garden. This convention is the
closest thing to it I have been to since. I had
binoculars; I was out to see what this curious
fellow was doing. I ended up coming to Jesus
Christ. There was no follow-up; my little church
had no concern. I was only followed up because
Billy Graham believes in literature. I received
a sermon pamphlet called Prayer by Billy Graham
that revolutionized my life at seventeen years of
age.

Before I say a word on literature (because
I am scared to speak on this subject; everyone
thinks that I and our little movement are "literature,
literature"), I just must share with you this
quotation that has meant so much to me. It will,
I believe, keep everything that has been said in
proportion, and I know every speaker will agree
with this quotation from Samuel Chadwick, one of
the greatest soul winners the world has ever known:

> The world concern of the devil is to
> keep the saints from prayer. He fears
> nothing from prayerless studies,
> prayerless work, prayerless religion.
> He laughs at our toil, mocks at our
> wisdom, but trembles when we pray.

I know that many times the devil has laughed at
me as I have stood on a street corner for twelve
and thirteen hours distributing Christian literature.

At the same time I know that the printed Word,
the Scriptures, Gospels, and books backed by
faith-believing prayer can be the greatest power
in the hands of the Holy Spirit of God.

Who can deny the power of the printed page?
I received a little pamphlet from one of our young
girls working in Nepal. It tells of an unknown
woman in the seventeenth century who gave a tract
to Richard Baxter. He was converted. This great
Puritan then wrote a book called <u>A Call to the
Unconverted</u>. Among the many responding to the
call was Philip Doddridge. This eighteenth
century hymn writer and leader wrote a book,
<u>The Rise and Progress of Religion in the Soul</u>,
which led to the conversion of William Wilberforce.
This man gave his entire life and wealth to end
slavery and to start a score of great institutions
including the Bible Society, which has probably
reached more people with literature than any other
group in the world today.

I want to say a word about production
because that is a part of literature. I believe
with all my heart that one of the greatest missionary
efforts of the past hundred years has been done by
missionaries, many of whom are in our presence
here today. As a very young man I must look up
to these missionaries who have translated and have
spent tireless hours to give us Christian books
in almost every language in the world today. An
incredible job has been done by the Wycliffe Bible
Translators, by the Bible Societies, and by a
multitude of unknown people, who perhaps have not
time to be "well-read" because they are giving
their lives to produce the greatest reading that
has ever been given to man--the Word of God. I
believe that we of the younger generation must
be thankful for the groundwork, the toil, the tears
that have gone on before us by well-known men
such as Carey and by unknown people whom we will
only meet in heaven.

Literature exists, books exist, the gospel
exists in more than a thousand languages. And

yet as you and I sit here with our Bibles, with
our New Testaments (some of them in many versions),
some of us with large libraries, fifty percent
of the world is waiting for its first gospel tract
that costs one-fifteenth of a penny to produce.
I believe that one of the greatest dangers for us
as young people is to listen to these men this
afternoon and agree, but not do anything about
it. Literature, unlike some of these other fields
mentioned, is something that we can work at right
now. How many of us have tracts in our pockets?
How many of us have a Gospel to give to a man we
might witness to even this evening? How many of
us are concerned at all about those around us,
many of whom have never had a Christian book?
You know, it is amazing that we buy books for our
own libraries. I believe in them and I hope that
you buy fifty books each during the convention.
While you're at it, buy my book on literature.

That is one of the powers of the printed
page: It endures long after the message is
preached. Believe me, when I stood in the streets
of India, sometimes all I had was five minutes
to preach, and that was it. One time a Communist
mocked a missionary in China, "You preach at us
and you leave us; but the Communists come and
give us the literature." How long do we have
to watch the Jehovah's Witnesses--the fastest
growing religious cult in the world--produce
fifteen tons of literature a day? How long do
we have to watch the Mormons, who, at the present
rate of growth, will have in fifteen years more
missionaries, all young men, than all the existing
missionary societies represented in this
auditorium today? How long do we have to watch
these propagandists, these dedicated, consecrated,
sold-out literature evangelists before we will
arise, load our pockets with literature, with
Bibles, and go forth to tell the world about
Jesus Christ?

I believe, young people, that God's greatest
desire for this convention is that you and I

determine to be active distributors of the Word
of God. Lenin, facing his revolutionaries who
overthrew Russia in a handful of weeks, said:

> Every atheist must be actively
> engaged in the distribution of
> atheistic literature.

I have articles here, but no time to read them to
you, that tell of the hundreds of millions of
pieces of literature with which these dedicated,
materialistic fanatics are flooding the world.
I ask you from the very bottom of my heart: Where
are those who will be willing to do that with the
Word of God? Where are those who will be willing
to work night and day, who will be willing to cry,
who will be willing to work the presses, who will
be willing to do the translation until everyone
in the world has had the opportunity to read the
Book we hold in our hand today? I believe it is
logical that what we have, that has regenerated
our lives, must be given to the whole world; I
beseech you in the name of the Lord to respond
with all your heart.

10. Evangelizing/Discipling/Church-Planting

ERIC FIFE: Introduction

Lord, it is almost a formality to begin our meetings in prayer. And yet we do not mean it to be a formality. Because we sense our need of your guidance, your insight, your strength, your power. We pray that you will help us all to live so in communion with you, so open to you, that when in eternity we must account for the way we spend these days, all of us who are on the platform will be able to account for it without shame. May those of us who sit in the seats likewise be able to meet you without flinching because we have been responsive to what you have to tell us. We pray in Jesus' name, amen.

This particular meeting, as you know, shall be taken out of the second part of a unit called "The Introduction to Missions." Yesterday we heard a number of people speak to us about the enormous complexity of the missionary task today, in regard to aviation, radio, education, literature, translation, the challenge of the cities, the work in business, and medicine. But we are convinced that whatever may be our labors in these technical fields, they are of very little value indeed unless they result in what we're going to have described to us today--evangelism, the discipling of men,

and the building of the church of Christ. Our
first speaker on evangelism is Mr. David Howard,
whom we introduced before, so we do not need to
introduce him again.

DAVID HOWARD: Evangelism

When we speak of evangelism as the heart
of all missionary activity, what do we mean? On
what authority can we make such a statement--that
evangelism must be at the heart of all the mission
of the church, that all of our activities must
somehow contribute to the evangelization of the
world? We really have only one final authority.
Our only and final authority is the person of
Jesus Christ. This afternoon we want to look at
Jesus Christ and what he has to say about evangelism
as the mission of the church.

First, by way of example Jesus showed us
what evangelism is. Second, by way of command
Jesus Christ made it very clear that evangelism
was to be the mission of the church. And third,
by way of provision Jesus provided all that we
need for the evangelistic activity which he placed
in our hands.

First then, the example of Jesus Christ.
As you read through the gospel accounts of the
life of Christ, you find it unmistakably clear
that Christ spent a major portion of his time
teaching and reaching people to bring them into
a proper relationship with God. He taught his
disciples how to do this, and he often spoke with
individuals, small groups, large groups, and vast
multitudes, teaching them about God and how men
could come into a proper relationship with him.
Take the book of John for example. In chapter
3 we find Jesus talked personally to Nicodemus,
explained to him what it means to be born again.
In chapter 4 Jesus sat by the well in Samaria,
talked to a Samaritan woman and attempted to show
her what it means to meet with God.

Incidentally, at this point I'd like to

make a plug for the book of the day, How to Give Away Your Faith by Paul Little. Chapter 2 in this book, which is the longest chapter and in one sense the most valuable part of the whole book (although the entire book is extremely valuable), is based on John, chapter 4. Mr. Little has presented here the principles which Jesus Christ used in evangelizing the woman of Samaria. He points out that the total scope of evangelism is seen in this particular incident. I commend this book to you without reservation as perhaps the most relevant book on personal evangelism for today.

In John 5 Jesus talked to the Jews as a group. In John 6 He taught a multitude of 5,000 whom he later fed with the five loaves and two fishes. Then in chapters 7 and 8 he spoke to the Jews as a group in the temple. In chapter 9 he dealt with a blind man and those who talked with him after the healing of the blind man. In chapter 11 he raised Lazarus from the dead and taught the significance of what he had done. And so on. Throughout the gospel stories Jesus made it very clear by his own example that evangelism must be the heart of the message.

Jesus was once asked this question: "What must we do, to be doing the works of God?" (John 6:28 RSV). Jesus answered, "This is the work of God, that you believe in him whom he has sent" (v. 29 RSV). The great work of God is that men and women should believe in Jesus Christ who was sent by God. The work of the church today is that men and women should believe in Jesus Christ.

Christ not only showed by example what our mission is, he also taught very clearly by way of command what is our job and our task as a church today. It is extremely significant to note the strategic location that the Great Commission, as it is given in each one of the four Gospels, holds in the ministry of Christ. Jesus Christ had lived three years with his disciples—training them, teaching them. He had performed the work of redemption by offering himself in sacrifice on the cross. He had performed the work of justification in rising from the dead. And then in that brief period of forty days between his resurrection and his ascension he was once again with his disciples. We know very little about what actually happened during those forty days, but each of the gospel writers gives us just a brief glimpse into what Jesus said.

To me it is extremely significant to notice what Jesus said on his first encounter with the disciples immediately after the resurrection. We find this in Luke 24. Christ had risen from the dead and met with a few individuals during the day--the women at the tomb, Simon Peter somewhere along the way, and two men on the road to Emmaus. But Easter Sunday evening he went into the room where the disciples were gathered as a group. This is the first time as a group that they had seen him since his death and resurrection. Jesus Christ showed them that he really is alive, and said "Look at me, I have flesh and bones, I am alive." We read in Luke 24:45 to 48: "Then he opened their minds to understand the scriptures, and said to them, 'Thus it is written, that the Christ should suffer and on the third day rise from the dead, and that repentance and forgiveness of sins should be preached in his name to all nations, beginning from Jerusalem. You are witnesses of these things . . . .'" (RSV). What was he saying? He was simply saying, "Now I have completed the work of salvation. I have done my job. I have suffered and died and risen from the dead. I am going back to my Father, and you take over from this point on. It's now your job to make this message known among all nations." This is the Great Commission. It's the first thing Jesus said to his disciples following the resurrection.

John recorded the same incident for us in John 20. Once again Jesus appeared to those disciples and said to them, "Peace be with you. As the Father has sent me, even so I send you"

(v. 21 RSV). The time is the first night, the day of the resurrection, as he met with those disciples. But Jesus gave the command in different words, according to John. The difference in the records of Luke and John may mean that Jesus gave this command twice the same night in different words so that they would not miss the point. "As my Father hath sent me, to seek and to save that which was lost, so send I you to seek and to save that which was lost." He did not want them to miss the point. He made it very clear that first night that this is now their job.

We turn back to Matthew 28, perhaps the best known of the Great Commission passages. There is one significant note that I would like us to notice. In Matthew 28:16 we read, "Now the eleven disciples went to Galilee, to the mountain to which Jesus had directed them" (RSV). Why do I emphasize Galilee? Because this shows that the incident recorded in Matthew is totally different from that recorded in Luke and John. The incident in Luke and John took place in Jerusalem. Now the disciples had gone to Galilee, a different location altogether. Jesus Christ met them there in Galilee and said to them, "All authority in heaven and on earth has been given to me. Go therefore and make disciples of all nations, baptizing them in the name of the Father and of the Son and of the Holy Spirit, teaching them to observe all that I have commanded you; And lo, I am with you always, to the close of the age" (vv. 18 to 20 RSV). The Great Commission. He had already given it. He had given it that first night in Jerusalem. But once again he was with his disciples in Galilee; he wanted to make sure they did not miss this point now. This is the central thrust of the church of Jesus Christ. He wants to make sure they get it. So he says it to them again in different words: "All power is mine; and I am sending you to make disciples of all nations."

Mark recorded for us the Great Commission in similar words, "He said to them, 'Go into all

the world and preach the gospel to the whole
creation'" (Mark 16:15 RSV). Mark did not make
it quite clear where this commission was given.
He simply said, "Afterward he appeared to the
eleven themselves as they sat at table" (v. 14
RSV). That is all we know as far as Mark was
concerned. But to me the significant thing is
that Mark included the Great Commission; this
meant that all four of the gospel writers, in
recording the story of the life of Jesus Christ,
recorded the Great Commission.

Did you ever stop to think about how many
incidents in the life of Christ were recorded
by all four gospel writers? Very, very few.
Not even his birth, as significant as that is,
was told by all four. It was only told by two--
Matthew and Luke. Mark and John ignored it.
How about the miracles? How many miracles were
recorded by all four writers? Only one--the
feeding of the 5,000. All the rest of the miracles
were recorded by one, two, or three, but not by
all four writers.

But of course all four gospel writers had
to include the death and resurrection of Christ
because this is the gospel. This is the good
news, the fact that Jesus died and arose from
the dead. And all four of the gospel writers
also included the Great Commission because this
is part of the gospel. This is the job that now
must be done by the church. Jesus died and rose
again. But what if nobody ever hears about it?
The church must now make this message known among
all nations. Not one of the gospel writers under
the influence of the Holy Spirit had been allowed
to ignore this commission. It had to be recorded
because it is part of the whole message.

Now we come to Acts 1 and the last time
that Jesus met with his disciples before he went
back to heaven. And so we find here his very
last words, "But you shall receive power when
the Holy Spirit has come upon you; and you shall
be my witnesses in Jerusalem and in all Judea and

Samaria and to the end of the earth.' And when
he had said this, as they were looking on, he was
lifted up, and a cloud took him out of their
sight" (Acts 1:8-9 RSV). The very last thing
that Jesus ever said to his disciples was that
they would be his witnesses to the end of the
earth. He knows something about human psychology,
does he not? Have you ever sat at the bedside
of a loved one who is passing away, and that
person speaks to you his last words? How fast
do you forget them? You will never forget them.
You will remember those words longer than anything
else that person ever said. Jesus knew that.
And so he chose this strategic point in his ministry
to say what to him was the most important thing he
had to say to his disciples, "You take over from
here on in. I'm going to my Father. You are now
my witnesses unto the ends of the earth." Those
disciples went back to Jerusalem with his words
ringing in their ears.

So Jesus Christ placed this strategic message
in the most strategic part of his ministry. It
is the first thing he said after the resurrection.
It is the last thing he said before he went back
to heaven. And he apparently said it several
times in between. So Jesus Christ taught us by
example what our job is, and he taught us by
strict and direct command what our job is.

But Jesus not only gave his example and
command, he made provision for this job to be
carried out. "You shall receive power when the
Holy Spirit has come upon you; and you shall be
my witnesses." So Jesus Christ has provided all
that we need in the person of the Holy Spirit.
He has provided for us so that we can be his
witnesses. He has said, "Stay in the city
[Jerusalem] until you are clothed with power from
on high." When that power comes, we no longer
have any right to "stay in Jerusalem." That power
has come so that we might go to the ends of the
earth with the gospel of Jesus Christ and make
it known as his witnesses to all mankind.

I wish we had time this afternoon to go
through the book of Acts. I suggest a fascinating
study that you can make on your own: Go through
the book of Acts and mark down every time the
Holy Spirit is mentioned. You will find the name
of the Holy Spirit more than fifty times in the
book of Acts. Then mark the times when the fullness
of the Holy Spirit is mentioned. You will find
that nine times in the book of Acts individuals
or groups were filled with the Holy Spirit. On
nine different occasions. And if you study the
context of those occasions, you will find that
on every single occasion, without exception, those
who were filled with the Holy Spirit immediately
witnessed for Jesus Christ. There is no exception
to that in the book of Acts. Every time they
were filled with the Holy Spirit, the direct
result was the giving of the message—that Jesus
Christ came, died, and rose again, and that he
can bring them into relationship with God—to
others. This is the major purpose of the Holy
Spirit in our lives. It is not the total ministry
of course. The ministry of the Holy Spirit is
vast. But when the Holy Spirit comes upon a man
and fills him, the immediate result is that the
man wants to speak about Jesus Christ. "When the
Spirit of truth comes . . . he will glorify me,"
Jesus Christ said. And this is what happened.
You will speak of Jesus Christ when you are filled
with the Holy Spirit.

This is the provision that Jesus Christ has
made. Here is our command. We have the example
of Christ. We have his command. We have his
provision. Now what are we doing about it?

Yesterday I was on the qeestion forum here
and was impressed as we discussed together and
tried to answer that question about the draft.
The question came up, How far should I go in civil
disobedience when I believe a decree of the
government is an immoral decree? I suppose there
are hundreds, perhaps thousands, of students here
this afternoon who would be willing to go to jail

if necessary for certain convictions that you have. You may be among those who have demonstrated against Viet Nam. Perhaps you have demonstrated against the draft. Perhaps you are willing to go to jail for your convictions on this. Let me ask you this: How many of you would be willing to go to jail if you had to break the command of the government in order to obey the command of Jesus Christ?

I know Colombians, very close friends of mine with whom I have been working for years, who bear in their bodies the physical scars and marks of persecution because they have disobeyed government decrees to obey Jesus Christ. There was a time in Colombia not long ago when they were forbidden to speak in public about Jesus Christ. They said, "Whether it is right in the sight of God to listen to you rather than to God, you must judge; for we cannot but speak of what we have seen and heard." And I know many Colombians who spent time in jail gladly and willingly rather than close their mouths and not fulfill the Great Commission of Jesus Christ. Some lost their lives as a result. I know many who had father, mother, brothers, and so on murdered because of their speaking of Jesus Christ.

You and I may be willing to go to jail because we do not want to go to the draft. Would we be willing to go to jail if the time ever came in this country, or wherever else we might be serving him, when we were told we could not speak for Jesus Christ?

Charles Wesley, one of the greatest hymn writers of all time, captured this thought of the centrality of evangelism as the mission of the church when he wrote these words:

> Jesus, the name high over all,
>   In hell, or earth, or sky:
> Angels and men before it fall,
>   And devils fear and fly.
>
> His only righteousness I show,

> His saving truth proclaim:
> 'Tis all my business here below,
> To cry, "Behold the Lamb!"

ERIC FIFE

It is almost an awesome experience to travel
through Colombia with David Howard and to see the
effect of evangelism on the Colombians not merely
in quantity, although he could, in fact, have
overwhelmed you with statistics of one individual
alone, but also in the quality of their evangelism.
It is unfortunate that some people have a very
narrow view of what evangelism really is. It is
at this juncture that we introduce Mr. Waldron
Scott, the Navigators' coordinator for Southeast
Asia who spoke at IVF Missionary Camp, where I
first met him a number of years ago, and who left
an indelible impression, not for his oratory but
for his realism and his honesty. Mr. Scott, who
has lived for the last ten years or thereabouts
in the Middle East, has been intimately concerned
with the business of making disciples. He will
speak to us on that subject now.

WALDRON SCOTT: Discipling

Last summer I was passing through Singapore;
it was a Saturday night. I heard a terrific noise
below my window. I went down to investigate and
found that the noise came out of a building. I
walked into the lobby and found that I was required
to pay a Singapore dollar to get any more information.
I paid my dollar, walked in, and discovered that
the noise came from nine different combos playing
at the same time. I don't know if you have that
here in America . It is an exciting experience
actually. I looked around the smoke-filled room
for a moment and discovered that about a third
of the students seemed to be dancing to one of
the nine combos, a third of them were sitting
around talking with their friends, and the other

third were just sitting around waiting for something to happen. So I went over to one of the young men. Above the din I shouted, "What's your name?"

He told me. He shouted back, "What's yours?"

I told him. I asked, "Where do you work?"

He told me. He asked, "What do you do?"

I said, "I'm a Christian missionary. I've been traveling through the Orient this summer telling people about Jesus Christ." It couldn't have been possible in that room, but I thought that there was deathly silence. It shows how the mind plays tricks on you.

But then after just a moment he turned and swept his arm over the room and said, "Well, Mr. Scott, there are 2,000 of us here dancing tonight, and we would all like to hear about Jesus Christ." It wasn't possible under the circumstances to tell them all, so I told that one. He trusted the Lord that night and entered the kingdom of God. Knowing that this kind of response is waiting out on the field is what makes so many of us eager to fulfill the Great Commission.

Now the subject that we have before us is a matter of discipling men for Christ. And this matter also takes its warrant directly from the Great Commission. As Matthew reported, our Lord commanded us to "go therefore and make disciples of all the nations." Now this seems clear-cut. He said to make disciples. Yet this mandate is frequently misinterpreted. Over and over again in conferences I've attended, in world congresses, in books, in sermons, in discussion groups, and what have you, the Great Commission is assumed so often to mean simply that we are to go out and expend our efforts in getting decisions for Christ.

But to get decisions and to make disciples are not the same thing. And failure to realize this has contributed significantly to our inability to fulfill the Great Commission. Not long ago in HIS magazine the story was told of a missionary who after an absence of several years revisited a former congregation in Colombia. The missionary

might have been David Howard. He was grateful
to note the presence of converts from past years,
but saddened to learn of the backsliding of
others. He wrote,

> The thought came to my mind, if only
> we had been able to hold all those
> who had ever professed faith in
> Christ, what a church there would
> be in Colombia today. The dropout
> problem suddenly loomed as a major
> factor in church growth. For
> advance is crippled by every
> retrogression. And backsliders
> do affect the inner spirit of the
> Christian fellowship.

Now what did our Lord mean when he told
us to go and make disciples? What precisely
was he talking about? The Great Commission
itself does not carry a definition with it. It
can be understood best by a description from
the lips of Jesus of what is a disciple. In
John 8:31 he said, "If you continue in my word,
you are truly my disciples" (RSV). A disciple,
in other words, is someone who follows through
in obedience to Christ. Are you a disciple?

Our Lord also said, "By this my Father
is glorified, that you bear much fruit, and so
prove to be my disciples" (John 15:8 RSV). A
disciple, therefore, is someone whose commitment
makes his life fruitful. Not just fruitful but
very fruitful, Jesus said.

Our Lord said again in John 13:35, "By
this all men will know that you are my disciples,
if you have love for one another" (RSV). A
disciple is a lover--a rare commodity in a
self-centered age. And many other passages I
could quote to you in the Gospels reflect a
similar thought pattern in Jesus' life. The
question comes, Are we disciples?

Are you a disciple? It does no violence,
therefore, to the Great Commission if I were to
paraphrase it like this:

Our Lord commanded, Go into all
the world and get me men who will give
me their total allegiance, men who
will acknowledge my lordship over
every area of their lives, men who
will produce, men who will love,
men who will sacrifice.

With that in mind, I invite your attention
to the motto of our convention: "God's men from
all nations to all nations." This is our job.
We are out to get this kind of man. It is not
enough that there are 8,000 of us here who may
volunteer for overseas service. There are 8,000
men in Japan, Korea, Indonesia, Australia, New
Zealand, and so on, all around the world, who
are waiting to be won to Christ and developed in
the faith so that they too can be God's men from
head to foot.

Now drawing primarily from my own experiences
over the past few years as a missionary to Arab
students in the Middle East, let me discuss the
way a missionary disciples men under three headings:
First, conserving the fruit of evangelism; second,
developing disciples; and third, multiplying
laborers.

As for conserving the fruit of evangelism,
I quote our Lord again. He said, "You did not
choose me, but I chose you and appointed you that
you should go and bear fruit and that your fruit
should abide" (John 15:16 RSV). Thus, when I went
out to the Middle East in 1960, I naturally began
with evangelism. But this evangelism, or more
precisely the way I went about this evangelism,
was predetermined in large measure by my conviction
that the fruit of the evangelism must be conserved.
It must remain. Therefore, rather than witness
haphazardly, for example, to whomever might cross
my path, I selected a single manpower pool--in
this case a high school. And within that large
high school I selected a single class--in this
case a sophomore class. I zeroed in on that
and began to win friends for Christ.

I thought that when these young Arabs began turning to Christ, they would already have the makings of a close Christian fellowship because they were already friends. In fact that's what happened. After fifteen months of witnessing among these Arab students, we had a little band of men united in a fellowship that required the minimum of attention to maintain because it was a natural grouping to begin with. They prayed together, played together, studied together, walked the streets together, grew in their faith together, and--insofar as was appropriate, in view of my balding hair and such other age differences--they made me a part of their fellowship. Now that was the initial step of conserving the fruit of evangelism. In reality it was simply preparatory for the more crucial matter, that of developing disciples.

There are at least two things that to me seem necessary to <u>develop disciples</u>. The first is a warm, honest, vital fellowship. This I have already referred to. The second is personal, individual attention. As the late Dr. Samuel Shoemaker put it, disciples are handicrafted, not mass-produced. In my case this meant giving hours and hours individually to each man who turned to Christ during those first fifteen months, even though it also meant a temporary curtailing of my own evangelistic activity. There simply weren't enough hours in a day to do everything. It became a question of priorities.

Now what did I do with these men? I don't have time to tell how we actually spent the hours and hours together. This sort of thing is known as follow-up, and the convention programmers have allotted special time in the elective of Personal Evangelism on Saturday and Sunday afternoons for discussion of the subject of follow-up. We'll talk about follow-up in more detail at those times--the "how" of it. But the point I want to get across now is that my follow-up took a great deal of time and meant a sacrifice of other

legitimate pursuits. You ask, Why spend so much
time? The answer is that it takes only nine months
to give birth to a new baby, but it takes well up
to eighteen years of close personal, individual
attention to bring that baby to maturity. By
maturity I mean a point where his character is a
credit to himself and his family. By maturity I
mean the point where he can be expected not only
to reproduce and have more babies but also to take
care of the babies.

That brings us to our third step--<u>multiplying
laborers</u>. The first step is conserving the fruit
of our evangelism. The second is developing
disciples. The third is multiplying laborers.
Our Lord himself is the one who taught us that
the key to the missionary enterprise is not
necessarily money, equipment, techniques, programs,
or ideas, as valuable as these are. The key, he
said, was laborers--laborers of quality and laborers
in quantity. "Pray, therefore, the Lord of the
harvest," he said, "to send out laborers." And
what we pray for we should work for.

Let me pose you a question. Suppose you
had just three years to live, and the whole world
to win. How would you spend your time? How would
you go about it? Where would you begin? This is
precisely the situation that Jesus Christ faced
at the beginning of his ministry. Part of the
answer was given by David Howard a moment ago.
Jesus spent a great deal of his time personally
out in evangelism. And yet again and again through
the Gospels you can see that the focus of his
attention was on a few chosen men. He stayed up
all night one night in order to get clear in his
mind with whom he should concentrate his hours
and hours of personal attention. He came up with
twelve names. His approach was to develop disciples
in order to multiply laborers in order that the
whole world might hear the gospel.

Disciple-making, therefore, is important
not only because it develops Christian character,
by which God is glorified and men are attracted

to Christ, but also because true disciples are
productive and reproductive. They multiply
themselves, not only adding to the number of
laborers available to the Lord of the harvest,
but adding greatly to the number of people out
of every nation who hear the gospel. Writing
to his son in the faith, Timothy, Paul says, "And
what you have heard from me before many witnesses
entrust to faithful men who will be able to teach
others also" (2 Tim. 2:2 RSV). From Paul to
Timothy, to faithful men, to others also. From
one to one, to a few, to the many. Now there
is one of the most effective patterns of outreach
ever utilized in the past 2,000 years. It is a
pattern that can be followed not only by full-
time Christian workers but also by all of us,
even those of us who intend to serve God overseas
in a so-called secular capacity. No matter what
our job, no matter how heavy the demands of our
time, it is always possible to win at least one
man to Christ and to begin discipling him with
the view that he should reach and train others
also.

I saw this happen as I taught school in
the Middle East. That little band of men I told
you about did not become flaming evangelists
overnight, yet in due time as they grew in the
Lord and their lives began to evidence the fruit
of the Holy Spirit, they began to win their friends
to Christ. Today in a half-dozen cities in the
Middle East there are similar bands of young men,
all the product--and, I might add, the natural
product--of that first group. This is the kind
of thing we can expect to continue for the next
thirty years because these men--the men in this
initial group--have matured. And having matured
in their faith, they are going to continue to win
and add others to Christ the rest of their lives.
They are going to multiply because they are also
discipling the men they reach. And the men they
are discipling are in turn going to reach others.

Today in the Middle East we have a growing

number of third-generation Christians. I don't
mean to use the word third-generation in the old-
fashioned sense. I mean young Arabs who have been
led to Christ by other Arab students and who are
being trained by those Arab students to reach still
other Arab students. To put it more personally,
I am a missionary who has become a spiritual
grandparent. And I am well on the way to becoming
a great-grandparent and great-great-grandparent
in the Lord. All this has to do with numbers
because disciple-making has an important enormous
potential for numbers, for muliplication, just as
the millions of people on the globe today have all
been descended from a single pair of parents. Yet
behind this quantity stands the whole concept of
quality which has been at the forefront of our
thinking so much during this convention. Our Lord
defined discipleship in terms of obedience, love,
character, purity of heart, and willingness to
sacrifice in similar qualities.

In June of last year an open war raged in
the Middle East for a few days. This conflict
had a traumatic effect on the lives of the young
men I've just been describing because some were
Syrians, some were Jordanians, others were Lebanese.
And each one had different views, mostly reflecting
the views of their national countries, on the
political situation and the whole Arab-Israeli
problem. I had left the area a few months before
the war broke out to take my new assignment in
the Orient. I confess that when the war started,
I wondered in my heart how it was going to affect
these fellows, whether under its emotional impact
they were going to falter or stand firm in their
faith. Then I got a letter from one of them.
He said, "Scotty, a few days before the war as
we saw it approaching, our fellowship was strained
because we fell to arguing about the political
issues. But the day it began in earnest, we all
gathered together, not knowing what the future
held. We covenanted that, come what may, as long
as there were men left on earth we would stay

together and pray together.

When the war ended, these young men separated temporarily from the fellowship of western Christians and planned and executed a special training program of their own for younger believers. Moreover, sacrificing financially, they gave themselves to seeking out refugees, particularly those refugees that they had previously led to Christ before the war, and helping them. This, I believe, is discipleship. And in it is much of the romance and deep satisfaction that comes from working in overseas countries. Writing to the disciples that he himself had made, Paul said, "For what is our hope or joy or crown of boasting before our Lord Jesus at his coming? Is it not you? For you are our glory and joy" (1 Thess. 2:19-20 RSV).

One final word. If making disciples is such a significant part of the missionary enterprise, how is it reflected in our training? What does it take to make disciples? Can a stream rise higher than its source? Can we make disciples if we are not disciples ourselves? Are you a disciple--Christ's man from head to toe? In the words of Jeremiah, "If you have raced with men on foot, and they have wearied you, how will you compete with horses? And if in a safe land you fall down, how will you do in the jungle of the Jordan?" (Jer. 12:5 RSV). To make disciples we must first be disciples. Eric Fife has said that the missionary must be taught and be teachable. He must be a living example of obedience. Perhaps your greatest contribution in 1968 to the total worldwide missionary enterprise will be the personal resolve you make this week to be a true disciple of Jesus Christ this coming year.

ERIC FIFE

We'll let the word go back to our churches and our campuses that we take evangelism seriously-- the making of disciples--and the church of Jesus

Christ. It is on this subject that Dr. Glasser
will speak now.

ARTHUR GLASSER: Church-Planting

Evangelism is something intensely personal.
Troubled disciples marked the beginning of Christians
coming together. Interpersonal relationship,
disciplining the life of another, learning how
to walk in fellowship one with another. But God
has an objective beyond evangelism and beyond
discipling of converts. That objective is the
planting of his church. "I believe in the holy
Catholic Church" is the way the Confession puts
it. What does this mean? How does this bear on
missions?

I must confess the privilege that is mine
to speak on a theme such as this. And yet I would
like to bear testimony to the anxiety that I have
experienced because one of my tasks at this
conference so far has been to read through the
scores of questions that have been sent forward
for the panel. It was through reading these
questions that I became aware of an area of need
in this whole matter of the church. What does
the church really mean? What is involved in
planting the church?

I'll not speak of the existence of the worldwide church today, nor of the glorious triumph of
the church tomorrow, nor particularly of the methods
of church planting, though they are exciting. In
Northwest and Southwest China we had the experience
of going to an area, preaching the gospel, and
watching the response. And then we trained the
converts, watched them grow in grace and in the
knowledge of Christ. We saw them come together
and sense their oneness in Christ--the fact that
they could be an expression of the body of Christ,
something collective in an area. To see the church
planted--to see the church organized--to see the
church going out with the gospel to the surrounding
countryside.

As a result of the questions I have been reading, I thought it better perhaps to alter things and seek to evoke a mood, to deal with some of the hard issues related to this matter of the church of Jesus Christ.

First, the focus of the church--this world. The universe is at war, cosmic war, against a God-forsaken dark power. Originally the dark power was bright and good and glorious, but he went bad. He envied his Creator and then he rebelled against him. And in his banishment he took with him many principalities and powers--all given him by God, but now used by him to oppose God. The result, civil war. Satan, the adversary. He is the power behind death and disease and sin. He is behind so much of the meaningless and pointless suffering of man. The god of this world, the prince of the power of the air. The great manipulator. Millions are living under his control. And his weapons are false and phony ideas, as George Verwer reminded us. Distortions of the truth, half-truths, downright lies. He is a liar and the father of lies. He has duped and blinded and enslaved and tricked men into prostituting their strength and their days in following destructive and selfish ends.

Now the painful fact is that you and I happen to be living in his domain. We are in enemy-occupied territory, if you will. The rightful King is Jesus Christ. Long years ago he came. The devil knew of his presence. He tried to defile him and was unsuccessful. Then he murdered him. But by that death that Jesus Christ accomplished, he grappled with the awful power of Satan and destroyed him to deliver all those who through of death were subject to lifelong bondage. Christ did a mighty work at the cross and then left this planet to return to his Father. He is going to come again, of this we are sure.

Now, why are we gathered here at Urbana? Because we have come to know the true King. We are eager to be active on his side. We want to know what he wants us to do in the war. C. S. Lewis put it this way:

> Our true king wants to organize
> us and get us moving out in a great
> big worldwide campaign of sabotage,
> particularly helping others to
> escape from the devil's grip.

This is evangelism. And the devil hates biblical
evangelism because thereby he loses control of
men. They escape his net, his power. They reflect
his rule; they follow his enemy, Jesus Christ.
The Lord says, Get involved in the work of the
resistance. We are going to rob the strong man
of his prey. The devil hates follow-up, too. He
does not like to see those who escape and join
the other side become strong and mature and
productive. He does not want to see that all-out
surrender to Jesus Christ. Oh, no. Because he
realizes the tremendous possibility for opposition
to his power wrapped up in one man controlled by
Jesus Christ.

But what Satan particularly hates is that
which Jesus Christ particularly loves--the church.
Because it is by the church, we are told in
Ephesians 3, that the purpose of God's redemption
is to be accomplished. It is in the church that
the results of evangelism are conserved, that
believers are trained, that they become strong,
and that they in turn evangelize the nations.
We have been hearing of the churches throughout
the world. Do you realize that more than two-
thirds of the members of the Christian church in
all of the younger nations--Asia, Africa, Latin
America--have come to Christ through the activities
of the church? All this exciting revival and
growth in Indonesia today is due to the fact that
at long last something has started moving. Not
isolated individuals but a corps moving out in
the will of God.

When we left China in the summer of 1951,
hooted and hounded out of the place, regarded as
the off-scouring of all men, what did we leave
behind? We left graves of missionaries and their

children. We left Christians. We thank God for
them. We left strong disciples and we thank God
for them. But what particularly gave us joy?
The fact that we had planted in China the church
of Jesus Christ, the Word of God in the Chinese
language, churches with strong leadership. And
the Lord saying, I'm going to thrust you, not
as individuals but as collective units into the
crucible of revolution because I believe that in
the midst of that sort of situation you can glorify
me.

All this brings us to the question, What
is the church? Some months ago a man in Sumatra
came to Christ. He testified, "When Jesus found
me, I found him. I found peace, but I also found
brothers, fellow believers, a Christian community."
Conversion is something personal, but it leads to
something collective. You cannot really live the
full-orbed Christian life by yourself. You must
share that life. You must enter into the corporateness
of the Christian church, because becoming a Christian
means joining Jesus Christ, entering a family,
being incorporated into a building, becoming a
member of a body. The church is no mere association
like a club of people with common interest. It
is something living. It is an organism. It has
as its head, Jesus Christ. We are all different
and we are all members of this complex body.

There's no such thing as churchless Christianity. The church is not some burdensome
appendage attached to the Christian faith. We
have heard so much about the church. But is the
visible, organized church the real church? We are
acquainted with independent congregations, families
of congregations, denominations, if you will. But
are they the church? Questions such as these were
put to the panel. We have not yet grappled with
these questions. In a sense, we started to today.
And Warren Webster said, "You can't say of any
local congregation, that is the church." You know,
there is a hiddenness to the church. The church
is a hidden reality. In the final analysis it

is known only to God, for only God knows those
who are his. Only he knows those here whose lives
are hid with Christ in God.

The Reformers struggled with this problem:
Where is the church? They struggled with its
hiddenness. They came up with this answer--I
think it's tremendous:

> The church is hidden, yes. But it
> has its marks, whereby the true
> church gives itself away.

We should know what those marks are, the marks
that reveal the presence of the true church in
the midst of other organizations. Calvin said,

> Look for the marks. When they
> are present, you have the church.
> When they are absent, you have
> something other than the church.

What are those marks? The old Heidelberg Catechism
said,

> The gospel purely taught are the
> sacraments rightly administered.

And these can be expanded in the following fashion:
Do these who profess Jesus Christ gather regularly
to hear the Word of God faithfully proclaimed?
What is their regard for apostolic teaching? What
do they do with Holy Scripture? Have their members
tied themselves by ties of order and discipline
so that they might guard the deposit of the
apostolic truth, so that they might manifest a
quality of life to which they hold one another
by the disciplinary process? Do they administer
baptism and the Lord's Supper? Do they administer
these ordinances that have the dimension of mystery
in patterns laid down by Scripture? Are they a
worshiping community? Do they make much of Jesus
Christ? Are they a listening community? Do they
make much of listening to the Word of God? Are
they a witnessing community? Do they proclaim
the gospel of the grace of God? Are they a serving
community? Do they roll up their sleeves and
seek to ameliorate the raw nerves of human society?

During the 1930's I was a brand-new Christian

caught up in a wave of concern for the biblical
standard of the church, its purity, its holiness,
its obedience, its glory. In those days there
was such sowing of seeds of doubt, such stabbing
at true faith. We had a desire that God would be
glorified, that churches would be established in
which, by his grace, the marks would be manifest.
We preached on the street; we gathered in store-
front locations; we worshiped the Lord. Just a
few weeks ago I had the privilege of returning
to one of these congregations. Now it was large;
they had a fine building. Young people have been
sent into the ministry, sent overseas. Other
churches have been multiplied from that one church.
The elders met with me. We reminisced of the old
days. Then they prayed with me. They were concerned
for the glory of God. They were going to turn the
pulpit over to me. And they cried out to God for
help that the one who would stand in their pulpit
would proclaim the message of the grace of God.
Then we filed into the sanctuary. They took me
just up to the pulpit and then very graciously
gave me the nod, "Go up, preach." Then they sat
in a row in front of me. The elders and I guarded
the pulpit, jealous for the glory of God. A large
congregation assembled in front of us. Such a
vast throng. Such a response to God's truth.
And in my heart I said, "I see here the marks
of Christ's reign. Here is a church moving in
the direction of the New Testament ideal. What
a sharp instrument for the evangelization of this
world!"

People say, "Ah, the church militant. What
a joke! We know how it's in retreat. We know
of its weakness." That is true, but don't be
fooled by all the glib talk about the failure of
the church to meet the needs of our time. It is
easy to misunderstand the purpose of the church.
Return to the enemy of whom I earlier spoke.
Recall his persistent, ceaseless, truthless efforts
to penetrate the church, to defile the church, to
divide the church, to overwhelm the church. Civil

war. Satan versus Jesus Christ. Local churches are God's outposts in enemy country. They are central and crucial to his strategy. There God's people gather to hear the Word. There they renew fellowship with one another. There they learn how to serve Jesus Christ and to sabotage the works of the devil.

In World War II an Allied underground was in the Nazi-occupied countries of Europe. And the different parts were in touch with London by radio. In France all went well at first. True messages were received. Down in their underground cells they got the word; they did the deeds. But then something went wrong. The Nazis secretly gained control of the central-receiving apparatus in Paris. The resistance started to receive wrong messages. Whole groups were betrayed and their members led to death. The parallel is painful and obvious. We speak not without reason of dying and dead churches.

Now, do you love the church? The business of missions is planting the church. The more the better. In every level of society. In every population center. Not made just of old people nor just of young people, but of families representing the life of a people in each and every place. The church in the academic world expressing its life in worship in ways different from the church in the industrial world, the political world, the residential world. Churches, not missionaries and not foreign missions. Churches must bear the brunt of evangelizing the world in our generation. If you reject togetherness, you reject Jesus Christ. If you live in isolation from the church, you will be impoverished, weakened, and eventually overcome by the enemy. How effective is a soldier who will not participate in the collective life of an army? How good is a fellow that endorses Inter-Varsity but will not identify himself with a local chapter? Be suspicious of all those who stress just missions and omit the church. Be suspicious of all those who stress just church and omit missions. Get the vision of which the Scriptures speak: the church and the mission, the church reaching out with the gospel to the uttermost part of the earth.

In conclusion, I have been silent on the social dimension of the church. The church must work for freedom, dignity, and justice of course. We are to be the salt of the earth. But listen. Even if this world could be transformed into a social paradise by human engineering, that accomplishment would not constitute so much as the first step in the true mission of the church of Jesus Christ. Jesus Christ will build his church, and the gates of hell will not prevail against it. Let us thank God that by his grace he has brought us into this eternal fellowship.

ERIC FIFE

A few months ago my physician told me I was showing signs of stress (people in Inter-Varsity noticed it long before), and he said to me, "Just don't get excited."

I said, "You do not understand the nature of my work. How can you be a Christian without being excited?" The devaluation of the pound, the Arab-Israeli war, the Viet Nam war--nothing takes place in the world that does not have an impact on the mission of the church. This is an exciting business.

11. Commitment to God and His Work
by David Adeney

  In the few months that I have been back
in this country, I have had the privilege of
visiting a number of universities in the East
and in Canada. To me it is a tremendous joy to
be back again with the Inter-Varsity Christian
Fellowship. I am so thankful for the privilege
of being with you tonight.

  As I have traveled around to different
universities, I have discovered a new element
on the scene--student power. I have seen this
discussed in magazines and campus newspapers. I
was at the University of Wisconsin during the
demonstration against Dow Chemical Company.
When I was at McGill University, the students
were in an uproar because the authorities had
taken disciplinary action against the editors
of the student campus paper who had published
an exceedingly obscene article.

  Student agitation is an accepted fact
of academic life today in many countries. Before
leaving China, I remember watching students
marching behind a banner on which were inscribed
the words, "Go where the revolution needs you
most." Just before leaving Hong Kong in July,
I watched high school students join the rioters,
waving their little red notebooks and singing

their songs in praise of the invincible words of Mao Tse Tung." Everywhere students are on the march.

Students are idealists. Students are impatient. Students feel that progress in the world today comes too slowly. They are frustrated. They feel that their elders are not doing a good job. And sometimes they seek to express themselves in perhaps rather violent ways.

Some time ago I was with a group of students in Seoul, Korea. Many students--at the end of a day of great agitation, suffering, demonstrations, and violence--lay dead on the streets. I will never forget the remark of one student who turned to me and said, "Today, our fellow students have shed their blood for a political cause. What have we done for Jesus Christ?"

It is not enough to enjoy the great meetings of this convention. It is not enough to be stimulated by the addresses. It is not even enough to sing beautiful hymns of dedication. The question must come to us again and again: "What have we done for Jesus Christ? What is going to be the practical result of our gathering here tonight?"

I once heard the criticism that Inter-Varsity is only "conference Christianity." If this were true, if Inter-Varsity were known only for its great conferences, it surely would be failure. But, thank God, the conference can be a time of vision, a time when we see God's plan and purpose and then, by the grace of God, go out and act. Men of God--that is the key. God's men and women going out into the world to make men know that Jesus Christ is the living Lord, that God is not dead, that we his servants, even if a minority, place confidence in the power of God and in the presence of our Lord Jesus Christ.

Today we hear of various types of power: student power, black power, Communist power, and so on. How often do we hear about Christian power? How often do we hear about people in the universities

coming and asking us about the power of Jesus
Christ?

Our Scripture reading this evening (Acts
4) brought a very significant question before
us. This is the question the Jews asked the
early disciples: "By what power have you done
this?" The Jews had thought that Christianity
was finished. They had assumed that when Jesus
of Nazareth died, that was the end. But suddenly
they were confronted by a small group of people,
relatively unknown and insignificant, who
demonstrated a baffling power.

"By what power have you done this?"
Certainly those disciples did not possess economic
power, nor political power, nor even great intellectual power. But they demonstrated such power
of God in their lives that it was said, With
great power they gave witness to the resurrection
of Jesus Christ. Later they were described as
the men who turned the world upside down.

I will always remember a conversation with
a Harvard student some years ago. I told him a
little bit about how God had used one group of
students at a Chinese university. Sincerely
amazed, he turned to me and said, "I never knew
Christianity could be so dynamic!"

It is a tragic thing that people today
do not regard Christianity as dynamic. It is a
tragic thing when they say of us, as this student
said, "I thought being a Christian was something
ordinary." God grant that in this convention we
may see afresh the power of God, that we may meet
with Jesus Christ, that we may gain a new vision
of what God is doing in the world, and that we
may see the tremendous privilege of being God's
men fro this generation, facing the problems of
the age in which we live.

Do people come to you with questions? I
believe that whenever Jesus Christ is being
revealed in the lives of students, people should
be asking questions. If your fellow students are

not asking you questions, it's not because they don't have any. As I travel through various countries of the Far East, again and again I find students asking me questions. In spite of the spread of materialism, in spite of general indifference, there are students who are concerned with the present moral violence. There are students who are asking, "Is there an answer?"

Recently I was up in the far northeast of India. A very small group of Christians there felt that they had to do something to make Christ known to their friends, so they had special meetings. Then they went to a very strong Hindu teachers college, the Rama Krishna Teachers College, and got permission for me to speak about the Christian view of life. At the end of my lecture the Hindu students sent up their questions:

"Tell me the way."

"How can we realize God?"

"How can we know we are sons of God?"

"You Christians only believe in one life; we believe in many lives. How can a man be purified in one life?"

"Why is it that God seems so much nearer in Christianity than in other religions?"

"I feel I am in the darkness, with no center for my life; with a moral code, but no strength and purpose in life."

"Do you believe a spiritual understanding of Jesus will help us out of the dangers of this materialistic world?"

In Singapore about a hundred Christian students had such a vision for making Christ known that they arranged a university mission. They advertised in a campus newspaper, they sent out notices, and they visited practically every student on campus. Hundreds of students came out to those meetings, and many stayed to ask questions. On a previous occasion, a Muslim engineering student there had told me he felt materialism was advancing on every side and asked the vital question: "Why does God not speak to man?"

Oh that men might tell that God is speaking to man today! God should be speaking through us who are his servants.

In the Philippines a Roman Catholic student said to me, "Do you believe that Christianity, if properly applied, can save society? Do you believe that Jesus Christ can enter into the problems of our day?" Have we a message for our day?

How would you have answered a Communist official in a police station who said, "You Christians! You believe in Jesus who lived two thousand years ago. What is the relevance of your faith to the scientific age in which we live?"

I turned to him and said, "Frankly if I believed only in a Jesus who lived two thousand years ago, if that were all, I wouldn't be a Christian!" To me the heart of the Christian faith, the very center, is that God has spoken; he has revealed himself in Jesus Christ. The Christ who lives. And it is by his risen power the early disciples' lives were changed.

What kind of Christians can answer the questions of today's students? Let us look at the disciples and see the wonderful picture we have from our Scripture reading. Do you see them there in Jerusalem, and later on spreading throughout the Roman world? What was the secret of their success?

a. The Fact that they knew Christ to be the living Lord.

There was tremendous conviction in those disciples' lives. It was not based on mere perpetuation of a memory, but on the fact that Christ's promises had been fulfilled. What he had said would happen had indeed happened, and Christ Jesus had triumphed as the living Lord. The disciples now lived in society convinced that Christ was with them. They lived in society

full of hope, confident that God was working.
They lived in society with an authoritative word
concerning the future.

b. Their lives were transformed by their encounter with Christ.

It is not enough just to know about the
resurrection. We must have an existential faith,
which means we are personally involved with the
object of faith.

Existential faith goes deeper than
intellectual assent to historical fact. A man
who has faith in historical evaluation can say,
"Yes, I agree with Gibbon, the great historian,
who said that if those early disciples had not
been absolutely convinced that Jesus was living,
Christianity would not have outlasted the first
century." If you are an historian, if you study
the evidence, you can see the tremendous power
behind that point. The disciples' lives were
transformed.

But why were they transformed? Because
they had personally encountered Jesus Christ.
Their faith was more than intellectual; it involved
their whole persons. Friends, today in this
convention I believe our greatest need is for
each of us to go beyond just saying creeds,
repeating facts we believe, to a current realization
of what it means to know in our hearts that this
is truth. The living Christ is with us today.

I was invited to the Philippines to lecture
in a very old Roman Catholic University, dating
back to about 1500. The head of the theological
department there introduced me by saying, "Mr.
Adeney is going to speak on 'Encounter with Jesus
Christ.'" Then, to my amazement, he turned to
those students and said to them, "This is a very
important subject in a day when there are so many
baptized non-Christians in the church."

Baptized non-Christians! Is it possible?
It is indeed. We thank God for all that church

fellowship means to us. But it is possible to belong to a church and yet not know Jesus Christ ourselves.

I think of a student who turned to me one day and said, "When I came to this conference I was only half a Christian."

"What in the world do you mean, half a Christian?" I asked.

"Well," he said, "when I was in my home church I used to stand before the young people and talk about the things of God, but deep in my heart I knew I was a hypocrite. I could say things which really didn't mean anything to me. Now, though, at this conference, I have met with Jesus Christ."

c. Their message was Christ-centered.

They were men who spoke with conviction concerning the living Christ. Now there are many problems that Christians must consider today. The Christian must be able to understand the questions of the non-Christian world. The Christian must have an intelligent grasp of the happenings and the thinking of his day. The Christian must be able to talk to others about their problems. But, eventually, the Christian must be able to present Jesus Christ clearly because, surely, without the knowledge of Christ there is no Christianity.

The president of a Filipino university asked, "Can you have Christianity without Christ?" He had just been to China. He had seen the enthusiasm of the Chinese youth. He had seen some things that he admired--a certain puritanism, a certain moral standard. And he came back and saw the lack of discipline, the corruption, in his own country. So he turned around and said, "Look at this--has Christianity failed?" If, in an atheist society, you can sometimes, along some lines (I know this is only from some aspects), have a higher degree of public morality than in a country which calls itself Christian, has

Christianity failed?

Senator Salonga of the Philippines spoke to this question at an Inter-Varsity banquet: "Christianity has not failed. Rather, people have not tried Christianity. They haven't really come to know what Christianity is. Christianity without Jesus Christ as the Savior is no Christianity."

That which distinguishes Christianity from all other religions is its emphasis on the person of Jesus Christ. Confucius gave a great moral ethic, but Confucius had no message of forgiveness of sin. There is no way of escape from sin against heaven, he said. Buddha had nothing to say concerning a personal God. His emphasis was, that which is must be dissolved into non-being. He knew of no personal salvation to an abundant life. A Muslim student wrote to a newspaper, "How can we know the forgiveness of sin?" Mohammed, with his profound idea of the great holiness of God, had no answer for the question at stake. But Peter the disciple of Christ simply affirmed, "There is none other name under heaven given among men whereby we must be saved" (Acts 4:12).

Again and again those early disciples pointed to the person of Jesus Christ. "We cannot speak anything else," they said. They were forbidden to speak again in the name of Jesus. Even their lives were threatened. But they responded, "We cannot help speaking--we must speak in the name of Jesus Christ."

In contrast is today's tragic lack of certainty, which I believe results in a lack of authority. This past week I listened to a lecture by Mr. Edward McLain, professor of philosophy. Reflecting on "Morals and Religion," he analyzed the religious situation. At the outset he quite frankly told us that he was not a Christian. During his talk he quoted from many different religious leaders. Finally, in his--to me, tragic--conclusion, he said, "Protestant theologians are in chaos. They do not know what they believe. Roman Catholics are becoming increasingly uncertain. As for the

Fundamentalists--why bother? They don't concern
us." Now these are the words of a non-Christian
These are the words of a man who has evaluated
the religious situation. And he continued, "If
the people who call themselves Christian are not
sure what they believe, if they believe in the
existence of God, but are not sure about the
character of God, then they have nothing to say
concerning morals." We must know Christ personally,
we must speak with conviction, and we must keep
a Christ-centered message if we would speak with
Christian power.

d. They were determined to obey God regardless of the cost.

The disciples spoke with courage, tremendous
enthusiasm, dedication, and, at the same time, a
willingness to suffer. Think of the way in which
those disciples counted the cost. They saw what
lay ahead of them. They were not promised an easy
life. When they came to Jesus Christ to follow
him, they knew that it would mean suffering. You
remember Paul's words, "Take your share of suffering
for the gospel in the power of God" (2 Tim. 1:8
RSV). There is going to be suffering. It is not
going to be easy. We rather shrink from the idea
of conflict, but Jesus Christ never suggested that
men and women could be his disciples without
suffering, without paying a cost, without facing
difficulties, without entering into conflict.

What about our groups on campus? Are they
groups in which the power of God is revealed?
Or are they just another campus club? If you
want to play chess, you join the chess club. If
you are interested in biblical Christianity, you
join Inter-Varsity Christian Fellowship or some
other evangelical group. Are we merely a group
of clubs instead of being God's army, instead of
being God's men and women with an objective and
a power?

As I have thought of those early disciples,

again and again I have said, "Oh God, forgive me
for the times when my life has been lukewarm,
when my witness has been less than clear and less
than full of enthusiasm and courage." God is
looking for men and women today who love Jesus
Christ and are not ashamed to confess him. A
Chinese philosopher once said to a group of
nominal Christians, "If I believed one-tenth of
what you say you believe, I'd be ten times more
enthusiastic about it." Why should we be afraid
of being enthusiastic in our service for the Lord
Jesus Christ? The church was never meant to be
a club for Christian gentlemen, but, rather, a
barracks for training Christian soldiers, so
said D. L. Moody.

Imagine what would happen if your I.V.
group or your church were suddenly transported to
Communist China. Living in Hong Kong, I meet
people who come out of China. I read letters
from others. I wonder if you realize that if
you were suddenly placed in Communist China, you
would be surrounded by a group of terrifically
enthuasiastic young Chinese who consider themselves
part of the greatest nation on earth on the march.
They have purpose and dynamism. You may depreciate
the amazing fanaticism of the cultural revolution
and the Red Guard, but you should realize that
there is a real discipline there. And there is
a real enthusiasm. If you were there you would
immediately land up in an indoctrination group,
and people would quote to you sayings from Mao
Tse Tung, morning, noon, and night. You would
hear testimonies of what they had accomplished
through believing in his name, and they would
look to see what you believed. If you confessed
Jesus Christ, you might well end up in prison
or a labor camp.

I read a letter just recently from one
who had suffered very greatly. This Christian
wrote:

> What a loving, faithful God
> indeed! Once more let us experience

>afresh the lesson of faith and
>taste afresh the difficulties of
>life. Although there is no more
>big book to read, yet how sweet
>it is when the Holy Spirit is with
>us himself. We live in the grace
>of God's love.

In such conditions, would we show a similar courage?
Would we demonstrate the faith that characterized
the early church, without which the church can make
no impact on the world today?

e. They lived in a united fellowship.

The company of the early believers was
"of one heart and soul, and no one said that any
of the things which he possessed was his own
(Acts 4:32 RSV). The earliest attacks on the
church were against the fellowship, because that
fellowship was its strength. If the fellowship
could be destroyed, the church would lose its
power to witness. Ananias and Sapphira sought
to bring hypocrisy into the church (Acts 5:1-11).
The feud between the Greeks and Hebrews (Acts 6)
threatened division on racial basis. Later on,
Corinthian Christians argued, "I am of Apollos,"
"I am of Peter," "I am of Paul," "I am of Christ."
(See 1 Corinthians 1:12.) And divisions hindered
the witness of that church at Corinth.

I venture to say that if we were facing
persecution, a great many of our petty divisions,
these foolish things that divide us and water
down our witness, would be done away with. God
is looking for students who are united in their
love for Jesus Christ. God is looking for groups
that are honest, sharing together in their fellowship
and their love, not merely saying, "We are united."
We do not just need organizational union, but,
rather, a deep fellowship in the Spirit of God.
When the disciples were united in that way, nothing
could stop them. Oh that God would give us that
unity in our witness on campus!

f. They were led by dedicated men
who were guided by the Holy Spirit.

At the head of the early Christian group
were spiritual leaders, men who had given everything,
men who were prepared to go to all lengths--to
death, to prison, to whatever was required to make
Jesus Christ known.

I have a feeling that today we are in danger
of a kind of conditional surrender to Jesus Christ.
We say, "Lord I will follow you, but let it be in
this particular way. Let me choose the way in
which I serve." However, in the early church we
find that the Spirit of God worked in unexpected
ways. And one thing about those early disciples
was that they were willing to follow the Spirit
of God wherever he led them.

Think of Luke the doctor. I don't suppose
Luke ever imagined that he would become Paul's
companion and do literature work. But I doubt
that he complained because he was not continuing
in his medical practice. I remember in one
country a young medical student who graduated at
the top of his class, with a promising medical
career before him. God spoke to him, "I want
you to enter into the student work." And, burdened
with the need of the student world, this young man
turned aside from that medical career to serve
God as a staff worker in I.V.C.F.

I think of John Sung, who got his Ph.D.
in science when few other Chinese had such a
degree. "He should be back teaching in a university,"
was the natural thought. But God spoke to him in
an unexpected way. John Sung went back to China
to dedicate himself for Christ, to burn out his
life for God as an evangelist. I have met so
many leading Asian Christians who say, "It was
through John Sung's witness that I became a
Christian." And I think of churches all across
southeast Asia which were brought into being
because that young student gave his life to Jesus
Christ to serve just as God chose and as God guided.

I do not say that there is no need for
university professors, doctors, or other professional
people. Of course there is. But the crux of the
matter is that we should not assume the scope of
our vocation is limited by the scope of our training.
We should not say, "Because I started as an engineer,
I will be an engineer all my life." We should not
say, "Because I have had this particular course
of training, God certainly will use me this way."
God may. God very likely will. But the question
is, are we ready for God to enter into our lives
and say, "I want you in this particular place, in
this particular type of work"?

Twenty years ago a young OMF missionary
came to live in our home. She had a Ph.D. from
an American university and could have been a
teacher back home. If you were to visit her today,
you would find her one of the most loved and highly
regarded Westerners in Taiwan. And you would find
her giving her life. Respected by the government,
she has been asked to be the adviser to a large
school for delinquent boys. They come to her at
all hours of the day or night, and she is giving
such a witness to Jesus Christ that people are
being drawn to him. They know her past training,
and God has used it. But her power comes not
from her training but from her willingness to
say, "Of all that I have, nothing that I possess
is my own."

God wants to use you. Don't spend time
arguing whether you should go into vocational
witness or missionary service. Remember, the
answer comes, very loudly and clearly, that both
are needed. We must penetrate every level of
society. We must advance on all fronts. The
dedicated professional witness is tremendously
needed as well as the full-time missionary.

I think of two engineering professors in
the Far East today. They are men who are highly
respected in their fields, men who have a reputation
for the quality of their teaching. They are also
men who have made a great impact for Jesus Christ

among the students in the universities where they
teach. In fact, I think they do more teaching
and preaching about Jesus Christ than most pastors.
There is a need for this kind of Christian
professor.

But there also remains a tremendous need
for those who can do a work which you cannot do
if you are bound to eight hours of secular work
every day. There are certain aspects of the work
of the church of Jesus Christ which require people
to give themselves for full-time missionary work.
I would ask you to collect some folders from the
I.F.E.S. missionary booth. In "Service in Asia
Today" you will see what Asian Christians are
saying about the types of people that are needed,
even whether they are needed or not, and what
opportunities there are.

The world must see some people giving
themselves wholeheartedly to their profession,
glorifying God in their work and at the same
time unashamedly speaking about Jesus Christ.
The world must also see other men who could have
succeeded in some secular profession, but God
has called them to go overseas as evangelists,
or literature workers, or medical men, or whatever
it may be.

**g. They understood the times
in which they were living.**

We should be like those early disciples
who had a real grasp of God's working in history.
Turn to the fourth chapter of Acts (verses 24-30)
and read the prayer they made when they had been
threatened and told never again to speak in the
name of Jesus Christ. Listen to how they prayed.
They took their words from the Old Testament,
but they saw these promises of God being worked
out currently. And they proclaimed their utter
conviction that God was indeed at work in
contemporary history behind the acts of men.
Convinced that God's promises were being fulfilled,

they saw themselves caught up in those very
promises of God.

Oh friends, today is a wonderful time to
be alive! I can never thank God enough for being
able to live in Asia at this time. During these
past twenty-five or thirty years, as we have
seen changes, as we have seen the development of
the pressing problems of our day, we have also
seen something of the excitement of the youth of
Asia . I suppose that fifty percent of all people
in Asian countries are under 21. Only twenty
percent are over 40. These young people are
facing terrific problems. And oh how I long to
see Asian Christians, with their brothers and
sisters from the west, working in one team--one
in Christ Jesus. Those whom God calls to go to
other countries should be there, because there
must be an international witness serving under
the leadership of local brethren, a witness giving
itself utterly, completely, to the service of
Jesus Christ.

Are we going to see this today? I know
that times have changed, conditions have changed,
missionary methods have changed. You may discuss
these things at length. But there is one thing
that has not changed: Basically, the greatest
need for the potentially successful missionary
is a complete and utter dedication to Jesus Christ
himself. Without that, however good your methods,
however fine your organization, you can do nothing.
"Without me," said the Lord Jesus, "you can do
nothing." ·

Do we possess the power of God? What could
this power mean in the lives of the thousands of
students gathered here? What impact could it
have in your university? What could it mean in
some country overseas if you go back experiencing
the power of the Spirit of God?

Notice (Acts 2:4) it is said of the disciples
that all were filled with the Spirit. Paul said
that if any man has not the Spirit of Christ, he
is none of his. Then he went on to say that the

same Spirit that brought again our Lord Jesus from the dead, that same living Spirit dwells in the believer (See Romans 8:9,11).

If you know that experience, if you know the power of God in your life, if you have experienced the love and forgiveness of Jesus Christ, if you have given your life unreservedly, completely, to him--what great things God can do through you.

You will go back into conflict, back to face today's burning issues and to identify yourself with those who are suffering. You will go back to campus realizing that there is no easy, pat answer for the questions of our day. You will go back realizing you must learn to understand those who are critical of the Christian. You must love them and learn from them, and yet maintain such a conviction and humility--speaking not in pride, not saying that you have learned anything, but being ready to give an answer in all humility and reverence concerning the faith that is in you.

Then God will take us and use us, and we shall have people coming to us and asking, "What is the power of Christ? Tell me about it." And then very humbly, by the grace of God, we shall be able to speak with authority concerning the living Lord, whose we are and whom we serve.

12. The Missionary Vocation
by Warren Webster

ERIC FIFE: Introduction

God is speaking to me this evening and I
am persuaded that he is speaking to many of you.
He is beginning to show us how much we owe. And
in this day of sophistication or pseudo-sophistication,
whichever way you look at it, we need to be reminded
of how much we owe.

A very close friend of mine said to me last
week, "I feel the Fundamentalists have cheated me
out of the movies for fourteen years."

And I said to him, "Yes, that may
be true and maybe they've cheated me. But I am
glad at forty-six years of age to be able to look
back to the time from when I was sixteen on, and
be able to say that there was nothing that I was
not prepared to give up, and there was no street
corner on which I was not prepared to preach for
Christ's sake, out of a sense of what I owed him."

Our closing speaker this evening, as you
know, is Mr. Warren Webster, a man who has turned
down many rather attractive opportunities for
distinction here at home to serve fifteen years
in Pakistan. He spoke at the last convention in
1964. We believed then that he had a message
for students and we still believe it, and we wait
for him now to hear what God has to say to us
through him.

WARREN WEBSTER

In the last 150 years the church of Jesus Christ has literally exploded around the globe. Already in this congress we have seen the extent to which, in the past century and a half, people have become Christians and churches have been planted. As a matter of fact, we are told that in the past 150 years more people have become Christians and more churches have been started around the world than in the previous 1,800 years of church history. And today the 900 million people who statistically are counted as Christian total more than the number of people in the entire world at the time of the beginning of the modern missionary movement. It is a thrilling thing for us to be workers together with God in the consummation of his purposes in his world in this age.

I want to tell you a story about a friend of mine, Dr. J. T. Siemens. Born of missionary parents in India, he himself spent at least twenty years there in the service of Christ, only to be called back to the States to the position of professor of missions at Asbury Seminary. I think he has one of the most unique and enviable teaching posts that I know. He is required to spend one quarter of every year abroad so that he can keep his finger on the pulse of contemporary missions and be able to communicate effectively about missions to his students and to the Christian constituency in America. Because he travels a great deal, largely by plane, as an evangelist and missionary, he has interesting experiences. One happened some time ago on a plane, when he was seated next to a well-dressed young man, and they began talking together.

Incidentally, here is a tip if you want to have an opportunity to witness to the people that you travel beside: A psychologist observed that if you sit down with someone and don't begin talking the first five minutes on a train or a

plane or a bus, you probably won't speak during
the whole journey. And possibly you have known
that to be true. As Christians who are interested
in opening opportunities of witness, it is good
to find an opportunity to chat at the beginning.

Well, as these two men began to talk
together, the young man said, "I happen to be in
big business."

"Well, I also am in big business," Dr.
Siemens replied.

Then the young man said, "I cover the
entire United States in connection with my business."

Dr. Siemens replied, "Well, as a matter of
fact, I've traveled all over the world in connection
with mine."

At that, the young man was feeling just a
little bit outdone, so he continued by saying
what he thought would probably clinch the
conversation: "Well, I'm in partnership with
my father and he's a millionaire."

By this time Dr. Siemens was smiling a
bit as he said, "I also am in partnership with
my Father, but he's a multimillionaire."

At this, the young fellow looked up with
evident surprise and curiosity and said, "Say,
who are you, and what sort of business are you
in, anyway?"

Then Dr. Siemens, with fitting and, I
think, proper pride, turned to him to say, "I'm
a Christian missionary, the world is my parish,
and I'm in partnership with my heavenly Father
who owns the whole world."

At that the young man turned to him with
evident sincerity to say, "Sir, you're not just
in big business. You're in the biggest business
in the world."

Tonight, young people, I want you to know
without any shadow of a doubt that those of us
who are involved in the cause of Jesus Christ are
caught up in the greatest things that happen in
life. May God grant that we never forget our
high and holy calling to be his servants and his

ambassadors in these days. In the words of the
scripture passage which was read this evening,
may we remember that God, who in Christ reconciled
the world unto himself, has also entrusted unto
us, people as weak and fallible as we, the message
and the ministry of reconciliation. And that is
what it means to be a missionary, to be an ambassador
of Christ, in the greatest enterprise in the world.
The greatness of our mission stems from the greatness
of God himself, and from our privilege of being
workers together with him in the fulfillment of
his purposes.

Now this is true for all Christians who
recognize their responsibility as witnesses and
fellow laborer. But if it is true for all
Christians, I am confident that it is uniquely
true for those who are on the moving frontiers
of witness, those whom we have traditionally called
missionaries or the ambassadors of Christ.

This evening my purpose is not to speak
with you along familiar lines about missionary
qualifications, nor even sbout the motivations
for missions. These things will be treated,
perhaps, in succeeding messages. But this evening
I want to speak to the great question asked by
Christians and many non-Christians, both here and
in Africa-Asia: Do missions and the missionary
vocation have any validity in today's world?

I think we must confess that it seems
fairly obvious, as far as we can interpret history,
that the Western orientation and domination of
the world is coming rapidly to an end. I am not
so confident that those people speak truth who
conclude that therefore the mission enterprise
of the church of Christ is also diminishing.
Time and again in recent years we have heard that
in this revolutionary world the missionary movement
is outmoded and is going to end soon. We have been
told by critics of missions and the church that
the great surge of Christianity around the world
in the last 150 years is just an accident of history,
an epiphenomenon of the political and economic

expansion of the West. And that as the West is coming to political retreat, so also it is inevitable that its religious manifestations, meaning the church of Christ, will also begin to diminish and fall away.

It has been asserted that Christianity was and is the handmaid of imperialism. This is one of the most blatant falsehoods current in the world, and we need to say that it is just that. It does not take a very deep knowledge of history to point out that for the most part the missionary expression of the Christian church has succeeded not because of but in spite of the efforts of imperialistic governments and political powers.

In India, for example, not only in William Carey's time but in succeeding decades, the East India Company did not want any missionaries there at all and made it difficult for missionaries to be there and made their ministry almost impossible. Likewise, in Indonesia, the former Dutch East Indies, the church is only now claiming areas through witness and conversion that were closed by the Dutch government while the Dutch were there. The European colonialists did not give the church opportunity to enter certain islands and certain groups of people lest the missionaries disrupt the natives' primeval splendor.

No, the mission of the church is not a form of religious imperialism. We might be accused of that type of imperialism if we were guilty of hoarding to ourselves the wonders and benefits of the gospel of Jesus Christ. Imperialists are those who keep for a few the wealth and riches that should be shared with many. This has never been the fault of the church of Christ in recent eras. If the church were trying to keep the gospel to itself, then we might be guilty of this charge. But not as long as we go to share it with a needy world.

A recent author in Asia, an Indian diplomat-historian by the name of Dr. Panikkar, has suggested that the spread of Western civilization and Christianity have gone hand in hand and that both will decline together. But the point that he has failed to realize is that today the church has become a worldwide body. It may very well be true that Western political institutions in foreign countries are on the decline. I confess that though I am proud to be an American, I carry no brief for any particular nation or political system. I have gone abroad as a representative of Jesus Christ, and it just happens that by accident of birth I am also an American. The wonder of the church's outreach in this age--and one reason that it will not quickly come to an end--is that while Western nations are diminishing, Eastern nations, and with them the churches rooted in them, are rising. We have already seen that the church in Japan, most notably, and to a lesser extent in the Philippines, in Indonesia, in India, and, of course, in Europe, is beginning to pick up some of the missionary responsibility which of necessity lies not upon the church in one land but upon the church in every place. Today I think we must distinguish between the gospel of Jesus Christ as a universal message and the national forms that it takes in particular areas.

I think it is time that we remind ourselves that Jesus Christ was not a Westerner, but he was born midway between East and West in order that he might be the Savior of both. The Christmas season reminded us of his birth that took place in a tiny little land which serves even yet as a land bridge between Asia, Africa, and Europe. By race and human ancestry he was neither white nor black. But he was born of the almond-colored descendants of Shem, so that with respect to time (for he came in the midpoint of redemptive history) and place (that bridge at the center of the earth), and with respect to both color and race, his position will always remain central in the history and the life of mankind.

I think we not only need to remind the

world that Jesus Christ was born in Asia but we
ourselves also need to distinguish and help others
distinguish between the gospel and Christianity.
For many, if not most, of the accusations hurled
against the Christian enterprise are hurled--and
sometimes justifiably so--against things which
are not germane nor relevant to the gospel itself.
They may be Christian, but are not essential.
What is the distinction? Can we validly make
it? I think we can and we must.

The gospel, after all, is God's gracious
provision for salvation through Jesus Christ to
all men in every age and climate who submit
themselves to him in faith and trust. Christianity,
on the other hand, is the human response to God's
divine message. The gospel is the power of God
unto salvation--divine, pure, universal in its
application. But Christianity is the local
expression of the gospel as it takes root first
in the soul and then in a soil of a given locality.
The gospel message is universal. The forms of
Christianity are local and often provincial.

And unfortunately they are compounded with
local custom and tradition and human fallibility.
While I can say with Paul that I am never ashamed
of the gospel of Jesus Christ, I must confess
that I am frequently ashamed of things that go
on under the banner of Christianity or Christendom.
And I think that this is what one Asian meant
when he said, "We want your Christ, but we do not
want your Christianity."

Christ stands today with a universal appeal
to the hearts of men before whom he's presented.
I think that we would have difficulty imagining
Buddha or the person of Mohammad or Confucius,
or even Socrates awakening equal devotion in
people who live in the South Sea Islands, Sweden,
Norway, South America, in the desert belts of the
Middle East and North Africa, in Japan, Scotland,
or in Wales. Yet this is precisely the attraction
which Jesus Christ radiates in every culture,
because he came to be the Savior of the world.

Our message proclaiming him has not changed and will not change until he comes to consummate this age. But we are living in changing times, and you and I as Christians must change in our thinking or be completely left behind.

There was a time when missionaries going from England to India took perhaps eighteen weeks. Today they make the trip by jet in seventeen or eighteen hours. Formerly, perhaps even in the early part of this century, out of a dozen missionaries who would go to the field, three or four might have died after two years. And after five years probably only half of them were left. Many missionaries used to succumb to tropical diseases before they could even learn the language and begin to preach the gospel, and surely before they could get much of the Bible translated into local tongues. But in the last decade or two, momentous changes have taken place in the world, changes which are so radical and far-reaching as to constitute a revolution in world affairs. Our message has not changed, but our methods may have. I think there is nothing sacred about nineteenth-century missionary methodology, though we honor the devotion and sacrifice of those pioneers. If we continue to operate the same way they did, we may not fulfill what God expects of us in this age.

So I'm thinking with you tonight about the validity and expression of the missionary vocation in today's world. You need not fear that if you become missionaries you are soon going to be out of a job. The mission of Jesus Christ will not end until Christ himself returns. Stacey Woods in a recent article in the Evangelical Missions Quarterly said:

> Under no circumstances is there
> any possibility of world evangelism
> and the need of missionaries ceasing
> until the return of Jesus Christ.
> There has not been nor will there
> be any revocation of the Great

Commission until that day comes.
Some of you that are in space technology or those
of you in the biological or other sciences may
well find your occupations and vocations outmoded;
technology changes that fast. But those of you
called to a Christian vocation in a missionary
dimension need never fear that it will be outdated,
for the gospel of Christ is eternally contemporary
and the relevance of his message will last as
long as the world remains.

I would not pretend to assess for you tonight
the precise eschatological significance of the
day and the conditions in which we live, but I
cannot help but agree with Bishop Newbigin when
he says that, rightly understood, the end of the
mission is the end of history.

This gospel of the kingdom will
be preached throughout the whole
world as a testimony to all
nations and then the end will
come.

He goes on to say that according to the New Testament,
the completion of God's purpose for the world waits
upon the completion of the mission. The fact that
our Lord has not yet returned is itself evidence
that the mission is incomplete. It is at this
juncture of history and into this type of a world
that God has entrusted unto us the message and
ministry of reconciliation. Just where and how
you find your place as an ambassador beseeching
men on behalf of Christ to be reconciled to him
may depend upon the bent of your heart in these
sessions this week.

It is not only the theological and
eschatological necessity for missions today but
also the continuing need in men's hearts that
makes the gospel eternally relevant. Some of
you have become sophisticated in the studies of
sociology and anthropology. Perhaps your studies
of comparative religion have left you with doubts
about the spiritual need of peoples around the
world. If so, I can only suggest that you take

a look inward for a moment, into your own heart, and take stock of your own spiritual needs for forgiveness, for cleansing, for guidance, and for power. Then, as Dr. Siemens has suggested to us, multiply that factor by three and a half billion. This will give you some index of the deep spiritual needs of the world. After Dr. Siemens had returned from India, someone asked him at the close of a service, "Do the people of India really need the gospel of Jesus Christ? They have lots of religions there. Aren't they getting along all right without Christ?"

And Dr. Siemens replied in words that I think you and I can use: "No man anywhere is getting along all right without Jesus Christ."

The mission is validated by men's continuing needs for what Christ is and can do.

The mission is also validated today because of the church's need to express Christ. Recently I stood in Burma talking with church leaders who had no missionary friends to help them in these days, to work with them, to work under them. I asked them, "If conditions should change in your country so that co-workers from abroad were once again permitted, would you want them, or would you need them, or have you passed that day?"

And though we were standing on a hill where they have five seminaries and Bible schools as training institutions for their church, the president of that seminary said, without even pausing, "Of course we would want them, because we are incomplete without them."

Many churches around the world have said what the church in India said in a recent theological conference. "First of all, we need and want missionaries because of the immense task confronting us, one that we cannot fully handle by ourselves at the moment. But second, if the day should come when there is no practical need for missionaries, we would still need them so as to express the universal character of the church of God in our land."

Yes, the mission today and the missionary calling are validated from an eternal perspective. However, we must make some changes in our thinking about the missionary vocation. As churches in the West, undoubtedly we need a new understanding of what mission means and the forms that it may take. There was a time when we thought of the mission as something "out there." We talked about "dark continents" and about "regions beyond." We still use these terms, but, as a matter of fact, there simply are no more regions beyond, in the sense of unknown areas of the earth's surface, that have not been explored or discovered. After a hundred years of missionary contact, Africa is no longer a dark continent in the old sense. Mission is no longer simply a matter of crossing geographical frontiers. But basically the work of mission is that of crossing the frontier between faith in Christ and unbelief, wherever we find it. As such, the missionary frontier, the conflict with paganism, is present in every land.

Here in America the mission field surrounds us. It surrounds us in the presence of friends who come from other countries for business and industry and study. But the mission field is also present in the pagan areas of American life, which need to be re-Christianized.

Since the church has become a worldwide fellowship, it has injected a new dimension into missionary thinking. This new dimension is disruptive for some, but it must be reckoned with. The home base can no longer be one or two countries in the West: the home base for mission is every place that the church is. The dear saints in Boston used to think of Japan as the very end of the earth. But I can tell you that from the standpoint of the Christians in Tokyo, the end of the earth is much more apt to be Boston or Philadelphia. And this points up the fact that we need to conceive in a renewed way the necessity of the whole church bringing the whole gospel to the whole world. And that is why today progressive mission societies

are not only thinking about but also doing something
about the internationalizing of their missionary
fellowships. And that is why on every hand we
welcome the entrance of national churches from
every continent into mission.

We not only need this new understanding of
what the mission field is. I think we need a new
interpretation of who a missionary is. In a youth
camp, when I was last in the States, I asked,
"What is a missionary?" And I remember the reply
of one girl who said--and I think I couldn't put
it better--"It seems to me that a missionary is
just an obedient Christian, and that every obedient
Christian ought to be a missionary." Of course
she was speaking in the broad sense. What she
really meant was that every Christian ought to be
a witness, and this is undeniable on the basis
of the New Testament.

This does not mean that every Christian
will go abroad. I think it is not expected that
there will be a mass migration of every American
Christian going off to another country. David
Bentley-Taylor reminds us in one of his little
pamphlets that since God has caused you to be
born in this particular cultural context, the
likelihood is that he expects you to spend most
of your life of service here unless he gives a
very clear indication and a rather persistent
conviction to the contrary.

There is another sense in which we need
the whole church taking the whole gospel to the
whole world. We need the witness of the whole
church in each place. And that is why lay work
is being emphasized. The layman can never replace
the professional ministry--the minister, the
pastor, or the missionary. Because it is the
ministry's role to train the layman and serve as
a guide for him. But, on the other hand, let
us remember that the laity, into which many of
you will come, of which you are a part, is the
frozen credit of the church which needs to be
thawed out today and put to work around the world.

When we talk about the missionary vocation, we are not limiting it to ordained ministers. Many people go as nonprofessional missionaries without any mission board support, and I think the role of these people is most effective in closed lands where the church is not free to carry on other types of witness.

The thing that makes a person a missionary is not his ordination or his training, but the fact that he goes with a sense of divine compulsion to communicate a message. You do not become a missionary simply by going to teach in a mission school or to work in a hospital, I think, unless you also go with a sense of having a message to proclaim and the determination to do something about it.

The role of the missionary also has been somewhat misunderstood. Some people think that it is up to missionaries to reach everybody for Jesus Christ. This is patently impossible. The truth is that the role of the missionary is not primarily to save individual people, though he will do that. Rather, he is to provide the permanent means by which souls may be saved, that is, by planting churches.

This thought has been underlined by a Roman Catholic missionary thinker in Africa, who said:

> The foreign missionary is not
> meant to convert a country. That
> is for the home missionary. That
> is the job of the local Christians
> in that land. The foreign missionary's
> job is to create a cell which will
> then evangelize a society from within.

These are some of the changes we should make in our thinking about missionary vocation. We must ponder these and implement them in our missionary outreach.

We must also lay foundations for a missionary vocation. This is highly important. It is the kind of thing you can read many books about, but if you have not experienced it you will never

succeed as a missionary. By foundations I mean
those basics of new birth and regeneration through
Jesus Christ, of walking in the light as he is in
the light, of learning to pray powerfully, and of
seeking both divine gifts and divine guidance from
his Holy Spirit.

Recently I read an article that said there
are two ways in which you can be a success as a
missionary today. One is to have unlimited
financial resources. And we all know groups that
give an apparent vestige of success by the way
they use their funds. The other way to be a success,
the author said, is by being a man of God in whom
the holiness of God's Holy Spirit is found and
recognized.

The foundations must not be laid lightly.
If the foundation is weak, the superstructure will
fall.

This evening my function is not to call
you to a particular place but to call you to a
lifelong dedication to the person of Jesus Christ.
And I am content to leave in his hands the direction
as to where you shall work out that vocation, whether
it be here or abroad.

I do want to suggest to you, in an atmosphere
of realism, that the missionary vocation is still
a difficult vocation. It always has been and I
think it always will be, because it involves a
spiritual warfare. But the difficulties today
are of a different dimension than they once were.

I was glad that Dr. Miller mentioned Dr.
Zwemer's speaking at Johns Hopkins University and
having to leave the meeting in tow of the student
who was taking him on to his next meeting. Dr.
Zwemer himself had chosen his mission field on
the grounds that he thought it was the hardest
witnessing place in the world, and he had presented
this to the student. The young man wanted to know
if that was really true. Dr. Zwemer said, "Well,
I don't have time to convince you now while we're
dodging traffic, but if you let me write it out
for you I'll send it tomorrow." So the next day

Dr. Zwemer sat down and wrote a letter to this
medical student in which he said something like
this:

> Arabia is the hardest mission field
> there is for the following reasons:
> (1) The climate is almost unbearable.
> One hundred degrees in the shade
> is common. Frequently they report
> one hundred degrees Fahrenheit
> at midnight; it stays hot all
> night. (2) Arabic is the hardest
> language of which I know anything.
> (3) You probably cannot expect
> any converts to Christianity in
> your lifetime. All you can do is
> serve and love, and let results
> come as God sends them. (4) In
> addition, our mission has no money.
> We're not supported by any church
> board and we have to raise our own
> funds. (5) New missionaries must
> promise not to marry for five
> years. Life here at this time is
> too primitive for women and children.
> Let me know what you decide.
> Sam Zwemer

That young medical student, Paul Harrison,
read that letter, and then wrote a reply: "I'm
your man." And he went out to Arabia to become
one of the greatest missionaries.

I would be less than honest if I let you
think that the sacrifices of today's mission are
in those dimensions. I recently visited some
of Zwemer's old stations along the Persian Gulf,
and saw that most of his followers today have
air conditioners--which is not to criticize them
but to applaud their realism. But this fact remains:
the era in which the sacrifice and difficulty of
missionary life was measured in terms of tropical
disease and great dangers to health has not entirely
passed; these problems are just not at the forefront.

Today the problems and obstacles are more apt to
be psychological and spiritual, and many people
find that they cannot take these pressures or
have not been prepared for them. Douglas Webster
says that the missionary vocation is a permanent
invitation to misunderstanding. And misunderstanding
itself is one of the hardest things to bear.

Webster goes on in an article in the Evangelical
Missions Quarterly to point out that the era of
missionary heroes also probably has nearly come
to an end. That does not mean that missionaries
still do not have to make sacrifices, but that in
relatively few places today does the missionary
occupy the center of the stage. And where through
force of circumstances he still has to do so, this
is not something of which to be proud. It simply
indicates the lack of success in bringing into
being a truly indigenous church. Today most of
you going out into missionary work will be working
with and under national Christians, and you should
be thankful that the church mission has progressed
to the point that we can now go out in that
capacity. But this introduces new problems.

The church mission today is difficult
because so much is demanded that cannot be
anticipated ahead of time. I know you young
people like clear-cut job descriptions. Well,
let me give you one here. It may not fully satisfy
you, but it indicates the type of missionaries
that they are looking for out in the Anglican
diocese of Polynesia. They pulled no punches in
their Church Gazette in listing qualifications
and disqualifications such as these:

> Ability to mix with people,
> mix concrete,
> wade rivers,
> write articles,
> love one's neighbor,
> deliver babies,
> sit cross-legged,
> conduct meetings,
> drain swamps,

       digest questionable dishes,
       patch human weaknesses,
       suffer fools gladly,
       and burn midnight oil.
Those are the qualifications. Now here are
disqualifications:

       Persons allergic to ants, babies,
       beggars, chop suey, cockroaches,
       curried crabs, duplicators, guitars,
       humidity, indifference, itches,
       jungles, mildew, minority groups,
       mud, poverty, sweat and unmarried
       mothers had better think twice
       before applying.

There is no typical missionary vocation
that I can outline for you. But you can be very
sure that you will be called upon to do many
things you never anticipated or prepared for.
It is a difficult vocation, yet a glorious vocation.

Let me conclude by suggesting that in the
modern twentieth century, it still may prove to
be a dangerous vocation too. Mao Tse Tung said
on one occasion, "A revolution is not an invitation
to a tea party." And I think the same must be
said of the missionary enterprise. The gospel
is, by its very nature, revolutionary, and conflict
is inevitable. Herbert Cain in an article tells
us that the Christian missionary of the present
day will need more than an average share of courage,
both physical and moral. He must learn to live
with tension, and also with danger. Some missionaries
may get hurt, but this should not surprise us. We
are engaged in a spiritual battle, and war always
involves danger and death. In spite of the dangers,
we must continue to send out men and women of wisdom
who understand the times and the nature of the
conflict in which they are engaged. Men of courage
who will speak up when all other men are silent.
Men who will dig in and stand their ground when
others are retreating. Men who will go the second
mile and stay on the job long after the sun has

gone down.

Young people, it is only because the job is difficult that it interests me and that it causes me to commend it to you. I believe that you are ready to do even difficult things for the glory of God. I want no easy job myself. Life is too short to be frittered away that way. Trotsky said that he who wants a life of peace and quiet has simply chosen the wrong generation in which to live. Many of you remember the words of the martyr, Nate Saint, who wrote, "I would rather be dead than live a life of obscure ease in so sick a world."

With one final illustration I must bring my message to a close. Some time ago in India a Christian missionary was addressing a group of Indian university students. The majority of them were not Christians. He sought to present clearly and persuasively the claims of Christ. After the meeting many of them came up with questions; some sincere, some trouble-makers. Near the end one fellow pushed into the group rather impatiently and, pointing his finger at the missionary, said, "Why don't you Christians go home, anyway? We Communists are going to win India." The missionary was a gentleman; he turned to him to inquire patiently what he meant. And the young man said, "I belong to a Communist cell group in this university. We spend all of our spare time writing literature. We have our own press and we print it, and on our holidays we go out to distribute it. We have learned to eat, drink, sleep, and are ready to die, if necessary, for Communism. But you Christians, you only give leftovers!"

When I heard that story I said in my heart, "O God, save me from giving the leftovers of my life, of my energy, ambition, talent, and strength. Help me to remember, in the words of the Scripture, that Christ died in order that those who live might stop living for themselves and live unto him who for their sake died and rose again (2 Cor. 2:15).

Of all who confront the church at this
crossroads of history, I am confident that we can
outthink them, we can outlive them, and we can
outdie them. But there is no other way. Jesus
said, "Whoever would save his life will lose it;
and whoever loses his life for my sake and the
gospel's will save it (Mark 8:35 RSV). Dietrich
Bonhoeffer told us that when Christ calls a man,
he calls him to come and die.

You will never be a missionary until you
have died to yourself, until you have died to
your own ambition, to your own pride. And some
of you are willing to do that; that is why you
have come to this convention. You are realistic
and you are sincere.

This week as you look the facts of missions
in the face you can react in one of two ways. You
can either go ahead and go on living for yourself,
or you can say with Paul: "Christ died for all
in order that those who live--and I am one who
lives; I am alive in Christ--might no longer live
for themselves but for him who died for us. And
I will live my life wherever he wants it to be."
And then someday you will stand in his presence
to hear him say, "Well done, thou good and faithful
servant. Enter into the joy of thy Lord."

And I would echo the words of Charles Spurgeon
who once said, "If God gives you the privilege of
being a missionary, don't stoop to be a king."

13. Ambassadors for Christ
by Francis Steele

PAUL LITTLE: Introduction

Dr. Francis Steele was a staff member--
one of the early ones--in the Inter-Varsity
Christian Fellowship in Indiana, Michigan, and
in Ohio. He served on the faculty at the University
of Pennsylvania and was working as an archaeologist
in the university museum when I was a student there.
God called Fran from the field of archaeology,
where he had made some significant discoveries,
to become the Home Director of North Africa
Mission. For a number of years now God has used
him in the lives of many across this country,
North Africa, and other countries to communicate
the gospel and to present opportunities for
evangelism in the Muslim world. He will bring
us the message of the evening.

FRANCIS STEELE

I am told that today students are beset
by enormous volumes of knowledge and information
and threatened by all kinds of power that this
information conveys. And I am told that some
students--Christian and non-Christian--are
dreadfully upset. We have so much information.
We have so much power. But we are so insecure,
unsure of ourselves, fearful, and whatnot. You

know, this situation reminds me of a group of
little toads sitting around a puddle. One of
them exerts great energy, spits about three inches
into the puddle and--big splash! He has tremendous
joy! "Look what I did!" he says.

This is analogous to our overestimation
of our power in comparison with God's. Certainly
we have a great deal more information today than
we had some years ago. But what we know now in
comparison to what God knows makes even our present
knowledge insignificant. Do not let the fretting
and the confusion and the fearfulness of the
non-Christian today infect your life and dim
your vision of God.

Now let us get three things straight as
we address ourselves to the subject before us,
Ambassadors for Christ: If you are a Christian,
you are a witness; you have been called; you are
under orders.

If you are a Christian, in the biblical
sense, if you have received Jesus Christ as your
Savior and Lord and, by faith in his work upon
the cross and glorious resurrection, have been
born again into the family of God, you are a
witness, you have been called, and you are under
orders.

A WITNESS

Biblically, if you are a Christian, you
are a witness. I wish somebody had told me that
many, many years ago. I arrived at a university
as a Christian, but was not well taught and not
even particularly obedient to what I did know to
do. I was not a joyful or happy Christian at
Cornell University. I knew something about
witnessing but I did not know the biblical
definition of a witness. I thought that to be
a witness (if I "gave myself away," disclosed
to them who I was, exposed myself to them as a
Christian) for Jesus Christ I had to be prepared
to answer any question that any student might

raise. And I knew full well that I was not prepared
to handle those questions. So I decided to not
be a "witness."

I was just kidding myself. The boys in
the fraternity knew that I was a Christian. In
a very general way I had identified myself
personally with Jesus Christ. But I was a Christian
who was a negative witness to Jesus Christ. By
identifying myself with him genuinely and biblically
and paying respect to his name, I was a witness all
the while I was at the university. But I was a
miserable witness. Why was I never told years
ago that I was inevitably a witness? Why was I
told that I had the right to decide whether or
not I chose to witness for Jesus Christ?

We do not have that option--to be or not
to be a witness. Did you know that? All the time
you have been there on campus trying to hide from
people very modestly or shyly declining to engage
in this or that activity, you have been witnessing
negatively to Jesus Christ. I did not know that
when I was a student. I thought a witness was a
lawyer. No one helped me to distinguish between
the two. I think it was Dr. Vance Havner who said:

God wants witnesses, not lawyers.

Don't argue, testify.

Although I did not know the Lord Jesus in a
personal way, which would have given me the
ability and joy to share him with others, I was
a witness. And so are you.

CALLED

Tonight as one small pebble in the enormous
stream of evangelical communication, do not expect
to divert the stream that insists on using the
word <u>call</u> for a lot of things that are not biblical.
There is no biblical justification for the suggestion
that you are "called" to a mission society or to
a field or to a people or to a type of work. This
is not directly a "call." Rather, it is guidance
from God. I challenge you to find a verse in

scripture which clearly teaches that God calls
you as an individual to a mission field, mission
society, country, or a people.

In five verses in Matthew 4, two almost
similar situations use two different words to
demonstrate the biblical sense of God's call. As
he passed by the seaside, Jesus saw two men fishing
and he said to them, "Come, follow me." Then,
passing further on, he saw two others fishing.
He "called" them. The biblical call is to the
person of Jesus Christ. We are called to him.

You know, in one sense I think it is quite
appropriate to suggest that everybody in this
building tonight has been called potentially,
because you have heard the gospel from this
platform and I am sure that you have been studying
it in your Bible studies. So the invitation of
God in the person of Jesus Christ has been extended
to you. You have been called to give your life
to Jesus Christ.

Now if you are not a Christian, if you do
not know that you have answered the call of God
in Jesus Christ and given yourself to him personally
for his salvation through his death and resurrection,
then there is only one message for you. That is
not a so-called missionary call, but the offer of
salvation in the person of Jesus Christ. You must
be born again into the family of God, you must
accept the summons of the commander-in-chief
before you can engage in battle in his army.
You must be clear about that.

Let me mention something to you who have
not yet answered that call to God's service and
to you who have answered it--this answer is your
first and last independent decision. (Excuse me
if I seem to contradict our dear friends on the
platform.) I insist that you do not have any
other decisions to make after you have decided
for Christ. God invites you in Jesus Christ to
give your life to him. When you answer that call
your decisions end.

UNDER ORDERS

When you answer God's call you are then
under orders. From this time on you are to do
what God wants you to do. I like that, don't you?
I have no fear of giving up liberties, my own
puny personal liberties, if it means that I give
myself into God's hands. He saw me in my deep
distress, he loved me in Jesus Christ, and he
called me to himself! By the work of the Holy
Spirit, I gave myself into his hands. Now it is
his will, not mine; his decisions for me, not my
decisions for him. Is it not better that way?

Many of you probably came here convinced
that the day of foreign missions is over. Others
perhaps wondered if the need for missionaries is
rapidly diminishing. Now I must tell you that
missions and missionaries are still much needed.
Is there still a dissenter in the crowd? Or have
you been convinced by the testimony of the Word
of God and the testimony of the servants of God
that there will be need for soldiers until the
last battle is won and the war is over and the
commander-in-chief himself comes. There is still
plenty of need for soldiers.

But what if means and methods change? The
message and the messenger blessed of God have
always been the same. There never has been a
place in the plan of God for promoters of western
culture or for perpetuators of alien ecclesiastical
or denominational distinctives. Neither free-
wheeling individualists indifferent to national
culture nor inhibited lackeys of a moribund national
church can do the job intended for ambassadors of
an everlasting kingdom whose message is supra-
cultural, international, and, in fact, eternal.

One of the missionaries to France under
our board is a splendid Christian, who formerly
served his government of South Viet Nam in France.
He was released from diplomatic service to join
the North Africa Mission. When he came to us,
he wrote for our magazine a little article, "I

was an Attache, but now I am an Ambassador for Christ." He is doing a tremendous job for God in France. God's mission work also demands ambassadorship.

The need of mankind is unchanged. Man is alien to God, hostile to his will, and deserving of a holy judgment. And man is incapable of escaping this predicament by his own efforts. The remedy of grace remains the same--personal faith in the Son of God as redeemer and Lord according to the explicit dictation of scripture. So also the means to communicate the gospel of grace is still what it was when Christ first commissioned his disciples long ago: God has chosen to use men to reach men.

But what will shatter our conservative complacency? What must God do to cut the ties, some conscious and most unconscious, which bind us to our private plans, our comfortable situations, our colorless lives of Christian mediocrity? What do we need to tear away the scales from our eyes so that we can see the world as it truly is-- hopelessly lost and doomed to inevitable eternal judgment by an holy God? What do we need to feel the heart anguish of the blessed Savior who wept for stubbornly rebellious people yet steadfastly went to the cross to bear the punishment for their sins? How can this sublimely pure love penetrate the coldness of sterile theology and move us-- move us irresistibly into acting out God's will?

Columns of frightening statistics will not do it. Living hearts are rarely moved by dead figures. Pitiful pictures of naked, starving masses will not do it either. The feeble stirrings of an uneasy conscience are quickly stilled by a few dollars for "the cause." Statistical facts about scores of needs are helpful to a limited degree. But they cannot, by themselves, provide an adequate motivation.

Somehow God will have to convey to us an unmistakable consciousness of his awful sovereignty and his indescribably powerful compassion expressed in the matchless person of his blessed Son, so that our hearts and minds and wills will be given unreservedly to him. Somehow the Holy Spirit will have to transform this mundane world before our eyes into a terrible battlefield for the eternal souls of lost and dying men, where glorious victories can be won for God by those who are willing to plunge in, regardless of the cost, with only one desire--to glorify our precious Lord and Savior.

Here is how one Christian put this in poetry:

> Passionately fierce, the voice of
>   God is pleading,
> Pleading with men to arm them for
>   the fight.
> See how those hands, majestically
>   bleeding
> Call us to rout the armies of the
>   night;
> Not to the work of sordid, selfish
>   saving
> Of our own souls to dwell with Him
>   on high
> But to the soldiers splendid, selfless,
>   braving,
> Eager to fight for righteousness,
>   and die.

In the light of the spiritual needs of the world and the neglect of the church, what would you consider a mighty work of the Holy Spirit among us during this conference? This is a question I will let you seriously and prayerfully consider. (I have been praying intensely about this for six months.) We have been thrilled by singing together the great hymns of the church. We have had our hearts warmed by magnificent exposition of scripture. We have been stirred by the enthusiasm of exciting reports from the mission fields of the world. We have been stirred. But have we been moved? What must the Holy Spirit be free to do in order to perform his will for the everlasting glory of God the Son in this conference?

May I submit to you that if 1,000 young men and women in this audience, who previously had had no intention to go overseas as missionaries, were led of the Spirit to (1) decide definitely for foreign service, (2) determine to take immediate steps to get to their fields, and (3) persist in this course of action until they reach the place of God's divine appointment, that indeed would be a mighty working of the Holy Spirit here to meet the needs of the world. But let us not settle for a few hundred decision cards soon to get lost in a file drawer somewhere. Let us not have a big group stand on their feet under the emotional spell of the hour and then sit on their hands for the next forty years. Let us expect a great thing from God for his glory and then ask him to do it.

Perhaps it will help our understanding of the biblical concept of ambassadorship if we retrace Paul's experience on the road to Damascus. And perhaps as we expose our hearts to God's Word he can use this experience, through his force which spans the centuries, to lead us to a similar experience.

There are three accounts of Paul's experience. The first, in Acts 9, is the record of the event as it took place. The other two, in Acts 22 and 26, are occasions upon which Paul gave personal testimony to this experience. We will confine ourselves, for the most part, to the third account in Acts 26.

Four things happened here. First, Paul was confronted by the glory of God. (Now that is the necessary place for us all to begin--for both non-Christians and Christians.) Second, he was converted to the God of glory. Third, he was commissioned by the God of grace. And fourth, he committed himself to the grace of God.

In this description we find a man, who was not only highly religious but also highly educated, on a mission which he deemed to be in the service of God. He thoroughly knew the Bible of his day,

at least he knew it intellectually. He did not
understand it, but he had been trained in it in
the schools of his day. And he was a zealous man.
He was on a mission, stimulated by his idea of
what glorified God: the extermination of "heretics,"
the Christians. As he traveled the road to Damascus,
the well-known dramatic experience suddenly took
place. Paul was confronted by the glory of God.

Notice especially two aspects of this
experience: a light and a voice from heaven.
Surely a man as well-trained as Paul appreciated
the significance of the light and the voice, because
many times in the Old Testament record God had
revealed himself to his servants in the same way.
The light was a symbol of the holiness of God, of
the burning purity of his holiness. The voice
identified this physical phenomenon with a person.
The light conveyed the character of God; the voice,
the authority of God.

So Paul responded as indeed any one of us
would have under similar circumstances--by falling
flat on his face before this evident manifestation
of the God of the universe, the great Jehovah of
the Old Testament.

Then the voice from heaven asked a deeply
puzzling question, "Why do you persecute me?"

Paul was persecuting Christians in order
to glorify God. Yet unmistakably the voice of
the God of glory asked this question. So his
answer, though it seems illogical to us, is easily
understandable: "Who are you, Lord?" (v. 15 RSV).

Then came this tremendous declaration, "I
am Jesus whom you are persecuting."

Paul was converted to the God of glory.
Here was a man whose whole course of life had
been set in one direction--in order to glorify
God he would exterminate those Christians. All
of a sudden he discovered that the One whom he
despised and detested, whose followers he planned
to exterminate, was in fact the Lord of glory!
This is conversion. Turned all the way around
in the opposite direction---converted to God in

the presence of the glory of God.

Now please do not misunderstand. It is not necessary for you to pass through an identical experience in every detail to come to the same end. I do not know how God will choose to reveal himself and his glory to you. But I know the source. It is here. If you will expose yourself in expectant faith to this revelation of God in his Word, God will most certainly reveal himself to you in such power as to leave no doubt whatsoever. God identified himself as "the high and lofty One who inhabits eternity, whose name is Holy" as he revealed himself to Isaiah. Although your experience may not in physical details compare recognizably with that of either Paul or Isaiah, it will be identical in its essentials, and that is the place to begin.

Christians, I am positive that numbers, perhaps hundreds, of you on campus now are living as dull, fearful, unsatisfied, and unsatisfying Christian lives as I did for four years. And oh, dear friends, I plead with you, stop. This kind of life is not necessary any longer, not one second further. As God reveals himself and his glory and his authority, he will set things straight. Paul was converted to the God of glory.

Then notice especially in these verses that the initiative, the power, the authority, and the responsibility lies with God to fulfill his purpose. The Lord continued, "But rise and stand upon your feet; for I have appeared to you for this purpose . . ." I love that word purpose. It is a wonderful word. Stop to think: Certainly God has a purpose for my life. In his infinite wisdom, grace, love, and compassion he has gone to such pains to provide my salvation that it is unthinkable should he not have a purpose, not just a general purpose, not just to set me in a certain category, but to win me into close fellowship so that he can reveal day by day through intimate communion his will for that day.

God has a purpose for your life. And let me assure you that God's plans and purposes for us are far more wonderful than those we set for ourselves. And God's purposes are attainable (you can almost never say that for the goals you set for yourself). Furthermore, God's purposes are perfect because in his infinite wisdom and love he has made you as you are for his will as it is. He wants to bring you and his will together so that you can glorify him and enjoy him forever. This fact gives wonderful comfort and encouragement: "I have appeared to you for this purpose. . ."

"The subject of each of the succeeding verbs is God. God undertakes to perform his purpose in you. He does not just lift you from the ground and dust you off and say, "Well, now, get with it and do the best you can under the circumstances; I am on the sidelines to cheer you on." No foolishness like that! God calls you to himself in love for the fulfillment of his purposes. He desires to offer abundant provision for you.

One of the most marvelous, nearly incomprehensible statements in scripture is that God desires to have fellowship with us. We are told this in John 4:24: "God is a spirit, and they that worship him must worship him in spirit and in truth" for the Father seeks such to worship him. He desires fellowship with us. If I neglect, deny, or disobey God's invitation to fellowship, I am displeasing him in addition to hurting myself. God is the subject.

"I have appeared to you . . . to appoint you . . ." "Appoint" means literally to choose, to select, and to use. God chooses and makes you a witness (or a servant, in a literal sense). Everything that our brother Mr. Stott has been telling us, from our study in 2 Timothy, about the hardship and servitude of the Christian life is true. But it is glorious servitude, because it is serving him. But it is work. God has appointed us to serve him and to bear witness.

We come again to that confusing word "witness."
(At least I was confused. And perhaps you are too.)
The scripture makes it quite simple. To what should
you bear "witness"? "To the things in which you
have seen me and to those in which I will appear
to you" (Acts 26:16 RSV). What had Paul seen with
the eye of faith in that vision of brilliant light
greater than the noonday sun? He had seen God.

If you have not seen Jesus Christ genuinely
and currently, you do not have a witness. You
are a witness, but you do not have a witness.
Perhaps your initial enthusiasm has grown cold,
and you are fearful and easily embarrassed and
ashamed. Perhaps you have no witness any longer
because you have nothing to say about what you
have seen in the past.

We are told sometimes, "Well, you don't
have to say anything anyway. It is the silent
witness of the Christian person that influences
people." Have you ever heard that before?
Nonsense! The symbolic witness apart from the
verbal witness is at best confusing. And we have
here a good illustration of that in visual aids.
Look at the flags above the platform. About a
dozen of them have a symbolic witness. But their
symbolic witness is meaningless without interpretation.
Now observe the green flag with the white writing.
That one has a verbal witness: "There is no God
but Allah. Muhammad is the apostle of God." The
Arabs are not ashamed of their belief. Their
statement of faith is spelled out explicitly on
their national flag. That is a verbal witness.
There is no mistake.

If you do not have your word to sustain
your life, your life is virtually meaningless.
But also if your life does not back up your word,
there is probably even worse confusion because
then both your life and word are meaningless.
God said to Paul, I want you to give personal
"witness to the things in which you have seen me
[past] and to those in which I will appear to you"
[in terms of a current experience of Jesus Christ].

May I tell you a story, which probably many
of you have already heard, which is an appropriate
illustration of this point. There was a young
couple, who were mediocre, average Christians.
One summer they were invited to a Bible conference.
It was tremendous. Bible studies they had never
heard before, fellowship in prayer with other
Christians, testimonies--the whole atmosphere
was terrific. So of course when they got back
home, they were simply bubbling over with
enthusiasm. They passed on their testimony about
the wonderful conference for some months until
nearly everybody had heard, and occasions to give
their testimony became less frequent. On these
rare occasions they found that the details were
becoming rusty, so they decided to write it out
to make sure they got it straight and not confuse
the testimony. On even less frequent occasions
they would get it out and read it.

Many years passed and some relatives were
visiting from across the country. Conversation
got around to religious things, and the couple
said, "Oh, did we ever tell you our testimony?"

"No, I don't believe you did."

"Well," the wife said, "John, would you
please go and get our testimony?" So as an
obedient husband he trotted off upstairs and
searched for it. He came down with a badly mouse-
chewed document.

"Look dear what the mice have done to our
testimony," he said.

That was not a testimony; it was an archive!
It should have been buried years before. Their
current life did not back up their past genuine
experience.

But seriously how many of us are trying
to live today on an experience that is rapidly
becoming so remote that it is nearly lifeless.
Under those conditions you are a witness, but you
do not have a witness. Yet, even if you have not
had the advantage of theological training or Bible
training in order to undertake the "ministry of

explanation," you have a witness if you have
genuinely met with Jesus Christ currently. And
do not worry about all the theology professors
with their long white beards and the strings of
degrees after their names. Not one of them can
refute or disprove your genuine, current testimony:
"I have seen the Lord. I was with him this morning.
He spoke to me through his Word." You have a
testimony and a witness. And God undertakes to
make that testimony effective. This is his promise.

Now all of this promise was still potential.
It was still in prospect because there is one
more important point. Paul went on in verse 19
and said, "Wherefore, O King Agrippa, I was not
disobedient."

I have heard this saying (I wish I could
give credit to the source), "If you and I were
obedient to one-tenth of what we already know of
Scripture, our lives would be utterly different."
Sometimes as Christians we are misled into thinking
that what we need is more information. Thank God
for the Bible studies. But, please do not
misunderstand me, I do not think that our primary
need is more Bible studies. If we were obedient
to what we already know, even one-tenth of it,
our lives would be different. Paul said, "I was
not disobedient."

Notice that in the Greek "obedience" has
to do with hearing. The word for obedience is a
form of the verb "to hear," with positive reaction;
disobedience is "not to hear."

Although I never had the privilege of
serving in the navy, I am told that the response
of a seaman to an officer is quite important. If
you are given a command and say O.K. or something
of that nature . . . none of that. They have
places for people like that. The proper response
is "Aye, Aye, Sir" which means, "I have heard and
will obey."

That is the response God expects from you
and me. On the basis of his revelation of himself,
lovingly in Scripture, he expects this response

from us, likewise in love: I have heard, I
understand, and I will perform.

> I do not ask, O Lord, a task to
> do beyond my skill,
> I only seek, my God, that I may
> know thy perfect will.
> Little is much if but the task
> I do thou shalt appoint,
> And so whatever life brings of
> good or ill,
> Give thou to me the will to choose
> The strength to do, thy will as
> unto thee.

14. God's Man for Our Time

AKIRA HATORI

A question that I was asked to answer for
you, dear brethren, is, What kind of missionaries
does Asia need? My sincere answer is--anyone!
This, the world's largest missionary convention,
thrills me. I think of Christians in Japan who
are not zealous enough to evangelize their own
people. But I am thrilled to see intellectual,
promising young people here, some of whom at
least are willing to go out to the foreign mission
field. I feel like bowing down before you right
now and saying, "Thank you."

Come to Japan and Asia, anyone whom the
Lord sends out. This is not only my personal
feeling. I am sure many of the evangelical
Christians in Asia would share the same view.
Dr. Benjamin Chau, a Chinese medical doctor in
Singapore, wrote in one of the Overseas Missionary
Fellowship magazines,

> Asia does need almost every and any
> kind of missionary, not necessarily
> only the specialist or the best
> qualified.

I say "anyone" now. But when I was younger,
there was a time when I had some heart-burning
resistance toward Western missionaries. I was
against their living in big Western houses. I

was against their having maids. I was against
their eating Western-style foods all of the time.
I was against their going away to their summer
cottages when the work was the busiest. I was
against everything. But the Lord dealt with me
and helped me and took away this resistance from
me. My days of resistance are gone; although I
still have a real allergy to lazy and proud
missionaries. Now, however, I remind myself that
if there are any faults or shortcomings in a
missionary, the Lord himself through his Holy
Spirit can tell him and correct them.

Now I would say again that we need, in
Asia generally and in Japan specifically, anyone
whom the Lord sends out. Coming out to a mission
field, any mission field, is not a simple thing
nowadays. In addition to your own willingness,
there are many sequences of red tape you have to
go through such as arrangements for your family,
church and mission board affiliations, screening
and training, your decision as to your place of
service, and the matter of getting financial
support. When the Lord wants to send you, he
will send you in spite of this complex procedure
of becoming a missionary. Sometimes he will send
you regardless of your academic attainments,
professional status, and technical abilities.

Some years ago I was attending a missionary
conference at Mt. Hermon, California. After an
evening message one young man came forward to the
platform and turned to the audience and said,
"I have been praying about missions for a long
time. I have kept the sense of God's call in me
for a long time. But now this evening I realize
that I haven't turned my key on. I haven't started
the motor. But I do now. The Lord helped me."
This young man came to Japan, though the Lord later
guided him to Brazil from Japan. If your engine
is on, if your motor is on, the Lord is surely
going to guide you. The most important thing
is your once-for-all commitment to the Lord.

Step out, and the Lord will guide you.

And do not be afraid of stepping out and going out
because the Lord goes with you and guides you.
Do not make too high standards or qualifications.
Do you want excuses for not committing yourself
to the Lord Jesus Christ, who came down to save
you, who died on the cross to save you? Has he
not promised to go with you and guide you?

Even without any special qualification,
your mere coming out to a foreign land will give
you many advantages. For instance your foreignness
will stand out clearly. You know we are strangers
on this earth. Our citizenship belongs in heaven.
We are here wholly and solely to be the Lord's
representatives, to do his will on earth and to
evangelize the people. In order to do this you
always have to be a stranger on this earth--and
you can be a stranger in a foreign land easily!

A missionary should be single-minded and
single-hearted in his desire to do the work of
the Lord and to love the people. He should not
be tied down by his desires and lavish ambitions.
I tasted this single-mindedness when I came to
America seventeen years ago. I did not quarrel
with anybody because I did not have enough
vocabulary to do so. I did not gossip about
anyone because I did not have any vocabulary for
that. The only vocabulary I had was biblical.
So the only thing I could talk about with people
was the Bible and salvation. And you would be
like that in a foreign land.

I know a missionary who came to Japan
with B.S., M.A., and B.D. degrees from good schools
in America. Yet he was a child with the Japanese
language. However, he went out on street corners
to distribute tracts. He visted home after home
distributing tracts, using a simple, short
Japanese sentence, "Please read it." Even using
this short sentence in Japanese he made a mistake
and said, "Please be my bride." But do you know
what the people of that little town started to
call him? In a very loving way they called him
"Mr. Christ." And he became a very successful

missionary in Japan.

Please do not rely on your high academic attainments, professional status, or technical abilities. Please commit yourself to the Lord and come. Come, anyone whom the Lord sends out. His sending is the first qualification for the kind of missionary we need.

Second, we need <u>anyone who can communicate the gospel of Jesus Christ</u>. One day a teacher of one of the new religions of Japan visited me.

"I would like to know about Christianity," he said.

"Well," I answered, "Christianity is love."

"And so is my religion," he replied.

"Christianity is purity," I said.

"So is my religion."

Then I said, "Christianity can make you happy."

"Yes," he replied, "my religion can make you happy, too."

So finally I said, "Christianity is Jesus Christ. He is God incarnated. He came down and died on the cross to take away your sins, and he rose again to give you new life.

This teacher stared at me, stepped up to me, and asked "Is this all true?"

"Yes, all true."

Then, broken in tears, this man cried, "I want to believe in Jesus Christ. My religion did not give me any peace, joy, or purity. I want to be made new!" He opened up his heart and received Jesus Christ.

Japan needs Christ. Nothing else. You know the other summer almost all the liberal missionaries in Japan gathered together and discussed their mission work in Japan. The conclusion of their conference was, "We are not to make Christians out of Japanese. We are to help Japanese be better Buddhists if they are Buddhists. We are to help Japanese be better Shintoists of they are Shintoists."

We do not need this kind of missionary. We want Christ preached. We want Christ communicated.

We want to see the lives of Japanese transformed
by the person of Jesus Christ. Your ability as
an electrical engineer might be very useful and
necessary to help radio and television evangelism
in Japan. Right now I need an engineer like that
in Tokyo. But regardless of your high academic
attainments, professional status, and technical
abilities, we need anyone who can really communicate
Christ to us. Can you communicate Christ to others?
Have you ever communicated Christ to others? Come,
anyone who can communicate Christ.

Third, we need anyone who has the compelling
love of Christ for us. John the evangelist exclaimed,
"See what love the Father has given us." No one
can resist a genuine love. Love can break through
the thickest heart wall.

Miss Burnett, an elderly missionary
lady from England who led me to Christ and made
a disciple of Jesus Christ out of me, was a hard
trainer. She insisted on my going out every
afternoon to visit homes and to preach in the open
air. But she loved me. When I got sick, she
visited me every day. Sometimes I pretended
that I was asleep when she visited so I could
save some time for her, and I will never forget
her big smile when she saw my pretendedly-sleeping
face.

One cold night I had a tent meeting and
came back late, and there at the doorway was Miss
Burnett, waiting for me with warm underwear for
me. Later I found out that she had waited in
the cold outdoors for more than an hour. She
did not want to miss me when I came in.

She gave me all the money she had saved
up in order to send me to America. She gave her
life to Japan. She did not give service for
merely one year or two years or three years--
but she gave her whole life to Japan and loved
Japan and became a part of Japan's soul. And I
can say with sincerity that because she loved
me, I have been sustained to be a witness to the
Lord. Her compelling love is still lingering

in my heart. I have never had a day pass without thinking of that dear lady.

Come, anyone whom the Lord sends. Come, anyone who can communicate the gospel of Jesus Christ. Come, anyone who has the compelling love of Jesus Christ for us in Asia. We evangelical Christians in Asia and in Japan will welcome you with gratitude.

I make one request of you tonight. Would you step out and say to the Lord, with sincerity and reality, "Here am I, send me"? Thank you.

ERIC FIFE

The voice from Asia has rung sincerely. On your behalf I want to thank Hatori Sensei for his ministry. Next we shall listen to what God says through the lips of Mr. Emilio Nunez of Central America.

EMILIO NUNEZ

The image of American youth projected by television and newspapers in America is quite different from the picture we have here in Urbana. To see you coming to this convention, to see you paying attention to missionary messages, to see many of you taking notes of these messages, and to listen to you singing praises to the Lord has been a refreshing experience and a tremendous blessing to my soul. Tonight because of you I feel more enthusiastic and more encouraged to go to my own country, to my own people, to continue my ministry for the glory of God.

Through the years the Lord has been teaching me some lessons with regard to my preaching and teaching. And one of the lessons is that I should resist the easier impulse to criticize my fellow workers and rather do the harder work to encourage them and to help them in their ministry. So it is with a sense of my own need that I have come tonight to say something about the qualifications

for foreign missionaries. I recognize that these
qualifications are for myself, too, because the
color of the skin makes no difference. These
are qualities that any Christian worker, either
a foreigner or a national, must have in order to
succeed in his missionary task.

My subject tonight is The Successful
Missionary. I want to be positive as far as
this may be possible. It has been my privilege
to know many successful missionaries through the
years, and I would like to mention some of their
characteristics.

First of all I have discovered that the
successful missionary is <u>willing</u>, even anxious,
<u>to get acquainted with the people</u>. In obedience
to the Lord's command he goes where the people
are. The successful missionary is not just a
resident in a foreign country, living always in
a well-protected missionary station and waiting
for the people to come begging for an interview.
Rather, the successful missionary goes where the
people are and lives among them to communicate
the message of redemption.

It is possible for a missionary to spend
all his life in the security and comfort of his
home on the mission field without having a real
interest in the people whom he professes to serve.
A young American missionary who works among the
Navaho Indians in New Mexico said recently, "Some
American missionaries have built walls around
themselves." I was impressed by this. There
may be many missionaries around the world living
behind walls of prejudice, frustration,
indifference, or the literal walls of a home
that is inaccessible to the people.

The second characteristic of a successful
missionary is that he is willing <u>to learn from the
people</u>. He should be a learner, getting lessons
from the people. That an American missionary is
supposed to learn lessons from the people (besides
the language) is usually overlooked in the United
States. A common idea is that a missionary goes

as a teacher for a people who live in complete darkness and ignorance. And the missionary may give the impression that he is sacrificing himself, working among ignorant people--without realizing that these same people consider him a child with regard to their own culture! Sometimes it is interesting to see a missionary laughing at the people and the people laughing at the missionary. This represents a lack of communication.

At the Congress of Evangelical Communications held in Lima, Peru, last September, Dr. Jacob A. Lorentz, an anthropologist for the American Bible Society, talked to us. He told us that American missionaries usually are well prepared and well trained with regard to the contents of their message but that they are little trained in the best ways to communicate this message. I think Dr. Lorentz is right. New missionaries know their Bibles--and praise the Lord for that--and they may even know a great deal of theology and the original languages of the Scriptures. But, humanly speaking, all this knowledge is not enough to communicate effectively the Christian message in a foreign culture. The knowledge of a people's way of life is the key to effective communication. And this knowledge includes the psychology, the soul, of the people.

A people's soul is open only to the missionary who lives among them, and learns their language, their traditions, their customs, their ideas, and their values. If the missionary is indifferent to the culture in which he lives, if he pays no attention to public opinion in the local press (there are missionaries who do not take seriously the local newspapers), he is not interested in the best literary and artistic expressions of that people, how can he know the thinking and the feelings of the people?

Actually we need more missionaries who are willing to go study in our universities. I know that not all missionaries need to go to the universities there, but at least some of them

should go to our universities to know what is going
on among the intellectuals in Latin America. We
need more missionaries who are willing to learn
from the people.

It is unfortunate that candidates and
appointees to the mission field usually are exposed
here in the United States only to the opinions of
American missionaries and pastors. And as newcomers
to the field they may be instructed only by their
elder missionaries, by those who have been on the
field for a long time. The advice of these
missionaries is of great value, of course, but I
believe that the new missionary should be open
from the beginning of his ministry to the suggestions
and ideas of the national leaders. I know many of
our national leaders may not have all the formal
education of the foreign missionary, but the national
leaders know, far better than the missionary, their
culture and their work.

In the third place the successful missionary
is willing to work with the people. I am grateful
for the American missionary who, at the beginning
of my ministry in Guatemala twenty-three years ago,
taught me that the Christian ministry is work.
It is hard work, not just a hobby. People expect
a great deal from a missionary because, according
to their reasoning, the missionary has the training,
the financial support, the equipment, and the
time to do the work. The successful missionary
is willing to work with the people.

Reverend Philip Armstrong quoted a national
leader's saying, "We want missionaries who will
come to work not on us but with us." We Latin
Americans would say the same. We are praying
·that the Lord may send laborers, not masters, to
his house in Latin America. As never before it
is necessary to emphasize the concept of being
co-workers in Christ.

And we have to realize that to work with
a people on a fraternal level implies a respect
for our fellow workers and even a willingness to
accept their constructive criticism. Missionaries

are human beings, and we human beings resent criticism. Some national brothers have "fallen from grace" in the opinion of a missionary because these brothers were bold enough to speak the truth on behalf of the Lord's work. And I know some missionaries who have "fallen from grace" in the opinion of national leaders because these missionaries were bold enough to speak the truth for the Lord's sake.

To work with the people is different from working on or for the people. There is no room for paternalism in the biblical concept of Christian missions. The successful missionary does all he can to help promote the training of national leaders.

Some missionaries give the impression that they believe themselves to be the only ones who can do a good job on the field. They tolerate national leaders, not because they have a conviction about the important roles national leaders play in the edification of the national church, but because they feel obligated to follow the indigenous principle to avoid criticism by the national church or by their missionary society. But the successful missionary is willing to work with the people.

Finally I would like to repeat what Mr. Hatori emphasized in his message: The successful missionary loves the people. Love is exceedingly difficult to define but not impossible to feel and to manifest. Even people in the most so-called underdeveloped countries in the world are able to respond to a sincere manifestation of Christian love, and they are able to detect any lack of love and sincerity in the one who comes to them preaching the gospel of Christ. It takes more than knowledge and techniques to succeed in our dealings with the human heart. It takes love—the love that is the fruit only of the Holy Spirit in the Christian believer.

In a recent visit to New Mexico and Arizona a group of students under Dr. George Peters, Professor of Cultural Anthropology at Dallas

Theological Seminary, interviewed a well-educated
Navaho Indian, who is in charge of public relations
for all the Navahoes. We visited him in the
capital city of the Navaho nation. When Dr. Peters
asked this man what he believed would improve the
relations between the white man and the Navaho,
the Indian was silent for a moment. Then he said,
"The answer might be expressed in a single word--
understanding."

That answer was impressive to me. Understanding.
Action. What the Navaho expects from the white man
is what everybody in the world expects from his
fellow man--understanding. And we may add, the
understanding that comes from genuine Christian
love.

The successful missionary should live
among the people, learn from the people, labor
with the people, and love the people. Thank you
very much.

ERIC FIFE

As God continues to speak to us about
missionary qualifications, many of us perhaps
feel somewhat depressed by the sense of our own
inadequacy. We should be reminded of what Martin
Luther once said:

We can always be too big for God,
but we can never be too small for
Him.

George Verwer will now bring to us the closing
message.

GEORGE VERWER

I do not think I can explain to you how
difficult it is for me to speak. I have never
spoken in conventions like this in my life. I
have been out of America for almost eight years,
apart for a few weeks traveling to Mexico. Most
of my life and time has been given to personal
counseling and personal evangelism. So if you

think that I am not serious in what I say, I can
only ask you to somehow give me a chance to know
you personally. I would do almost anything
tonight to help even one needy person in this
auditorium.

I know of some young people who, when
reading a missionary biography, only become
depressed. I know some who, when reading the
story of the men who were martyred in South
America many years ago, only become convinced
that they will never make it. They read about
George Mueller and how he prayed for millions
of pounds to support his orphanages by faith,
and they do not even understand it and become
overwhelmed. And I think if I had been sitting
here as a freshman in college (I had been a
Christian only one year at that time) and I had
heard some of these challenges and facts and the
qualifications so tremendously presented by our
brethren, I just would have had to confess that
I could not do it.

Some of you already have come to me with
your problems. Many of you have admitted and
spoken among yourselves about the dichotomy I
spoke about in an earlier message, and you know
it is very real. My heart goes out to you who
are sons and daughters of missionaries and Christians
and strong evangelicals, to you who have been raised
from your very earliest age like my own children
on Bible verses. My son at six years has passed
out hundreds of tracts all by himself in a single
day. And perhaps some of you were doing the same
thing as young children. Yet now at the university
or at college somehow it is not real any longer.

You have looked at that decision card, a
very powerful card. I will admit that I am preaching
for a decision tonight. And I believe Jesus Christ
preached for a decision. He told Zaccheus to
come down. He told the blind man to put mud on
his eyes. Wherever he went, he called people to
make decisions.

But tonight it is with fear that I would

call anyone to make this decision without his
counting the cost. I think of the words in the
fourteenth chapter of the gospel of Luke where
Jesus said that we must count the cost. Before
you make a decision like this, before you put
your name on something like this, you must count
the cost lest you become like thousands of young
people (those of us on the platform know this is
true) who have signed their names, who have raised
their hands, yet who have never fulfilled that
commitment.

Yes I am afraid if I had been here as a
freshman, I would have been somewhat frustrated.
We speak about these qualifications. Who can
live like this? Recently I was reading Andrew
Murray's book on humility. And it made me want
to quit the ministry! I could not even understand
what Murray was talking about, much less ever have
it. And again and again as I have been reading
books by men of God and studying biographies, I
have felt so overwhelmed by it all--by the responsibility of the Christian life.

I want to speak especially to those of you
tonight who feel somewhat overwhelmed, somewhat
incapable. You have problems in your life. You
know that this dichotomy is very real for you,
and though you sing Onward Christian Soldiers,
you have never marched for Christ. Though you
sing, "Who will follow in his train?" you know
deep in your heart you are not following in his
train. The songs that we have sung, the hymns
that we have sung even in these meetings, carry
enough spiritual truth to drive us to the uttermost
parts of the earth, to drive us to the unconverted
men in our university--our commitment is real.

If the statements on this card became real
in our lives, we would become revolutionists for
Jesus Christ. Men would be won on our campuses.
Our chapters would become alive by the love of
Jesus Christ. We would be constrained to go, to
give, to love, and to experience the tremendous
reality that is in Jesus Christ. An atheist once

said to an evangelical Christian in the British
Isles,

> If I believed what you say you
> believe, I would cross Britain
> upon my knees on broken glass to
> tell men about it.

But when I was graduated from my high school
I was called the class clown. Everything was a joke
to me. I had more jokes and more witty stories
and more swear words and more things to keep people
laughing all night than anyone else. I always got
excited or suddenly interested when a meeting
ended early--because my Saturday nights used to
begin about ten. We would go over the river into
New York City with one of our girls--I had about
thirty-two of them when I was between twelve and
sixteen years old. (Don't laugh--some of you have
had far more than that.) We would begin to dance--
old-fashioned rock and roll. (The twist was just
coming in when I got twisted out by the Lord.
Praise God.) I would start dancing to a Guy
Lombardo record or whatever I could find to dance
to. I had loud speakers all over my room. They
automatically kicked on in the mornings and roused
me out of bed to jazz or something else. I lived
on music. And we would just start about 10 P.M.
I loved it.

When Jesus Christ found me I could not say
I was sad. I was fantastically happy. I had a
beautiful blond next to me in a seat at Madison
Square Garden. I was enjoying life.

Some people think you come to Christ only
when you are sad, overwhelmed, depressed, or have
a tremendous guilt complex. Then you come to
Christ.

No not necessarily. I want to say this
with all my heart: God pulled me out of those
night clubs. And he gave me something more real,
or I would never be here tonight. I loved dancing,
I loved music, I loved all the things of the world.
And even today if somebody played a juke box in
the corner I would have to hold my knees down.

But for the past nine years the only thing
that has kept me up as late as a prom night--and
it has usually been every other week or so--is
spending a night with believers in prayer and
worship to God. Spending seven or eight hours
in the presence of God and in worship to him.

I want to tell you that God is real. I
want to tell you that God is so real that, though
my friends said I would be back in one month, I
have not been back once in eleven years. I want
to tell you that God is so real he can make rock
and roll and all the poison, sugar-coated pills
of this world seem like dead stones in the middle
of a desert. I am convinced that Jesus Christ is
so real, that his love is so tremendous, that
when we really fall in love with him and really
experience his life, these things of the world
fall off without the ninety-nine negatives that
are often preached at us.

Many of you know that God is not that
real to you. You say, "Well, that's okay for
you. God found you in a night club. But what
about us Christian young people?"

I want to tell you about one of my best
friends. He was a student leader at Moody Bible
Institute when I went there as a student. In
the Student Council he met me. His name was
Jonathan. Jonathan was born on a mission field
and raised by missionary parents. Jonathan once
told me he had never kissed a girl in his life.
I told him that I would not even talk to a girl
on a date if I could not . . . never mind the
word I used. But I could not believe a fellow
could be like Jonathan. And from his very early
years on a mission field Jonathan has, to this
day, gone on for God. There was a time when his
commitment became very unreal. There was a time
when he almost became an agnostic, even in the
middle of Bible School. But as he met other
Christians, as he experienced reality and saw
that Christianity could be lived, that Jesus
Christ is alive in the twentieth century, he

recommitted his life to God and has become a
mighty man for God.   It is only because of Jonathan
that I have been able to go to Asia, because he
coordinates our work all over Europe.   He has
the same life, the same zeal; he has more love,
more reality than I do.   Yet he came from a Christian
home just like many of you.

Jesus Christ can meet every need.   Whether
God found you in the deepest ditch in Chicago or
as a missionary child, he can meet your need
tonight.

There are needs here tonight--needs in the
social life.   Billy Graham in his book World
Aflame says we are a nation of sex gluttons.   It
is true.   This is the biggest battle of your life
on campus, Billy said in the 1957 convention.
And if you do not win this battle, you are going
to lose all around.   I am convinced Jesus Christ
is sufficient for your sex battles, wherever and
whatever they may be.   I pray you will take some
of the Inter-Varsity books on this subject and
devour them.   But what they say will only become
a reality in your life as you experience the
sufficiency of Jesus Christ to meet your emotional
longings.

And when he meets your need, when you
experience victory, when you know reality, then
and only then can you be God's man and God's
woman on the mission field.

I am not talking about perfection.   I
have not come to offer you any kind of spiritual
pep pill.   I did not say, "Believe this, and
everything from now on will be perfect."   No.
Jesus Christ said, "If any man would come after
me, let him deny himself and take up his cross
and follow me."   Do you believe that? He repeated
that again and again in each of the Gospels.

There will be struggles.   There will be
battles.   Victory is not easy.   But there is
victory.   The book of 1 John says, "This is the
victory that overcomes the world, our faith."

And in a few minutes, though I do not

like it, though my personality rebels against it, I am going to give you the opportunity to express faith like Zacchaeus did when he came down from the tree. You are going to be thinking about it in these next few minutes.

My invitation to you tonight is not necessarily to become a missionary. You have to work out what and where you are on your knees before God. I do not believe that we as missionaries, so-called, are necessarily any more committed than the man who never moves out of his factory. I believe that with all my heart. If God calls you to a carpenter shop, remember Jesus was a carpenter most of the years of his life. As you work out your vocation and location and pray and seek God's will (and that is one of the greatest privileges we have--to know the will of God), then you can fill out that card, and with sincerity and faith you can mail it in or you can give it in.

But my invitation tonight is to those of you who want to know reality in your life at any cost. Maybe during these days at the conference something has been ringing in your heart. I cannot explain it to you. It will be as unique in one man as it is in another. I think we must throw away the cookie-cutter and stop pretending we are all going to get to the place where we cross our t's in the same way and place.

So the decision for one might be to know Jesus Christ. Maybe you do not know Christ. Maybe you came here believing you were a Christian, and now the Spirit of God has witnessed to you and you realize you have never been born again. I have known people going door to door with our movement to distribute a Christian book or testify personally for Christ who have discovered they did not know him--and they were converted to Christ on the door step!

Some here already have confessed faith in Jesus Christ. But my main invitation and appeal to you tonight, and I appeal to your logic more

than to anything else, is that you will come to
the end of yourself. I pray that you will be
honest and admit that you do not have reality,
if your heart and the Lord convict you that you
do not. You may admit that the dichotomy exists--
that what you say you are, what you sign that you
believe, what you sing, is not really operational
and functional and real in your life.

All of the reality will not come tonight,
but there has to be a beginning. I believe that
there has to be some kind of crisis in a life.
Most people experience many crises to weave their
lives for God. I think the idea that there is
only one special spiritual crisis for a man is
one of the biggest lies Satan can ever get us
to believe. The men of God whom I have studied
have had all different kinds of crises, and some
of them have had many.

But in every case their crisis was followed
by a process such as we spoke about the other day.
If you are not ready for the process, if you are
not ready to place importance on your quiet time,
then do not stand to your feet tonight.

If you are not serious about Bible study,
if you are not ready to get into God's Word and
let it devour you, then you are not ready to come
at all. You see, our problems are in our unconscious
mind. The dichotomy of our life is rooted in our
unconscious mind. We do things we do not want to
do. We say things we do not want to say. They
just come because those deep problems surge up
from our background, from our childhood. We
wonder, "Why did I say that? Why did I do that?"
And I believe one of the areas for the cleansing
powers of the Word of God is in the unconscious
mind. That is why you must be serious about Bible
study.

You say, "But I don't have time to get
into the Word at the university!" During my first
year at the university I did not know how I would
ever get any time for Bible study. I was running
back and forth across the campus, and I thought

I would never get enough time. But the only way
I got through all of the courses I took, including
Bible teaching from unbelieving professors, was
through spending hours on my knees.

I asked a Ph.D. from Princeton, "How did
you get through Princeton University and still
remain a tower of strength preaching the full
gospel of the Lord Jesus Christ?"

He said, "Young man, I spent two hours
every day on my knees, studying the Word of God.

You have to find time to get into the Word
of God. You will find it.

I prayed, "God, give me time." He did.
My physics teacher lectured about everything but
physics. So I took my physics book and covered
it with memory verses, hundreds of Bible verses
that God put in my thick skull by his grace--and
this revolutionized my thinking.

I am sorry to confess that at the age of
sixteen I began, among other things, to peddle
pornographic literature. My unconscious and
conscious mind was warped by the pornographic
filth that pours out in our country. But I can
confess today that because of the power of the
Word of God I have a new mind. I want to tell
you it is a liberty, it is a freedom, beyond
anything you can ever experience. That which
Jesus Christ can give, I believe, makes LSD seem
like a very inexpensive pill, to say the least.

Oh, young people, do you think I am just
saying this? If so, will you ask the 400 young
people from all over the world who are united
with me this year, who have lived literally on
top of me? Will you ask the 2,000 young people
from twenty-seven countries that have marched
with our movement?

The only reason these young people--
Cambridge men, Oxford men, Swedish boys, and
all the rest--have stuck it out is because in
their lives and minds God is real. God is real.
Men can actually live like the Lord Jesus Christ
in the twentieth century. There will be failures,

there will be sin, there will be violence, but
God is real. Victory can be yours if you love
Jesus and if you want it.

I want to speak for a few moments to the
girls. The majority of you are girls. I wish
my wife were here. Maybe you think I am burning
all out for Christ because I have a fanatic wife.
Well, my wife could not be more human.

To start with, she had everything against
her. She was from a broken home. Her father was
killed in Germany. She had to leave home and live
in an orphanage as a small girl.

So she had the major human problem: she
wanted love. She wanted marriage. She thought
that everything would be settled if only she were
married. And I know many girls are here tonight
like that. You would not dare think of going to
the mission field single.

My wife was converted before I met her,
but that had not solved all her problems. That
was only the beginning. (The Bible says that
the new birth is only the beginning. If only we
would realize that.) After I had met and had
fallen in love with her, and as we got to know
each other, to my surprise I discovered she had
some serious problems.

My wife's problems were three psychosomatic
illnesses: migraine headaches, back tension
pattern, and heartaches. (Many doctors say fifty
percent of our illnesses are due to psychosomatic
causes. This is the number one health problem in
America today.) With such physical problems, my
wife could not go to the mission field. She went
down to Mexico with one of our teams. She was in
bed every night with tears and every kind of
problem you could possibly dream of. When we got
back, she tried to get help from a book, Health
Springs Forth. But her problems remained.

So we knew we had to part. I had to go
to the mission field. We sat together in a lobby
of our school one night, and I told her that
though I loved her with all my heart, we would

have to break it off.

That could have killed her because she wanted to marry me more than anything else in life. This was the one thing she had hoped for. And her sickness got worse. She went to her room and did what everybody told her to do--"cast it on the Lord." But she picked up her pain the next morning and carried it all day.

At the end of the fourth day she realized the greatest truth in the Bible--that Jesus Christ is an all sufficient Savior. He is sufficient for all of our needs. He is sufficient for our emotional problems, for our intellectual problems. There in her room, in complete quiet, she bowed down before God (as I am going to ask some of you to do tonight). Then she said, "Lord, I believe that you are my victory. I believe that you are all that I need. I am ready to go to the mission field without George Verwer."

Peace and joy flooded her heart. And she was miraculously healed of all her sicknesses. And she has been pioneering on for Jesus Christ in difficult circumstances in fifteen countries since then.

You know, people say, "Be careful," and I am sure even tonight some are saying, "Watch out, this commitment business is emotion." It is amazing. We can get emotional about anything in America and nobody says a thing. I used to come home at six o'clock in the morning, singing shouting, doing all kinds of things. I was the craziest one in the school. I would get out on the football field and shout and play the drum and throw the siren around and do anything in the football game--and they elected me president of the class.

But if you begin to shout for Christ, if you have an emotional experience with the Lord in which he becomes real to you and you express your love for him, people will call you fanatic and say, "Be careful, the emotion is going to wear off." That is what they told me the night

I accepted Christ in the Billy Graham meeting.
But the emotion does not wear off if it is followed
up by continual interaction with the Holy Spirit
of God.

I could tell you stories about Communists
in London, girls from the backstreets of Paris,
boys from the Hindu temples of southern India,
young men who have taken two bottles of strong
poison to kill themselves before they found the
living Christ in reality--I could be here all
night.

Christianity is real, young people, but
I believe with all my heart it is real only to
those who come to the place where they say, "Lord
Jesus, you are all I want." It cannot be Jesus
plus this or plus that, not even Jesus plus
evangelism. With me, it could not be Jesus
plus Operation Mobilization. It has to be Jesus
Christ and him alone.

I am convinced that if you are willing to
come to the end of yourself and say, "Lord Jesus,
you are all I want," then God will begin to break
that dichotomy and you will begin to experience
a reality that you have never known in your
Christian life. I know this is true tonight.
And I pray that you will consider it, and act as
God leads you.

In Colossians 2 we read tonight, "In him
[Jesus Christ] the whole fulness of deity dwells
bodily, and you have come to fulness of life in
him, who is the head of all rule and authority"
(RSV). Please, young people, consider Jesus
Christ who can give you fullness of life--not
a dichotomy, not two people--a whole person in
him. And tonight, come to that place where you
say, "Lord Jesus Christ, you are my all. You
are my everything. I will follow you. I will
do whatever you want me to do."

15. With No Reserve
by Michael Griffiths

It has been good to be here. Many of you,
like myself, have made new friends. None of us
will ever be quite the same again because of the
world vision set before us here. But what will
you take away with you? What will you remember
most?

I would like to bring to you tonight the
words of our Lord Jesus: "Why do you call me
Lord, Lord, and do not the things which I say?"
(Luke 6:46). I would like to suggest some reasons
for this dichotomy--the piety of our lips and its
lack of expression in our lives.

The first reason is a very practical one:
Enthusiasm is easier than obedience. It is easier
to say than to do. The emotions are more easily
aroused than the will. It is easier to be stirred
by a religious meeting and to pray with fervor
than it is to overcome sloth and self-indulgence.
It is much easier to talk about winning the world
for Christ than to accept our responsibility to
go forth and tell people about him.

Second, it is easier to apply truth to
others than to ourselves. These words, "Lord,
Lord," are not spoken by a nominal Christian.
They are by an enthusiastic person, a person who
says not just "Lord," but "Lord, Lord." You know
the type. And maybe you will try to evade the
force of it. Don't assume that Jesus' words are

addressed to some other person; let us take his words as being addressed to each one of us. We are a mass at this convention, a multitude, but he cares for each one of us. He died for each of us. He has a plan and purpose for each of us. He has prepared beforehand good works for each one of us to walk in. He speaks these words to each of us individually, "Why do you call me Lord, Lord, and do not the things which I say?".

We are not going to have very much to show for our time if our faith stops with happy religious feelings, if we leave Urbana with only impractical aspirations. It is easy to feel that we want to serve Christ with all of our lives, but this nostalgia for a wholehearted life is not enough if the will is not involved.

It would be possible to leave with an emotional sense of glory. That is easy. It costs nothing. We could all go home saying we had had a wonderful time. We could boast of the 9,000 students and the $90,000 (pledged to IFES' foreign student ministry). But is that how we measure success? by the numbers attending and the feelings we have experienced? Or do we measure success in the lives of obedience issuing forth from this time together with God? "Continue in the things which you have learned"; rings in our ears. What glorifies God is not an emotional workout here, but continued obedience hereafter. It is easy to say tonight, "Lord, Lord," but it will be hard tomorrow and the days after to obey.

Is there any way of handing over our wills once for all? I don't believe God gave us a will that could be handed over or handed back in some easy act of self-surrender. The Lord wants sustained obedience. We are not to call each other to an emotional signing-away of our lives. It is not possible for a response like that to be more than a superficial emotional crisis. He wants a will continually obeying him. This is what glorifies him: repeated, joyous obedience to his commands. That is what "no reserves" means:

not a little religious fervor tonight, but a cold
determination to do the things he says.

When you're building a bonfire, you can
put on a bit of dry fern or conifer and get a
sudden flare-up. You can put kerosene on damp
wood and the saturated part will burn hotly.
But when the kerosene has burned out, all that
is left is a pile that smokes and smokes and
smokes. What a difference between this smoking,
soggy pile and a fire that burns steadily with
a bright light until there is nothing left but
white ash. What is Urbana to be to you: A
sudden flare-up of emotional excitement followed
by middle-age dullness and spiritual coldness
of heart? Or is it going to ignite a life which
burns brightly and steadily in obedience to him?

Here it is: "Why call ye me Lord, Lord,
and do not the things which I say?". The words
cast upon your hearts here at Urbana can be like
seed falling by the wayside. If this is the case,
then as you travel home tomorrow, "the birds of
the air" will already have begun to snatch them
away. Or the words may be like seed fallen upon
the rocks, springing up with a momentary "Lord,
Lord" enthusiasm, then dying away because there
is no root, no depth. Or maybe those desires and
aspirations will be choked by the busyness of
student life and the even greater busyness of
graduated life, married life, and all that follows.
Or it can be deeply planted in your heart, bringing
forth fruit thirtyfold, sixtyfold, a hundredfold.

Enthusiasm is easier than obedience.

The third reason for this dichotomy is
that we do not understand the implications of
calling him "Lord." The word Lord can become a
cliche, a pause for breath in the middle of a
stereotyped prayer, vain calling upon the Lord's
name. We can use it without meaning very much.
Yet, this New Testament word, kyrios, means an
owner of things, or an owner of people; a master
of slaves. It emphasizes the comparison between
the one who is the master and the one who is the

308

slave. The slave is one whose living body belongs
to his master, whose every small possession is
not his own but his lord's. Is that what you mean
when you call him Lord?

"Whoever shall call upon the name of the
Lord shall be saved." Calling him Lord first
brings us into the experience of salvation. "If
thou shalt confess with thy mouth Jesus as Lord,
and if thou shalt believe in thine heart that God
has raised him from the dead, thou shalt be saved."
What must we confess with our mouths? What must
we believe with our hearts? Believe in this man
who died in disgrace, discredited; this man who
seemed to be a liar and a fraud? Who could believe
in this man--a man who claimed power and died in
weakness, who claimed glory and came to shame?
The cross was the end. Who could believe in him
now? That God raised him from the dead is his
vindication. You must believe in your heart
that God has raised him from the dead. That is
basic, fundamental, to faith in him. Not only
faith in the heart, but confession from the lips
is to mark our belief. Jesus, that human man
Jesus, is Lord. The word Lord, as applied here,
carries all the weight of its Old Testament usage.
In the Greek version of the Old Testament it has
the meaning of Jehovah, the Covenant Lord of the
Old Testament. Will you confess Jesus as Lord?

If you want to acknowledge him as Lord,
tell someone before you leave this hall tonight
that Jesus has now that position in your life.
Remember how Thomas with all his doubts and problems
said when he saw the risen Christ, "My Lord and
my God."

There are others of us who long ago made
that confession. But we may have missed the meaning
of obedience. We have been Christians for our own
selfish enjoyment. We came to him to save us, to
help us. Maybe we have become Christians so people
will think well of us, or as a kind of eternal life
insurance, a fire-escape from hell. That is a
selfish Christianity--Christianity because of

personal advantage.

To call him Lord is to become a Christian
not for ourselves but him. It is his due. We
are not saved by what we can do, but by what he
has done for us. Now that we have come to him,
the stress is on what we, his slaves, must do for
him, our Lord.

Are some of you weighing whether to obey
his commands? Are you condescending to God, to
the Lord? You should be thinking about the future
in the way Moses had to think about it. "Take off
the shoes from off thy feet for the place whereon
thou standest is holy ground." We may not choose
between this course or that, between this career
and that. We stand before One who is Lord of
lords. If we call him Lord, it means that we
cannot say, "No, Lord." If you say no, then he
is not Lord; if you say Lord, you cannot say no.
All your time and energy is going to be given to
him. When you have a date, that is for him.
"He is my Lord" means a lifetime of obedience.

The implication of calling him Lord means
allegiance to him without conditions. I didn't
say without fear. Timothy was fearful. All of
us feel nervous when faced with situations where
we just cannot imagine ourselves at all. I once
took a course on tropical diseases. I felt I
had each one of them as I listened. All of us
have silly fears like that. Some are more
important fears. Some of our fears are understandable.
You may be called to places of physical danger.
You may feel scared even if it is not dangerous.
Don't worry. It is natural to feel like that.
Moses felt a reluctance, a hanging back, a feeling
of inadequacy. "Lord, I can't, I'm not the type,
I'm not the sort." Fears, perhaps. They are normal.
But no reserves. No secret conditions. You cannot
be like the man who said, "Lord, I will follow you,
but . . . ." You cannot say but. "Lord, I will
follow you. I will obey. I will train like an
athlete. I will work. I will meet with you each
day. I will flee from sin. I will keep the rules."

In your secret heart of hearts are you
making reserves and adding conditions? Perhaps
you will not go unless you can use your academic
training. God may want to use your academic
training, but you may find altogether new things
to be done once you get out to a country, things
you never realized were there.

My own life is an example of this. I used
to do lots and lots of children's work at home.
That was the way to work! I enjoyed it. The
Lord had given me a gift for it. I nearly went
out to train children's evangelists in Africa.
But in ten years in Japan I have spoken to
children no more than about three times. The
situation is different than I expected. There
are so few Christians. One cannot wait for the
seeds to grow up. A child cannot do very much
in a non-Christian home. The light of experience
reveals work among adults and students to be
important.

Examine your motives for insisting on
using your academic qualifications. Make certain
your desire to go as a non-professional is not
the result of pride. Are you prepared for the
sacrifice involved in living on charity?

Maybe the condition for some of us is
"not unless I can be married." All of us long
for that blessing--and it is a blessing to go
out two by two. But it can not become a condition.
And it is, of course, only a blessing with the
right girl. I want to say something to men.
A good girl will keep even a mediocre man on
the field and help him to be effective. But a
mediocre girl will bring even a good man home
with her. Remember that.

Maybe your condition is "not unless I
can keep the living standards I'm used to."

Now I would like to say a word to the
women. You will set the pattern of your homelife.
You can live in a Japanese house, sleep on the
floor, eat Japanese food, speak the Japanese
language, but your life with your husband and

children will naturally include some and exclude
others. Your attitude as the woman is the key
in this situation. The higher the standard of
living that is yours now (yours since your childhood
or yours if you have married and already built your
little nest), the harder it is to take it to bits
and move somewhere else. You want to take all
your bits with you. That may make a barrier
between you and others.

How easy it is to make this wall. You
stand in your house and look out through the
window. In Japan it is rather like it is outside
here, not quite ten below with the snow coming
down. When it is like that and the wind is blowing,
you think, "Shall I go out visiting this afternoon?
I'll make myself a cup of coffee." That sounds
bad, but it is worse than that actually. It is
not only that you may not go out, but that others
may not come in. I have seen missionaries who
could preach zealously, actively, keenly, but
somehow when someone came to their door there was
no warmth in their welcome. People who came there
did not feel that there was interest directed
toward them. There was faithful, earnest preaching,
but lack of personal welcome and love toward others.
You may shut others out if the wife insists on
setting up a home like the one she has known here;
if she does not want her children to sleep on the
floor; if she is reserved with visitors; if she
is jealous; if she wants her husband to herself.
She has got to be prepared to belong to the people.

I think of a lovely missionary family from
North America that is a challenge to all of us.
There are times when ten or twelve extra people
sleep in their house. (You can do that in Japan.
If you just put down a tatami, a mattress, you
can get lots of people in your house. Lots and
lots. And that is what they do.) Oh, it is chaos:
it is not very tidy. The house does not stay
spic and span or even neat. But what love, what
care, what concern. There are the funniest
people in that house--odd sorts of people. But

the family is prepared to spend hours with them.
I say, therefore, to you women, you will set the
standard. To the degree you are prepared to
integrate and identify, to that degree will your
husband be effective among the people. Do you
have reserves about your standard of living?

Do you have reserves about the length of
time you will serve? I know it is not necessarily
for life. When he is our Lord, he may always
change our orders, redirect us, send us off
somewhere else. But have you got this reserve:
"Well, I'll go for two or three years, and then
I'll come home." That may be the case, but are
you willing to go for life if that is his will?
Dave Howard told me that after ten or fifteen
years maybe you are still not really in and still
do not understand fully what makes people tick.
It takes time. Go visit a country for three weeks,
and you will write a book about it. But after
three years you realize how little you know. It
takes time to get into a country, into its culture
and its literature, to understand its people.
Are you willing, or have you got reserves? To
call him Lord means there are no reserves.

"Why do you call me Lord, Lord, and do not
the things which I say?" The fourth reason I'd
like to suggest for this dichotomy is that we
are not as biblical as we claim. We boast that
we are evangelicals. We believe the Bible to be
the Word of the Lord. But do we obey the Word
of the Lord? We say it's our guide in all matters
of faith and conduct. But is it? What are you
living for? Yourself alone--with an occasional
side glance at Christ? Do you play at Christian
service? Are you a passive spectator instead of
an active participator? Does the Bible really
direct your life?

What is the purpose and direction of your
life? You have heard Matthew 28:19,20, "Go
therefore and make disciples of all nations, baptizing
them in the name of the Father and of the Son and
of the Holy Spirit, teaching them to observe all

that I have commanded you; and lo, I am with you always, to the close of the age." Who is it addressed to? The Reformers said it applied only to the apostles. Later, others began to see this could not be so, because the promise is that Christ's presence will abide to the end of the age. If the promise goes on to the end, so does the command.

To whom, then, is it addressed? The commands are to make disciples, baptize them, and teach them. What does it say is to be taught to these new disciples? "All things whatsoever I have commanded you." Does that not include the command in this passage to "go and make disciples?" Of all his commands, you cannot forget that command. Everybody who is a disciple, who has been baptized in the name of the Father, the Son, and the Spirit, he is to be taught in all things. "All things" is to include going, making disciples and baptizing them, and teaching them. Otherwise it would have been wrong to make converts or baptize anyone since the time of the apostles.

Do you think you have the freedom to decide whether or not you are going to obey Matthew 28:19? Are you trying to make up your mind whether you will obey it? You cannot do that. If you are a well-taught Christian, you must obey. "Teach them to observe all things that I have commanded you."

"Why call ye me Lord, Lord, and do not the things which I say?" What are the things which the Lord came to do and that he wants us to do? In Matthew 9, earlier in that same passage, we see the crowds. When he saw the crowds, he had compassion on them because they were harrassed and helpless like sheep without a shepherd. Compassion was the first thing, but he did not stop there. He went on from compassion. "The harvest is plentiful but the laborers are few. Pray therefore the Lord of the harvest . . . ." He went on to intercession. Then it goes on to say that he sent out people to preach to the lost

sheep of the house of Israel. He came in order
to gather in the flock. First, his lost sheep,
"and then those other sheep I have whom also I
must bring." He came to initiate a harvest. He
came to initiate a program. He came to teach us,
he came to die on the cross, he came to rise
again. But what good is that if no one knows?
What good is that if the news of it is not taken
out to the ends of the earth? We have got to
bring in the lost sheep. We have got to start
the harvest. Is this not what our Lord came to
do? That is what he began. That is what we are
called to. We have all got to be involved in
this great charge that is set before us.

How can we putter about when we are called
to obey this command? How can we fritter away
the years purposelessly, pointlessly? How easily
these years--these lovely, wonderful, glorious
years as students--can be wasted in secondary
things. We can be so busy with the opposite sex
that we have no time for the evangelism of our
own sex. These years can be wasted, frittered
away. And they are such glorious years. Why do
you call him Lord, Lord, and do not the things
that he says?

Let me suggest some practical things which
you can do.

First, since it is hard to make decisions
here, set aside a day after you get home to review
the notes you have been taking, and start to read
the literature you have collected. On that day
begin to review. Make a note of what Urbana has
meant, what you have learned, and what you are
going to do because of it.

Take the prayer card you received and put
it in your Bible as the second practical step.
When I was a student, we had a student committee
that ran our missionary convention. A missionary
who had spent about forty years in India was at
our convention. He worked on the principle that
if the leaders do not go to the mission field
others cannot be expected to follow; so each day

he met with some member of the committee. We soon
realized he had a list of all the committee members
and was seeing us one by one. Each day in our
committee meeting we would check to see who George
had been to see that day. He said, "Take this
form (such as the one you have been given here),
and put it in your Bible." He did not say, "Sign
it now." He said, "Put it in your Bible. Pray
over it. Keep remembering it." There it was in
our Bibles, a small thing; but there are many
of us on the mission field today. We are scattered
all over the world, separated, but all there in
obedience to his call.

The third practical step comes from the
example of Christ's compassion and concern. You
must be interested in and concerned about what
goes on in other parts of the world. You must be
interested in what goes on everywhere. I like
to think of young William Carey, the shoemaker,
sitting in his shop with a map of the world.
Everything he heard of a country was something to
pray about. He would look at his map and pray.
Some of you are waiting for guidance. Perhaps
you have no guidance because you are not yet full
of compassionate interest for what goes on all
over the world. When I was a student we had a
slogan, "Know something about every place, and
everything about some place."

Students from overseas have spoken about
their sense of estrangement here. Somebody asks
where they come from and they say, "Togoland"
or "Surinam." The response is, "Oh yes, how
nice," because we do not know anything about
those places. We do not know anybody who is
there. We are not even quite sure where it is.
That is lack of compassion and concern. This
is the practical thing you can do: get informed.
Get hold of missionary books and magazines and
read them. Become concerned.

But don't stop there. The Lord didn't
stop there. The next step, you remember, is
intercession. Not only interest, but intercession.

"Pray ye therefore the Lord of the harvest." Pray,
he says. There were about 400 of us in the Christian
Union in Cambridge when I was a student. We had
thirty or forty prayer groups. Six of them prayed
for China at the time when China was just closing.
There must have been fifteen for different parts
of Africa. The student committee that I was on
decided that in order to avoid too many meetings,
we would meet every other week. So our group
used to meet every other week officially, but
every other week we met unofficially because we
found that we wanted to get together to pray.
We used to meet for breakfast on Saturday morning.
It wasn't much of a breakfast, just any odd bit
that we scraped together. A couple of us took
missionary magazines for East Africa, and various
ones of us had prayer letters from friends and
used them together each week for that part of
the world. Four of us became doctors and went
to Africa; three are still in Africa. Two of
us wanted to go to Asia, but one was turned down.

Pray. One of the practical results of
our gathering here will be prayer. Prayer for
the whole world would be too vague. Take an area
or some special kind of work that you are
interested in and pray for it. You start. Bring
in a friend, and another friend. Pray together.
This is something practical.

Next, get involved. Christ sent his
disciples to do something. This means today, not
tomorrow. We think about the missionary service
that we will do in the future. But the command
to "go out and make disciples . . ." means now.
It is easiest with your own age group, in your
own country, where you know the language, the
customs and the thought patterns. You have no
barriers of age and class; you are all of the
same educational level; there is a climate where
you can talk with others. I spoke to about 120
students at a university in another country (it
wasn't England; it wasn't Japan). I was looking
for missionaries for Asia. About halfway through

I asked, "How many of you have won someone here
at the university?" Only two raised their hands.
I had to change my message. If they could not
win souls in their own land, what good would
they ever be elsewhere?

What you are now is going to matter
tomorrow. You must win students here in America
and Canada today. The supreme missionary quality
is the ability to win souls. A Ph.D. is grand,
but can you win souls? We would rather have a
man who can win souls and have no Ph.D., than a
man with a Ph.D. who is not a soul-winner. This
is something practical to be involved in now:
evangelism--where we are.

In closing I would like to put one or two
other thoughts before you.

The final practical step is to <u>discover</u>
<u>where the Lord wants you to be and what he wants</u>
<u>you to do</u>. He does not want all of us to go
overseas, but you should realize that more of
you here will be called to the mission field
than from any comparable gathering in the world.

There are several reasons for this: First,
North America provides something like 60 percent
of the world's missionaries. And this gathering
is mainly North Americans.

Second, you are young people. If this
were a gathering of old fogies, we could not talk
like this. We have heard that it takes ten years
for some missionaries to get to the field. In
five years' time several thousand missionary
replacements will be needed. If half of you
could go within five years, you would no more
than fill these gaps. You people are already
older than 50 percent of the population of Asia.
You are old by their standards. Get cracking.

The third reason that many of you should
prepare to go is that you have had experience of
campus work. In many areas of the world there
are more women in church than men. The men
commute to the cities and have little to do with
the residential community in which the church

functions. To reach the masses of men in factories and offices, we need to meet them where they work. Your campus experience of meeting where you work each day in the lunch hour is exactly the training that will fit you for the changing situation confronting the church.

There is a fourth reason: we need some well-educated missionaries. While I was a member of the Japan Council of Evangelical Missions, we were looking for a man to check a Japanese translation of the Old Testament to see whether it was worthy. There wasn't anyone on the field at that time who was really competent in Hebrew. No one among approximately 1,500 evangelical missionaries! There is, therefore, an especial reason why you in IVCF have a responsibility: we have to reach intellectuals as well as non-intellectuals. We are not trying to reach just the intellectuals. But we must reach all strata of society. And you who are educated have a special responsibility for the educated in other lands. If a good brain is needed to teach theology here, a better one is needed to teach it in another language and culture.

The gospel must penetrate all levels. I have been delighted to see the guitar here. We need that kind of missionary too--people who can get others to sing, who can teach the gospel that way. Ordinary people, young people. We are going to need people skilled in television communication. We are going to need cartoonists. We are going to need people with experience in television. Where are they? Within five years you will be able to tune in your favorite program whenever you like. They will commercially produce a film and different languages can be added. We need evangelical Christians who can do that: ingenious people, the kind of people who can make up a campus newspaper, people who can produce a magazine, people with ingenious minds who can write verses. We need all sorts of people to get the gospel over

in the new world of mass communications. This is
an exciting and thrilling world to live in. And
so there are special reasons, if you like, why a
higher proportion of you here are needed abroad.
That is the last step: the step of preparedness.

Will you take these practical steps I have
suggested to you? Set some time apart to meet
with him and to think about this conference.
Put that prayer card in your Bible. Become informed
about the world you live in. Join a prayer group.
Work now to win people all around you. And look
forward--realize the needs of the world and be
ready to do. I am not going to appeal to anyone
to stand up now. We are concerned about the
years ahead. Our concern is not that you should
stand now and call him "Lord, Lord," but that you
should obey all of your lives. Do you want to
abandon yourselves wholeheartedly to him, to put
yourself at his service your whole life long, or
until he comes? Simply and sanely determine that
you will serve him, that there will be no reserves,
and no turning back.

Part V. Student Work Worldwide

16. Biblical Ideals in Worldwide Student Witness
by C. Stacey Woods

ERIC FIFE: Introduction

As we get larger and the organization
becomes more complex--I speak here, I'm sure,
for all the members of the executive committee
of Urbana--there comes a nagging feeling into
our minds that some of us will put our faith in
Urbana, and there is no magic charm here. There
is no magic charm and guarantee of blessing in
Inter-Varsity. This morning I read these words,
"Some boast of chariots, and some of horses,
but we will boast of the name of the Lord our
God" (Ps. 20:7). We have worked for three years
to make this convention possible. We have taken
almost endless pains to try to iron out the details.
But our faith is not in horses and chariots, good
though they may be. Our faith is in God and in
God alone. And because our faith is in him, we
expect great things. And we trust that you do
also.

Mr. C. Stacey Woods, General Secretary of
the International Fellowship of Evangelical Students,
will address us each evening at this hour to the
subject of student work worldwide.

C. STACEY WOODS: Standing for God's Truth

"Wherefore, seeing we also are compassed

about with so great a cloud of witnesses, let us
lay aside every weight, and the sin which doth
so easily beset us, and let us run with patience
the race that is set before us, looking unto
Jesus the author and finisher of our faith; who
for the joy that was set before him endured the
cross, despising the shame, and is set down at
the right hand of the throne of God" (Heb. 12:1-2).

I have chosen as the theme for these brief
evening talks Biblical Ideals in Worldwide Student
Witness. This evening we will consider the ideal
of standing or God's truth.

There can be both a true and a false
idealism. We are acquainted with the tragedy of
Nazism--men and women of ideals but, unfortunately,
false ideals. We are aware of the sacrifice and
zeal of many communist youth. Again a tragedy
because of a false ideal. Idealism can be both
good and bad.

I fear many of us today face an even more
tragic situation, not false ideals but the loss
of all ideals. Life has no meaning. What is it
all about? Who cares? There is nothing to live
for. There is nothing worth dying for. If this
ever should become part of your thinking, it
would be tragic.

The evangelical who retains some ideals
and awareness of life's meaning is not wholly
immune. We can be affected by our affluent society
and lose the biblical ideal of living sacrificially
for the Lord Jesus Christ, choosing instead to
indulge ourselves. We may lose the ideal of giving
up all for Christ's sake in order to preserve our
reputation, even while confessing to follow him
who made himself of no reputation. We may be
unwilling to be called narrow, even though that
is one description of the Christian way. We can
lose the ideal of standing for God's truth
regardless of the cost.

You men and women who are here tonight
are part of a worldwide student association with
some 35 national member movements. One common

bond is that each is a confessional movement:
each has a doctrinal basis of faith which is a
platform for all their evangelical activity.
Such a doctrinal basis is the only foundation
for true evangelism. Many students now, as in
the past, believe with conviction that this
expresses God's truth. Only a week or two ago,
I was meeting with five directors, four from
Scandinavia and one from the German movement.
It was a great joy for me to be again with those
five young Lutheran ministers, all of whom had
such strong conviction regarding biblical truth.

May I take a minute to tell you something
of what took place in the past? Years ago the
Cambridge Intercollegiate Christian Union joined
a great world student association which at that
time was biblical. Through the ensuing years,
however, the world association changed its doctrinal
position, for the watchword in that day was
"Evangelize the world in this generation," and
they felt the change was in the interest of evangelism
and missions. The Cambridge Union refused to
change its doctrinal position, in spite of pressure
to broaden out, give up this narrow biblical point
of view, and stand together with sincere people
with other viewpoints in order to preach the
gospel. Finally there came the suggestion that
they should withdraw from the world association.
They did. One university union stood against
the opinions of the entire world association and
the church leaders of that day because they had
an ideal. They believed their conviction was
God's truth and like Luther of old they said,
"Here I stand."

The stand of those students in 1910 resulted
in evangelism and contributed greatly to the
formation of the Inter-Varsity movement in Britain,
and later in Canada, Australia and New Zealand.
In Scandinavia a similar situation occurred.
There Professor Hallesby, one man with a group
of students founded his new movememt on a base
of biblical doctrine. This movement swept right

through the Scandinavian countries.

The movement in Germany did not even begin
until there were twenty-seven students brought
to the conviction that the entire Word of God was
trustworthy: trustworthy regarding such things
as the incarnation, the atoning death of Christ,
and his bodily resurrection. They said, "We
believe these things; therefore, we have a mission.
Now we have a message to proclaim to our fellow
students in Germany."

It is interesting to note that the great
call was to broaden doctrinal platforms in order
to evangelize. But if you study history, those
who did so lost their evangel, lost their
evangelistic zeal, lost, as it were, their
message, while those who maintained their doctrinal
ideal grew and were effective.

We need to realize that there have been
those with conviction in the past, and that we
are able to stand today because of their
faithfulness. They believed certain things to
be true, not in some dry, impersonal, doctrinaire
manner, but because a doctrinal stand expressed
loyalty to the Lord Jesus Christ. They were
convinced that love and obedience to the Lord
Jesus necessitated taking a stand on truth.

So through the generations of students,
we arrive at today. We, too, are confessing a
high regard for God, his Son, our Lord Jesus,
and his holy Word. But I wonder if in our
universities we all share this ideal. I wonder
if our loyalty and devotion to the Lord Jesus
will cause us to take a stand, a stand which
will give us a message to proclaim to other
students.

The verses we have read this evening picture
a runner laying aside every weight in order to
win a race. The race, of course, is terminated
as he finishes his course with joy, fulfilling
God's will. The model before the runner of that
race is the Lord Jesus who is the forerunner.
There is also in this picture a great cloud of

witnesses, those who have gone on before. I
wonder if we realize there are witnesses watching
us; a crowd of those who have been loyal to God's
Word, those who unswervingly have proclaimed
Christ's truth. They are looking at us today.

I trust that during these days you will
have a fresh vision of the unevangelized student
world, a fresh understanding of God's will, a
fresh conviction of what you believe and why.
Then in the strength of that conviction and in
the power of the Lord, go forth to preach the
gospel. May this be true of all of us for the
sake of our Lord Jesus.

STUDENT EVANGELISM

Our theme is The Ideal of Student Evangelism.
Yesterday we ended with the conclusion that
evangelism apart from true doctrine soon ceases
to be true evangelism. In Psalms 68:11 we read,
"The Lord gave the word; great was the company of
those that published it." What does it mean to
evangelize? It means to preach, to teach, to
persuade, to defend, to testify, to command in
relation to the good news of salvation through
Jesus Christ. This is done personally, man to
man; it is done in small groups; and it is done
by mass evangelism. Our ideal in student work
is for every Christian student to be a witness to
the Lord Jesus, seeking to speak to others, to
win them to him, and to intercede for their
salvation. Generally, a student's salvation is
a process that ends in a crisis. There is sowing,
there is watering, and there is reaping.

Let us look at some ways students are
seeking to evangelize. One of the newest efforts
is a reading room in Algeria, North Africa. It
is very difficult to preach the gospel here, yet
in this reading room Muslim students come to
study, to read, and to pick up a French correspondence
course on the Bible. In the evening the room is
crowded with students learning English with the

Bible as a text book. By these indirect means, students are being contacted, and the gospel is being proclaimed. A similar reading room in Rome is also crowded with students day by day, although the situation there is quite different. There, almost every night, students come together for evangelistic Bible studies or talks. The IFES staff worker might say, "See that person over there? We believe he'll become a Christian in two or three weeks. We're watching his response and see that he's showing an interest in the gospel. Come meet someone who came to know Christ only two days ago." By this means the gospel is going out and students are coming to Christ.

Or if you were to take a jet to Stockholm, that great cathedral city in Sweden, you might find a group of sixty or seventy students coming together for prayer and then going out, two by two, to call on students in their rooms and tell them about the Lord Jesus Christ. Throughout Scandinavia going out two by two, knocking on doors, opening up the New Testament, and presenting Christ, is providing an effective means of evangelism.

In Tokyo a large group of students distribute tracts which contain an offer of a correspondence course. Personal conversation with those showing interest, possibly an invitation to attend church, follows. Reports of God's blessing frequently result.

At Cape Coast in Ghana you could attend a lecture by Mr. David Bentley-Taylor, a visitor from England. You would be amazed at the high percentage of students from the university college who are present. You would also be surprised at the type of question asked following such a presentation of the gospel.

From Cape Coast you might go on to Comercy to a five-day evangelistic campaign arranged by students who invited their own speaker. During that five days ninety percent of the entire student body would hear the gospel presented at least once. The large number of students receiving Christ as

their Lord and Savior is amazing. There are so
many that the attendance at the weekly Bible study
has jumped to about 400. The work of the university
Bible fellowship in Korea continues because of the
tremendous sacrifice and discipline of the students.
An unusual approach to get hold of students for
Christ is often used. In many of these universities
you could attend a daily prayer meeting of intercession for the salvation of friends.

Evangelistic meetings in Germany are lectures
on a subject of contemporary interest without any
reference to the gospel at that meeting. But later
in the evening the Christian answer to the problem
is given. After the confidence of the students
is won, then the claims of Christ are presented.

In Dakar in Senegal the work is very
difficult. The nucleus of Christians come from
Nigeria, Ghana, or Sierra Leone. Here they are
working with Muslim students. The relaxed atmosphere
of a weekend camp, a lecture, and then personal
conversation concerning Christ is the pattern here.
In another country the public debate on Christianity
may be popular. But in every instance, in each
country, the seed is being sown and God is giving
the increase.

All over the world, from one country and
another, there are these trickles of students
coming to the Lord Jesus. When we see the work
in aggregate, we are amazed at what God is doing,
at the numbers coming to him. There are many
approaches, but it is always the same message.
The ideal in each case is for every Christian
student to be involved in the task of making
Christ known: at least one friend for whom he's
praying, one friend he's bringing to the Bible
study, one friend he's speaking to about the Lord
Jesus. If you are a Christian student and are
not personally, practically involved in this task,
you're missing God's will for you in your university.
The least that should be true of any Christian
student is that he is involved with some unconverted
friend, in prayer, in witness, and in care, seeking

to lead that person to Christ. In this way, the work of the gospel goes on.

THE GOSPEL PRESENTED WITHOUT CHARGE

Some of you may be interested in knowing more details about the IFES: its philosophies, policies, and the history of some of its member movements. At the Inter-Varsity Press book store is a paperback history of IFES. Look it over. An interesting possibility for some of you this coming summer may be to work with Inter-Varsity in Europe, including a four-week training course in Austria. Folders on this are available at the IFES booth.

This evening the ideal we are discussing is The Gospel Presented Without Charge. The Apostle Paul spoke of those who labor in the gospel as being worthy of support. He also spoke of himself as laboring with his hands that the gospel might not be chargeable.

One of the most exciting aspects of the IFES ministry around the world is that things happen without any headquarters' planning. We recently learned that something has come into existence: A few weeks ago I received a letter from Australia announcing a new Christian union in the newly formed University of New Guinea. Who was responsible? Several Australian grads, who are members of the faculty of that university.

University graduates, who have taken positions of teaching abroad, have been one of the most tremendous factors in the spread of our worldwide ministry. The graduates from British universities have been responsible for bringing student work into existence in Sierra Leone, Ghana, Nigeria, Kenya, and Tanzania. This was done without world strategy and without a great deal of expense. How did the work begin? The British grads invited students into their homes on a Sunday afternoon for a cup of tea and a biscuit, Bible study and prayer. Students got the vision

of what they could be as Christians in the
university. They took the initiative and moved
forward.

How did the work in Japan begin? It
began when an American IVCF grad, Charles Hummel,
then in the U.S. Army of Occupation, began a Bible
class for university students in that country.
The work in Singapore, the work in Malaysia
similarly owes its existence to graduates.

Another factor has been the existence of
the work of the Scripture Union in the schools.
There have been Christian boys and girls nurtured
through the SU who have seized the opportunity
for uniting for Christian witness on the campus
when they have gone to the university.

The way in which these graduates have taken
initiative has differed. In some instances, a
student has left his homeland, gone to the United
States or Great Britain to study, returned home
as a member of the university staff in his own
country, and there gotten a student group started.
In other instances, graduates as expatriates from
countries have taken positions abroad and have
commenced this work. In still other cases--listen
to me--graduates from Canada or the United States
have spent an undergraduate year abroad studying.
There they have started a small Bible class, a
prayer meeting, and a new work has come into
existence. To me this is one of the most exciting
happenings of the Holy Spirit.

I could list country after country from
which we've received letters saying, "Is there
no possibility that students from North America
could give a year or two of their time, even
postponing graduation for a year, to study in
an overseas university and help three or four
weak Christian students get under way for the
Lord Jesus?" The opportunities are simply boundless.
This evening we have with us a member of the staff
of IFES, Miss Ruth Siemens. She wasn't always an
IFES staff worker. God has used her in a unique
way, as someone working abroad who has gotten

things under way for the Lord. I have asked Ruth
to come and tell us something of how God led her
when she was in South America.

RUTH SIEMENS

All through my student days, God was giving
me a real desire to be a missionary. But when an
opportunity actually came for me to go to another
country, it was rather a shock. I wasn't really
prepared for it.

About a year after my graduation from
college, while I was helping with an Inter-Varsity
missions conference on the West Coast, I was
invited to fill a specific teaching position in
Lima, Peru. After considerable conflict, I was
convinced that that was what God wanted me to do.
True, I decided to go for only one year so that
in case I didn't like it I could come back! But
I've been in South America for fourteen years and
I'm still enjoying it very much.

I found this time in Lima to be a rewarding
experience. A whole mission field was right there
in my school, which was attended primarily by
elementary and secondary grade children of the
upper class. I worked with these pupils, met
their parents, and was invited into many of their
homes. I am quite sure Jesus Christ had not been
taken there before.

A good number of these pupils, and at least
one of the teachers, received Jesus Christ, but
I soon realized that my main work in Lima was to
be with university students. The person teaching
me Spanish was a university student. She was not
a Christian, but we became good friends. Very
soon, we had a small Bible study going with some
of her friends. At that time I also decided to
audit classes at San Marcos University, partly in
order to learn Spanish more quickly, partly to
learn a little bit about a Peruvian university
from the inside, and partly to be able to make
more friends with university students. I met a

few Christian students in the churches who began
to help me. Among them were several outstanding
leaders who I know were sent to us by God. Some
now, twelve years later, are filling important
positions of Christian leadership in Latin America.

When my three-year contract ended, I decided
that this student group did not need me any more,
and that perhaps it would be God's will for me to
find a similar position in another Spanish-speaking
country. So I applied to a number of schools and
was disappointed to receive negative answers from
all of them. About this time I received an
invitation to become the principal of the American
school in Sao Paulo, Brazil. I had already turned
this down because I did not think that God expected
me to learn Portuguese after having struggled
through three years of Spanish. But that was
what he did expect! After seeing all the other
doors close, and having turned down this position
in Brazil twice, I was nearly out of money. So
I was relieved to receive a telegram from Brazil
for my final answer, and I wired "yes."

My second day in Brazil, I met the university
student who became the first president of our little
student group in Sao Paulo. He brought a Catholic
girlfriend with him who became the first student
in our group to receive Jesus Christ. These two
were married later, and today are very active in
our Portuguese publications program for university
students.

Although I was limited largely to the
group in Sao Paulo because of my responsibilities
at my school, there was a new full-time IFES staff
worker traveling throughout the country, and
several small student groups were started in
widely separated cities. After some time, when
he had to leave Brazil, the responsibility fell
to me to try to keep these student groups going.
I found myself flying very long distances on
weekends. My position, of course, allowed some
good long vacations and also enough money to be
able to make these trips.

Perhaps one question occurring to you is, How does someone in a profession make contact with students? I've already mentioned several of these. I think auditing classes in a university is one of the best. Another very successful way is to have a student live with you, if that is possible. I have had a student living with me who felt free to bring her friends home as often as she wanted to, and our apartment turned into a real student center.

I really thank the Lord for the privilege which he has given me to serve Jesus Christ as a non-professional missionary in Latin America.

WOODS

This is an illustration of what God might do through you, if you are open to his leading. Many of the student movements around the world began when Christian grads took positions abroad. There is an urgent need in many areas of the world for people with a bachelor's degree, preferably a master's degree, who will take a job abroad. There are extraordinary opportunities for teaching. Many universities in the Muslim world are wide open. What a wonderful thing if we could have one Christian faculty member in each one. Today, Indonesia is open. Thailand and the Congo are begging for teachers. Missionary schools are closing because they cannot get volunteers to give three years of their lives teaching abroad. The same is true throughout all French Africa. There are some opportunities for qualified teachers in the Communist world: it's a bit hazardous, but wonderfully exciting, and we have one person in such a post today. Teachers are accepted in Israel where missionaries are not allowed to work. Furthermore, dozens of universities in Latin Europe are pleading for American or Canadian students, strong in the Lord, who will give one year for study abroad and for work with Christian Italian or Spanish

students for Christ. God may give you the
opportunity to help the ideal of presenting the
gospel without charge come to pass.

SELF-SUPPORT, SELF-GOVERNMENT, SELF-PROPAGATION

"Apollos watered, but God gave the increase."
One of my deepest joys in international student
work is that we are not a one-man band, but that
all sorts of people are working together so that
national evangelical student movements may emerge
in the nations of the world. There are national
staff workers. There are students and graduates
of many nations. There are a growing host of
missionaries ministering to students. There are
non-professional people abroad who likewise are
working with us. None of these people is concerned
about building up IFES; rather, their concern is
to build up the work of the Lord Jesus in the
universities in order that student movements may
stand before the Lord in partnership with the
churches of their nations.

To me it is an inexpressable joy that
instead of competition in this work there is
cooperation. I believe competition in the Lord's
work is hateful in God's sight. The competitive
salesmanship of a free enterprise system has
absolutely no place in the economy of God. I do
not refer to the matter of efficiency but to the
spirit of competitiveness that exists when one
organization strives against another. Since
I've been here, I've heard about a situation
where an IV chapter was flourishing. Another
organization moved in. When asked why, the new
organization answered, "Any salesman knows you'll
get more sales where the competition is succeeding."
Now this is unChristian thinking. We are brothers
and sisters in Christ, working together for Christ
and his Kingdom.

The goal of their cooperation is the
emergence of a national movement in each country
with its own staff, its own committees, and its

own finances; each movement belonging to its unique
culture while subject to the abiding Word. The
degree to which this goal is realized is a wonderful
and exciting thing. A few weeks ago we received
a letter from Argentina saying that they will not
need nearly as much help in 1968. Word has come
from Ghana: "Thank you for the help given last
year. It can be less in the future. Our graduates
are getting behind the movement." A letter has
arrived from Germany accompanied by a large check
to help the movement in Japan. We can remember
when the German movement needed help to stand on
its own feet financially. The IFES began with
about eleven movements. Today there are thirty-
five national movements, and almost every one of
those is entirely self-sufficient. Each year the
amount we give becomes less and less as the amount
coming from within the nations becomes more and
more.

We are also concerned about the great
unfinished task. George Verwer made mention of
some of the desperate need in the world today.
Our work in Catholic Europe is pitifully weak.
In Latin America, in Africa, and in some countries
in Asia Christian work is very, very much stronger
than in Latin Europe. There the proportion of
Christians is pitifully small. In many places a
mere handful of students is trying to stand against
an enormous flood in student bodies of from 60,000
to 70,000.

In the Muslim world we are scratching only
the surface, just beginning to make an imprint.
We pray that God will soon give us an Arabic-
speaking national staff worker from the Near East.
Pray with us that we will be able to penetrate
that vast area soon.

Then there is the Communist world. For
the last three summers we've had groups of students
from Eastern Europe coming to us, and God has
blessed and saved some. Only a short time ago
I got a letter from a girl in Southern Yugoslavia
who had come to the Lord two summers ago. She

came back to us the second summer. Although apparently it is forbidden, she has a thriving Bible study group of women students meeting each week. We believe we are just on the verge of a breakthrough in many of these countries. In one of the countries of Eastern Europe this coming summer, we shall have one or two special student evangelistic campaigns. Naturally, I cannot say more.

Reaching French-speaking Africa is another whole task.

Although we are seeing God work, and national movements emerge, and cooperation among missionary societies, IFES staff, and nations increase, there yet remains much land to be possessed. As we lift up our eyes to look on the fields, we see a great harvest still unreached. But we remember and thank God that we are workers together. We are not empire builders. We are working for Christ and for his Kingdom.

ATTACKING THE CITADEL

On behalf of the IFES family, I should like to express thanks to God and heartfelt gratitude to you for the offering that was received last night for our pioneer work around the world. On the 26th of December, when I left Switzerland to come here, I had a very real concern. We had in faith expanded our staff in several areas of the world, and there was considerable financial need. Since arriving here, Mr. Adeney has told me of three urgent financial needs that have arisen suddenly in Japan, in the Philippines, and in India. From a human point of view, it seemed quite impossible for these needs to be met. Yet in his own wonderful and miraculous way, God has met these needs through you. I have only one request to make: As you have given financially, so remember the IFES ministry in your prayers once in a while, say once a week. This is the secret of God's blessing among students around in the world.

This evening I would like to speak on another aspect of this worldwide student ministry. I might call it "Attacking the Citadel." Sometimes a theological faculty or seminary is a citadel of God. Sometimes it is a citadel of Satan. The most strategic area in the worldwide strategy for the cause of Christ is our theological colleges.

You must understand that the situation in many parts of the world differs from that in Canada and the United States. Here, because of the separation of church and state, we have what could be called free theological seminaries or faculties. In Europe, where there are state churches, we do not have free university or theological colleges, except in a few rare instances.

Rather, we have state university faculties of theology. Theology is strictly an academic subject in these universities. As a result, professors compete for positions, not on the basis of their Christian commitment, but on the basis of their academic attainment. It is not being uncharitable to suggest that in many, many instances in Europe theology is a regular, almost secular, subject. The members of the staff or faculty are unconverted. This has a dire effect upon the church itself for these theological faculties produce ministers who have no true Christian faith and no true Christian message. As a result, the church in Europe, generally speaking, is spiritually poverty stricken, in spite of the biblical liturgy in most of these churches.

German theological thought, in particular, influences and dominates the world. This has continued generation after generation even though Germany is the seat of the most radical theology you will find anywhere. In science, first one theory and then another becomes popular; likewise theology, one theological fashion follows another. One prominent professor arises, becomes popular, and has his own following. Five years later the students flock after another professor. Because of this, there is a constant change in theological thought and emphasis, and little stability. The great tragedy is that German theological thought influences the theological seminaries of the world to an alarming extent.

One of the exciting happenings in the last thirty or forty years, however, has been the capture of several liberal, almost radical, theological seminaries for the evangelical cause. Chairs (or positions) in theology have fallen, one after another, to young men of evangelical convictions. They in turn have influenced their students. These students, as they were ordained, have influenced the churches, and an entirely new theological climate has come about as a result. Therefore, we believe in our evangelical work among students.

The theological student, you must understand, is a regular university student. He enters university as a freshman to study theology just as someone else enters university to major in biology. We must have a special approach as we work with these students. Rather recently there has been a new development led by a man from the United States. Dr. Harold Brown, who is the IFES secretary to theological students, is now trying to perform a "rescue operation." The task of attacking the seminary or the faculty itself is too great. The thing we are trying to do is rescue some of the students by helping them to understand what the Bible really is and what it teaches. It has been a wonderful and an exciting thing to watch.

For instance, only last summer we had a theological course in Italian Switzerland for ten days. We were crowded out by theological students. We had to turn some away. The opposition was terrific, and the debate sometimes bitter. Not two months later, the letters started to arrive. The seed had penetrated. There was a change of conviction, a change of thought. This is a heartening thing.

Dr. Brown does much correspondence and visitation and is traveling almost constantly. Because of his own theological attainments, he is being invited increasingly to give a week of lectures in one theological faculty or another. This is cause for much thanksgiving.

We hold theological reading parties on weekends. This coming summer we shall have three theological seminars, one in which the major language will be English, the second French, the third German.

We also publish a theological paper which some of you have seen, Themelios.

Largely as the result of our General Committee at Wuppertal, Germany, last summer, there has been a general call for assistance among theological students from Asia, Latin America, and Africa. Will you pray with us that in this special division of the work God will give us wisdom, provide the staff, and also provide facilities?

Another encouraging development is among pastors. The state churches usually provide money and the opportunity for ministers to take a refresher course. The normal thing, particularly in the German-speaking countries, is to go to one of the universities for a series of lectures. Now groups of ministers from the state church are coming to us and saying, "Look, we have the money. We'd rather not go to this university. Will you put on a two-week course for us?" This gives us a wonderful opportunity to serve the church. Personally I hope that both Canada and the United States will see similar developments for theological students and others who are theologically oriented. Theological students, just as other students, need much help.

As you consider this worldwide ministry and the unfinished task we have, think of the strategic role of the theological student and the theological seminary in the total cause of Christ and in the health, vigor, and ministry of his church.

Part VI. Centennary Tribute

17. Tribute to Samuel Zwemer and Robert Speer by William McE. Miller, Sr.

JOHN ALEXANDER: Introduction

Second Corinthians chapter 5, beginning at verse 14: "For the love of Christ controls us, because we are convinced that one has died for all; therefore all have died. And he died for all, that those who live might live no longer for themselves but for him who for their sake died and was raised. From now on, therefore, we regard no one from a human point of view; even though we once regarded Christ from a human point of view, we regard him thus no longer. Therefore, if any one is in Christ, he is a new creation, the old has passed away, behold, the new has come. All this is from God, who through Christ reconciled us to himself and gave us the ministry of reconciliation; that is, God was in Christ reconciling the world to himself, not counting their trespasses against them, and entrusting to us the message of reconciliation. So we are ambassadors for Christ, God making his appeal through us. We beseech you on behalf of Christ, be reconciled to God. For our sake he made him to be sin who knew no sin, so that in him we might become the righteousness of God" (vv. 14 to 21 RSV).

I suppose the most definitive work ever written on the history of missions, certainly the

most exhaustive and detailed, is that of Dr. Kenneth
Scott Latourette of Yale Divinity School. He called
this last one hundred years of church history "the
great century of advance." It is your privilege
to come upon the scene after an enormous price for
the expansion of the church has already been paid
by the pioneers. This year is the centennial of
two architects of that advance: Dr. Samuel Zwemer,
apostle to the Muslims, and Dr. Robert Speer.
Both are known for their concern with students
and with the mission of the church. Tonight it
is my privilege to welcome Dr. William Miller, a
Presbyterian missionary in Iran among the Muslims
for forty-three years, to pay tribute to these
two men and to tell us something about the impact
of their lives.

WILLIAM McE. MILLER, SR.

What a joy and privilege for me to be here
with you tonight. I am reminded of the first
great missionary convention which I attended
fifty-four years ago. That convention was held
in Kansas City, exactly at this time in the
Christmas vacation with 5,000 students, teachers,
and missionaries present. In back of the platform
was a huge map of the world. And above that map,
in large letters, were these words: The field is
the world, and Go ye into all the world and preach
the gospel to every creature. The men sitting on
the platform were among the greatest Christian
leaders of that generation. And towering above
the others were three men, great in stature, great
in spiritual power: John R. Mott, chairman of
the convention, Samuel M. Zwemer, and Robert E.
Speer. Tonight we unite with Christian people
around the world who remember with gratitude the
one hundredth anniversary of the births of Speer
and Zwemer. These men, at that convention as at
other gatherings, inspired thousands of students
to go forth into all the world and preach the
gospel to every creature.

That convention was sponsored by the Student Volunteer Movement for foreign missions, which had its watchword The Evangelization of the World in this Generation. This movement started in a very small way in 1883 at Princeton University where a half-dozen students and the sister of one met Sunday afternoons to pray that God would convert many Princeton students and call them to other lands and to tell the good news of Jesus Christ. Those prayers were answered. A revival came to Princeton. Many students believed in Christ and committed their lives to him. A number decided to go as missionaries and signed the Princeton declaration, "I am willing and desirous, God permitting, to become a foreign missionary."

Three years passed. In 1886 Dwight L. Moody, the famous evangelist of that day, invited college students to come to his school at Mount Hermon, Massachusetts, for one month of Bible study. Two hundred fifty students from 100 institutions in the United States accepted his invitation. One of those was Robert Wilder, the leader of the prayer group and missionary movement at Princeton. When Wilder got to Mount Hermon, he and other students who were hoping to become missionaries began talking to the other delegates. They had a prayer meeting every day. The number began at twenty, then grew and grew until on the last day of the month, ninety-nine signers of the declaration met to pray. While these were praying, the one hundredth man entered. One hundred students volunteering for foreign missionary service.

They decided to present this missionary challenge to other colleges. Robert Wilder and his friend John Forman spent the following academic year traveling to colleges throughout the United States. They visited 260 institutions; at the end of their tour 2,000 students had signed the declaration: "I am willing and desirous, God permitting, to become a foreign missionary." As a result, the Student Volunteer Movement for

foreign missions was established with that watchword:
The evangelization of the world in this generation.

When Wilder visited Hope College in Michigan
he found a senior there named Sam Zwemer, whose
mother had dedicated him to missionary work before
her death. Zwemer responded to Wilder's presentation
and signed the declaration. At Princeton, the alma
mater of Wilder and Forman, they met a sophomore,
Robert Speer, a brilliant student and member of
the football team. Speer's ambition was to become
a lawyer, like his father, and one day to become
a judge of the Supreme Court of the United States.
Hearing their appeal, Speer changed his plans; he
signed the declaration and devoted his life to the
service of Christ in missionary work. When one
of Speer's friends asked him what his father would
say about his change in plans, Speer replied, "I
had to do it. When are you going to decide?" His
friend became an eminent minister in the United
States. These men, one after the other, became
traveling secretaries of the Student Volunteer
Movement. They visited many colleges and appealed
to the students to volunteer. It is said that
during the year in which Speer was traveling,
1,000 more students volunteered for this service.

Robert Speer later went to theological
seminary. In his middler year in Princeton, as
he was practicing football one afternoon, a
secretary of the board of foreign missions of
the Presbyterian Church came to the side-line,
called him off the field, and said to him, "We
want you to come to New York and become a secretary
of the board of foreign missions." Believing that
this was God's call to him, Speer left his seminary
study and went to New York. At the age of twenty-
four he became a secretary of the board and continued
in that position for forty-six years. During that
period under his and his associates' inspired
leadership the number of missionaries of the
Presbyterian Church rose from 155 to 1,600.

Speer not only sat behind a desk and
carried on the executive work of his mission, he

also traveled widely and spoke in churches and
colleges throughout the United States. He was
perhaps that generation's most powerful speaker
to students. I will never forget an address he
gave at the student conference in Northfield,
Massachusetts, in 1912 when I first saw him.
His theme was from the fourth chapter of 2
Corinthians: "The light of the knowledge of
the glory of God in the face of Jesus Christ."
And as this powerful man, with his deep voice,
spoke to us of Jesus Christ, I saw, as I had
never seen before, the glory of Jesus Christ in
his face. Ever since then he has been to me
the most Christ-like man I have ever met. He
was perhaps the greatest Christian statesman
and missionary speaker of the world at that time.

     He visited the mission fields. Once he
traveled 1,100 miles across the plains of Northern
Iran in a horse-drawn vehicle in the bitter cold
of winter. He went to visit and encourage seven
of us in our missionary task in a pioneer station
on the border of Afghanistan. He spent three
weeks--at a time when he was very busy as one of
the leading religious figures in the United States,
not only in his own church but in the whole
Protestant community. His coming was like the
coming of an angel of God.

     He not only gave addresses, he also wrote
sixty-seven books--most of them about Jesus Christ
or about the work of Jesus Christ in the world.
His great volume is The Finality of Jesus Christ.
Jesus Christ was everything to Robert Speer. His
one passion was Christ and the work of Christ.
And at the age of eighty he went to receive his
reward.

     Samuel Zwemer, leaving Hope College upon
graduation, went to the theological seminary of
the Reformed Church in America at New Brunswick,
New Jersey. He was a burning torch. Very soon
he had persuaded the students and faculty of the
small seminary to raise enough money to support
a missionary of their own in India.

He and several of this friends decided to choose the most difficult mission field in the world, and after due consideration they chose Arabia, the heartland of Islam, unpenetrated by Christian missionaries. Because his church at first refused to support this mission, he and his friends raised their own support, went out to Arabia, and founded the Arabian mission. Later the Reformed Church took over the mission, and it has become one of the great missions of that church today. Zwemer and his friends labored in Arabia for a number of years, facing difficult stituations, until Zwemer was invited to make Cairo his base. Then from Cairo he went to all parts of the Muslim world, which includes one-seventh of the world population. He inspired missionaries in India, Indonesia, and China to make Christ known to followers of Muhammed (those who believe that Muhammed came and took the place of Jesus Christ).

He was a powerful speaker in British, American, and Dutch (Dutch was his native tongue) missionary conferences and churches.

I heard him speak in that Kansas City convention fifty-four years ago. I can picture him standing on the platform, appealing to us to sacrifice everything for Jesus Christ. He told us about William Borden, the graduate of Yale, who planned to go as a missionary to the Muslims in China but died in Cairo before he ever reached his field. He called on us to follow in Borden's steps, to give all to Christ. Many in that convention and in other meetings like it heard God's call through Dr. Speer to devote their lives to the task of evangelizing Muslims. Most of those who volunteered were influenced by Samuel Zwemer.

Zwemer not only influenced students from the platform, he also talked to people individually. He had pockets full of literature. Everywhere he went--on trains, buses, anywhere--he gave out his literature. It is said that while he visited John

Hopkins Medical School and rushed from one classroom
of medical students to keep speaking engagements,
a young medical student pursued him across campus
and said to him, "If you can prove to me that
Arabia is the most difficult mission field in the
world, I will go there as a medical missionary."
On the next day they found time to sit down and
discuss it, and Paul Harrison, fully persuaded,
went to Arabia to become one of the greatest
medical missionaries of the past generation.

Dr. Zwemer also wrote at least fifty books--
books about Christ, books about Islam, books to
inspire the church to go forward in her missionary
task. It was very hard for him to retire at the
age of seventy from a professorship in Princeton
Seminary; at that time he wrote a pamphlet, Life
Begins at Seventy. For fifteen more years he
wrote books, gave addresses, spent his all for
Christ.

His last public service was at a missionary
conference of Inter-Varsity in New York City.
Paul Little told me as we were coming on the
platform that he was in that conference and heard
his last address. Zwemer gave three addresses in
one day, and shortly after that he went to receive
his crown.

Only heaven will reveal how many people
were inspired to devote their lives to missionary
service through these two great servants of Jesus
Christ. They did everything in their power to
evangelize the world in that generation.

That generation has passed. You are now
living in another generation. God still commands
you to make known to all the people living in
the world today the good news of Jesus Christ.
Far more people who do not know Christ are in the
world today than were in the world when God's
call came to Wilder, Mott, Speer, Zwemer, and
their fellow workers. Your task is larger; the
church also is larger. God's trumpet still calls
for an advance. Can you hear God saying, "Whom
shall I send, and who will go for us?" Are you,

like the prophet of old, going to say, "Here am
I! Send me"?

Now we are going to express our gratitude
to God for these men and for others like them who
have finished their course and have kept the faith,
and who have worked to bring about the vast expansion
of Christianity about which we heard this morning.
In silence let us thank God for these men and
the great host of others like them who did all
they could to tell the good news everywhere.
Then are you willing to add, "Lord, here am I.
I will take up that task. I will devote my life
and all my powers to make Christ known throughout
the world, wherever you send me. Lord, here am
I, send me." Will you in silence say that to
your God?

With praise and gratitude for the privilege
of serving You, oh, Jesus Christ, we say, amen.

WHAT IS INTER-VARSITY?

Inter-Varsity helps students find the reality of God. Historically, IVCF was born in revival. Deeply concerned about spiritual needs in the university, students at Cambridge banded together in 1870 to form an evangelical witness. The spark ignited, the flame spread to Canada, then to the United States, and now into seventy countries, with forty member movements affiliated with the International Fellowship of Evangelical Students.

Since IVCF-USA was incorporated in 1940, the student population has nearly quadrupled. With leadership in both Christian and secular segments of society coming primarily from university graduates, the mushrooming university population is a vast and vital mission field.

The aim of Inter-Varsity Christian Fellowship is to establish groups of Christian students in colleges, universities, and schools of nursing whose purpose is:

To witness to the Lord Jesus Christ as God Incarnate, and to seek to lead others to a personal faith in him as Lord and Savior.

To deepen and strengthen the spiritual lives of students by the study of the Bible, prayer, and Christian fellowship.

To present the call of God to the foreign mission field and so help all students discover God's role for them, at home or abroad, in worldwide evangelization.

The triennial Missionary Convention is one answer to the question of missions leaders: Where can we get more missionaries? "Urbana" is a vast recruiting ground. Missionaries, challenged to full commitment at this convention, are serving in every part of the world.